U2 Show

We have always taken the design and production sides of our world seriously and we are delighted that now, for the first time, the definitive and fully authorised story of our touring history is being chronicled. U2 Show *offers a unique behind-the-scenes perspective of what it takes to put U2 on the road. It also stands as a testament to the many talented people who have worked with us to help create the band's reputation as a great live act. We hope you enjoy it.*

U2 and Paul McGuinness, Dublin 2004

U2 Show

Diana Scrimgeour

ORION

Contents

Pictures

Words

Foreword by Diana Scrimgeour

This project originated with a commission for a feature on the design of PopMart in June 1997, photographing the show in San Francisco and Los Angeles. Having been a photographer for many years, this marked the start of a new journey, and I spent the next five years at many different tour production rehearsals and shows on either side of the Atlantic, immersed in documenting how shows come together. By the time U2's Elevation tour was on the horizon in 2000, I fully appreciated the level of their contribution to and influence on the evolution of rock and roll shows. I spent a week in Miami for the Elevation production rehearsals and after the first show agreed the concept and support for this book with Paul McGuinness, which enabled me to document the tour throughout 2001 and spend the following two years doing research.

A 21st century rock and roll show is a hi-tech event. It is made possible by a team of skilled professionals who work 24/7 to achieve a very specific result night after night. There are no rules for how often a band must go on tour, but for those who have the wish and the wherewithal to mount a large-scale production and take it on the road, there is usually a period of a couple of years between the end of one tour and the start of the next. It is a constant challenge for show designers to find new approaches, and as the speed of technological developments accelerated through the nineties, the rock and roll show often found itself at the forefront of these developments, providing the perfect platform for demonstrating the latest in sound, video and lighting.

U2, arguably more than any other band, have been at the cutting edge of developing new technology in their shows. Their intelligence informs every aspect of their work, not least their approach to their live performances. This book illustrates their relentless commitment to perfectionism, and how this is demonstrated in their live shows. Their career has been marked by constant reinvention: pushing boundaries to improve their musical performance. Likewise with their show design, if a good idea is on the table then a way will be found to make it happen. ZooTV, PopMart and Elevation have all involved the invention and utilization of new approaches in sound, video and lighting to realise the band's vision.

U2 Show comprises three distinct parts: introductory texts, a plate section and a text section. At the front of the book, Michael Bracewell has addressed U2's shows in the context of the rock show as theatre and art, and Willie Williams has written a synopsis of the development of a U2 show from his twenty years' experience of overseeing their show design. The second part of the book is a major photographic record of U2's performing history divided into five chronological sections. The third part, introduced by Mark Cunningham's short history of rock touring, is made up of interviews with a selection of the band's closest collaborators. These interviews illustrate how U2 have contributed to the advancement of the live performance throughout the course of their 25-year career, and give a uniquely personal perspective on what is involved in the creation of a touring show. They trace the steps from the creation of a record to the interpretation and translation of the music into the live performance.

A bizarre aspect of any illustrated book about a rock show is that only the visual aspect can be recorded on the page. The music and energy of the live performance can only be a memory, conjured up by the images. U2 have toured every album they have released, and each time sound supremo Joe O'Herlihy has been responsible for interpreting the fidelity of U2's recorded sound at and during their shows. While his work cannot be illustrated here, his vital contribution is inestimable.

No book about U2 would be complete without reference to their humanitarian conscience and political awareness, which have underpinned their lyrics and performance since the earliest days. Their commitment to raising public awareness about socially unjust issues on a global scale has marked their career. This came up time and again when interviewing people for this book, and a section is devoted specifically to this topic.

It was always my intention to tell this story in the words of the people who make it happen. While the fulcrum of each show is U2, I have focused not on telling the story from the band's perspective, but from the world backstage. I have learned great respect for the many people who dedicate their lives to ensuring that the show must go on! A show is like an iceberg: the performance is the part you see above the water; the unseen 90 per cent below the water are the years of experience, preparation, design and construction which enable the whole to be realised successfully. Few books make reference to the discipline and extraordinary teamwork of the crew behind a successful show. I hope that this one will go some way towards redressing the balance.

U2 came onto the scene in the late seventies at a time when rock and roll touring was still in its infancy. Before then it wasn't common for bands to take their own productions on the road. U2's story, therefore, runs parallel with the growth of touring, and the people who have worked with U2 on the many aspects of their tours have learned their trade from the ground up, becoming in the process among the most accomplished and well respected professionals in their fields. Their recollections provide a unique window into this extraordinary world. Most importantly, U2's core team have been with them from the earliest years of their career: manager Paul McGuinness; sound designer Joe O'Herlihy; show and lighting designer Willie Williams; production manager Steve Iredale and tour manager Dennis Sheehan have worked together on every show since 1983's War tour.

Since the eighties the higher echelons of the rock and roll world have been creating shows of ever-increasing visual complexity and splendour. Through the nineties the development of technology accelerated and rock and roll shows became even more sophisticated, with audience expectations rising accordingly. The support structure for the tours developed into an industry. The individuals who became the first road managers (preceding today's tour and production managers) and those who started their sound and lighting companies in the seventies were the pioneers. For the most part self-taught, learning their technical skills and business acumen through experience, to this day these people remain the experts in their fields and cornerstones of the rock touring world. U2 were fortuitous in their timing. In the earliest years of their career they joined forces with some of the most experienced facilitators, from Chris Blackwell of Island Records and legendary agent Frank Barsalona to sound suppliers Clair Brothers and lighting/video suppliers Nocturne, who shared their experience and skill with the young Irish band.

U2's longevity in the transitory world of rock music is unique. They are the only band of their generation to have retained their original line up, to be still composing and releasing their own music and still be among the handful of performers able to sell out a world stadium tour. They are a band with a conscience and a message. Their particular combination of heart, mind, intellect and spirit makes for a thrilling and challenging live performance. This is U2's show.

Acknowledgements

First and foremost thanks to U2 for providing the inspiration!

Thank you to the band and Paul McGuinness for their authorization of this book. To all at Principle Management: thanks for your support and help, particularly in Dublin to Sheila Roche, Candida Bottaci, for her patience and good humour in dealing with the stream of requests, Susan Hunter, Aislinn Meehan, Cecilia Coffey and to Steve Matthews for great facilitation in the final stages!

Of all U2's crew members, I am especially indebted to Willie Williams for his words of introduction in this book and his belief in the project from its initiation, and to Steve Iredale and Joe O'Herlihy who have been extremely generous with their time, advice and support. Thank you all, and to the many other crew members who have extended their welcome to me (and my camera) on tour. You know who you are! I hope that this book does your work justice. Thanks to Regine Moylett, and at RMP to Louise Butterly, Nadja Mayow Coyne and Eavann McCarthy for their help with the archive, and Amanda Freeman for her help on the PopMart and Elevation tours.

Everyone who I interviewed for this book gave their time generously and enthusiastically, and I am very grateful for the opportunity to have met so many people with such a wide range of unique experiences. It was great fun, and thank you all for bringing this book alive.

Special thanks to Mark Fisher for all your very practical support and advice and for the use of your wonderful photographs. In the Mark Fisher studio, salutations to Adrian Mudd for your technical advice and for your help overseeing all the video grabs, and to Gillian Ward for co-ordination of all Mark's material. Thanks to those who shared photographs from their own collections, particularly Jeremy Thom, Ellen Darst, Frank Barsalona and Barbara Skydel.

For support and encouragement in the earliest stages of my rock photography career, thank you Andrew Zweck for provoking me into action and raising the bar, and Mark Cunningham for sharing the vision and facing the challenges together! Also special thanks to Jake Berry for all his help on so many tours over the years.

To the team who worked with me on this project, words fail me. You have all been so terrific in your commitment and devoting your professional expertise to realising my vision for this book. Thank you Katy for your artistry and skill and determination, Robert for bringing your special brand of editorial wit and intelligence, Emily for the endless hours working with me on researching the images and Rhonda for all your help on every aspect of the organization and the endless hours unscrambling the mountain of interviews! David Godwin, thank you for opening the door for me and for your unreserved help and guidance throughout. At Orion, thank you above all to Ian Preece for shepherding this book through its many stages, to John Mitchinson for originally commissioning the book and also to Trevor Dolby and Alan Samson.

Thank you to all at Flash Photodigital in London and to Peter Ryden for developing and printing assistance over the years.

For advice and collaboration in the early stages, many thanks to Ruth Katz, Catherine Owens and Maria Manton and, in the final stages, to Jane Vukovic.

Special thanks to friends who have all contributed unique advice and support: Julia Peyton Jones, Della and Dan Hirsch, Belinda LaViolette, David Darling, Wiz and Tom Deakin, Shaun Ford, Avril Rohou, Peter Sapieha, Simon and Debbie Taffler and Louise Reiser.

Above all, most love and thanks to my family: Hugh, Daniel, Alex and Sophie.

U2 and Rock Music as Spectacle by Michael Bracewell

On 12 May 1979, at the Dandelion Market beside Dublin's Gaiety Green flea market, an up-and-coming local band called U2 played an outdoor concert to a largely teenage audience. It would be the first of several similar events staged by U2 at that time, arranged so as not to disappoint those of the group's fans who were under 18, and consequently unable to see them when they played at the neighbouring, licensed, McGonagle's club. And in this little scrap of history, perhaps, can be found the beginnings of U2's founding attitude towards live performance.

U2 performing at the Dandelion Market, Dublin, c.1979

First, U2 are a band who pursue a particular, visceral intimacy with their audience. (Hence, you imagine, singer Bono's admiration for the Velvet Underground, Patti Smith and Morrissey.) Even fifteen years after their Dandelion Market gig, when the group were touring the epic, multi-media presentations of ZooTV to some of the biggest stadium venues in the world, their entire performance would be geared towards creating a one-to-one bond with every individual member of the audience. They don't want anyone to be left out of the experience.

Second, they are a group for whom performance is always in some way political – no matter to what extent they package those politics in extravagant display. So back in 1979, by playing the outdoor shows especially for their younger fans, U2 were also making a statement about access and exclusivity: that inherent in pop and rock, as the writer Dave Marsh has stated, is the drive to give a voice and a face to the dispossessed.

Third, U2 have pioneered the live presentation of rock music as a spectacle. And within the spectacle of a U2 show is a mass of technical, aesthetic and theatrical devices, the combination of which might be seen as part ritual and part rally: a sensory bombardment of sound and image not only to heighten the drama and the meaning of the music, but to enfold the audience within its world – to appeal to both head and heart; to thrill, but encourage the questioning of why we are thrilled. And again, back in 1979, near a flea market in Dublin, what better way of prompting all these notions than by playing raw, punk-based rock – as U2 were known for then – not just in a smoke-filled club but right out there on the street?

When U2 emerged off the back of the British punk-rock scene, they were part of a generation of groups who made confrontational and lyrically smart music. This was a generation which might be said to include, from Ireland, both Stiff Little Fingers and The Undertones. Raw-throated and guitar driven, yet seeming to stem from a much older sensibility of Irish folk music, these were groups for whom songwriting was steeped in both the traditions of romance and the political conscience of social realism. While Stiff Little Fingers were the more musically aggressive – more in tune with the two-chord energy of any number of first-generation punk groups, from 999 to The Clash – and The Undertones delivered a gorgeously contorted interpretation of the classic pop love song, it was U2 who seemed to possess an almost unlimited potential to work on a global scale within the medium of rock music.

Back in the late 1970s, the live music scene which had been created by punk was a complex network of clubs and halls – many of which were little more than shabby local discos, handed over for the night to what the management would bill as 'new wave' groups. Bands like Prag Vec, Reluctant Stereotypes or

Clock DVA appeared to be on an endless tour of such venues. But on one particular night, supported by The Blades at a club called the Baggot Inn, in Dublin, U2's performance caught the eye of a *Sounds* journalist who noted Bono's compelling style: 'You follow Bono with your eyes as he counts on his fingers or runs across the stage or spontaneously mimes something that is impenetrable but opposite to the moody, fat rolling sound …'

This was an astute piece of writing, for as U2 made the swift progression from their punk beginnings to a far broader, more monolithic concept of music, there would remain at its centre the vital tension between Bono's inherent theatricality and the urgent, galloping tempo of the group's musical style. In many ways, you could say that Bono's range and intensity as a performer are more than partially enabled by the sheer physicality of U2's chassis of drum- and guitar-powered rock. For there is a particular dandyism to Bono's performance, the disquieting style of which would be perfectly framed by the astonishing, rococo postmodernism of their later multi-media shows – ZooTV and PopMart – designed by Willie Williams, with further artistic and conceptual input from the legendary producer, musician and ideologue, Brian Eno.

On an evolutionary scale, the shows designed by Williams might be said to represent a highly developed form of rock theatre, calling on inspiration and influence from a vast range of media, from fine art to advertising by way of cinema and opera. Previously, the big rock spectacular had been known more for its bombastic attempts at heroism than for any particular sense of finesse and self-awareness. But there had been honourable exceptions within the history of rock theatre, which might be considered interesting precursors to U2's reinvention of the format.

While progressive rock music had foregrounded virtuosity, concept and structure – as evidenced, for example, by the live presentation of *Tales from Topographic Oceans* by Yes as a pseudo-classical piece in four distinct movements – there was also an attendant exploration of both technological innovation and a kind of generative improvisation. The Pink Floyd, as early as the late 1960s, would showcase tracks such as 'Instellar Overdrive' as epic excursions into audiovisual theatre; and Andy Warhol's *Exploding Plastic Inevitable* shows with the Velvet Underground were volatile fusions of light show, music, projection and film – 'It's, uh, going to be very glamorous', as Warhol pronounced in a shy mumble.

Miming the interior world of a drug-induced trip, such live shows were concerned with a disarrangement of the senses – rerouting perceptions into new circuitry, the shifts in which would, presumably, be further unbalanced by drug use. There was a sense of ritual and ceremony involved in freak-outs such as the 24-Hour Technicolor Dream, staged at Alexandra Palace, which might be described as either a secular form of communion or a social form of theatre: audience participation was total, declaring unity with an entire culture of beliefs.

In the early 1970s, however, rock shows by groups such as Peter Gabriel's Genesis, the Pink Floyd again and even a futuristic vaudevillian such as David Bowie would present a new, more structured interpretation of the genre. Genesis mined a peculiarly intense form of English fable, with Gabriel himself playing a range of startling characters on stage – a Green Man of folklore, for instance, with foliage extruding from his head, or dressed in a woman's scarlet evening gown and wearing a fox-head mask. In addition to this, the rest of the group would make use of such intensely visual devices as dressing in white under ultra-violet lights – the more to enhance Gabriel's extraordinary role as a performing vocalist. By the time of their bizarre narrative show The Lamb Lies Down on Broadway, in 1975, the group were even beginning to experiment with primitive holograms – thus allowing Gabriel, playing a gangland New Yorker called Rael, to appear simultaneously

Peter Gabriel 'appears' on stage in three places simultaneously as Genesis experiment with holograms on their 1975 The Lamb Lies Down on Broadway tour

on three different marks on the stage. Bowie, in more Gothic mode, had moved away from the earlier use of mime in his shows to seeming to inhabit the ruins of a city street. On the concerts caught by his *David Live* double album of 1975, Bowie seems like a cross between Frank Sinatra and Hamlet – a skeletal crooner, both the product and the prisoner of a rotting culture.

Such concerts were dismissed from fashionability by punks' initial dependence on low-budget (or no-budget) DIY performances, but they left a valid artistic and technological legacy which would be reclaimed by bands as diverse as Talking Heads and the Pet Shop Boys as a valid contemporary art form. Importantly, the new generation of rock groups who chose to work with the notion of live performances as spectacle and theatre – at the forefront of which are U2 – would become increasingly interested in making statements about popular culture itself.

With ZooTV the rock concert became a new kind of spectacle: 'A technological theatre for the Mass Age of popular culture.'

In the late 1980s, U2 achieved global status as a rock group known for emotionally powerful, anthemic music. Songs such as 'I Still Haven't Found What I'm Looking For', 'Where the Streets Have No Name', 'Sunday Bloody Sunday' and 'Pride (In the Name of Love)' could unite audiences in the biggest stadium venues. As tracks, they were heroic; they articulated attitudes of defiance and prayer in a way which the mainstream of popular culture absorbed with ease. In addition to this, U2's presentation of these songs – as filmed by Phil Joanou in *Rattle and Hum* – would be raw and comparatively stripped down. As *The Joshua Tree* had made U2 a multi-million-selling group, so they were concerned with an intense visual imagery – from their choice of album and single sleeve images through the entire presentation of the group and their music. A principal benefit of rock superstardom is that it grants you the financial leverage – within a business notorious for its fiscal conservatism – to maintain full artistic control of your creativity. And as their audience continued to grow globally, so U2 advanced their revolutionary exploration of the possibilities of live music. This idea of turning live rock music into a new kind of spectacle – a technological theatre for the Mass Age of popular culture – can be seen in U2's shows such as ZooTV (1993) and PopMart (1997) to achieve an unrivalled level of technical, thematic and theatrical sophistication. Even now, they are rather like watching a musical based on Marshall McLuhan's pioneering essays on the pleasures and perils of mass media. And yet they work first and foremost as pure entertainment. For rather than allowing the colossal scale of the presentations to impose on the performances of the musicians, the very stage sets and their various electronic conceits become tools for the group to utilize. In this manner, Willie Williams and the group create a live show that is in tune with U2's performance: the presentation of the music becomes in itself a political commentary upon the music. And it is to this tension that Bono adds the further inflection of his own, at times heavily stylized, dramatic performance.

Bono has always played with the notion of character in his performances: he comes across as the cowboy or the Devil or the boxing champ – and all of these characters might be said to be comments on his role as an artist and a vocalist. It is a game with identity which has appealed to artists as different in style as Jeff Koons, Cindy Sherman and Gavin Turk. It seems to replicate a comment by Marcel Proust, where he writes of the many gentlemen of whom he is comprised. And Bono, through the medium of U2, can not only play the roles of those different gentlemen, but frame the performances within the most spectacular and self-analytical of settings.

As punk had laid waste to the idea of the big, spectacular rock show having any relevance to the modern world, so U2 would reinvent the genre as a richly ironic, politicized statement about the way we live now. Loosely, ZooTV and PopMart could be said to articulate statements about the postmodern world –

describing that world back to itself as a perilous pleasuredome of seemingly infinite images and information, the accelerated accumulation of which might seem to threaten our perceptions, free will and fundamental human feelings. In this much, the U2 show is about acting out a passion play of good versus evil in a very blatant way. Why else might Bono, during ZooTV, achieve such a bravura performance as the Devil – played, incidentally, not as a swaggeringly satanic Mick Jagger, sinewy in black, but rather as a sentimental old impresario, virtually exhausted by the suffering he has given to the world. Occurring towards the end of the concert, Bono's extraordinary performance as the satanic creator of mass media comprises one of the most sophisticated theatrical statements to be made by a rock show. Following on from the visually simpler Rattle and Hum tour, the scale and complexity of ZooTV – its astonishing use of technology and the ergonomics of a concert stage – is literally breathtaking.

Role-playing on ZooTV: Bono as Mr MacPhisto

ZooTV started as an indoor arena tour in America and Europe, between February and June 1992. Willie then brought in the set-design team of Mark Fisher and Jonathan Park to help him realize the big outdoor version, called ZooTV Outside Broadcast in North America, which came to Europe as Zooropa, and subsequently went on to Australasia and Japan. The idea that the whole ZooTV concept could be open to ongoing adjustment was central to its vision, and part of the agility of the tour lies in the production's awareness of itself, and the honed acuity of its dialogue with the audience. The various legs of the tour would alter the content – with the Outside Broadcast leg opening with manipulated clip of George Bush Senior talking about the bombing of Baghdad, and the indoor leg opening with the Ronettes' 'Be My Baby'. From the audience's point of view, the experience was all-engulfing, with each version appropriating a different mix of glamour, desire or politics. This was never less than radical for a stadium and arena rock concert medium. In one version, we are confronted with the monolithic structure of the stage: scaffolding and lights, banks of video walls, layers of amplifiers. Beneath this massed technology, the musicians' instruments and playing area appear tiny. Already, the production seems to be making a statement about the totalitarian status of the rock superstar: that here is a show of power by the contemporary music industry, every bit as calculated to impress and dazzle as any political rally.

As if on cue, the monitors snap into life – and the amplified hum of their technology does make them sound as though they are alive – and our first contact with the temper of all this technology is the image of a stern and defiant youth, drumming out a call to arms. While no emblems are in sight, this is clearly a Hitler Youth – made as inspiring and heroic as only the meticulously honed glamour of Nazi propaganda could achieve. And in this context, as the overture to a wildly anticipated rock show by one of the biggest groups in the world, there is clearly a much broader point being made about the seductions of fascism. Presented with enough fanfare and pomp (the technology seems to be asking) will we allow ourselves to follow any party?

Just a few minutes into the spectacle of ZooTV, the capacity audience is being enfolded in a mixture of emotions. And again, right on cue, the questions begin to flash across the monitors: 'What Do You Want?' Here the visual reference seems to be to Barbara Kruger, the American artist whose work often takes the form of questions and statements and is largely concerned with issues of power and authority. As though to answer the question for us, the monitors begin to broadcast a dizzying bombardment of imagery – notions of pleasure and satisfaction, excitement, desire and glamour. The effect is as though Stalin had run the world's biggest advertising agency (which, in effect, he did) and as such this entire audio-visual introduction becomes a political statement about the desire systems and vulnerability of the consumer in an age of rampant cultural materialism. It is almost asking of the audience: Are you sure you want to support the economic system which is making even this concert – your pleasure – so desirable?

And this is a fairly loaded question for a rock group to ask of their audience. But ZooTV, as a U2 show, maintains its questioning of perceptions and desires in the technological age. When Bono channel surfs the local television stations between two songs he is making the radical act of reducing the supposedly heightened atmosphere of a rock show to nothing more than seeing what's on TV – an act which might remind you of the time when the avant-garde rock group Can would include in their stage sets an area for members of the band to stop playing and just watch TV or read a newspaper: at what point does banality become a part of spectacle? Acting out the role of the satanic god of television, Bono comes across as part pantomime villain and part messianic rock star. You feel that somewhere within his performance is an act of self-portraiture – not least as he teasingly suggests to the audience that they may one day be as wealthy and as glamorous as him. As filmed at the concert in Sydney, Bono's performance is astonishing – his presence is at once clown-like and operatic as he makes his bequests of information technology to the world, their significance finely balanced – as in reality – between a blessing and a curse.

ZooTV was audacious in both its theatrical style and its political ambitions. Its very success lay in the concert's maintained reinvention of itself to address both the countries where it was being performed and its topicality; in this the show became a broader commentary on its own context, always allowing the local political climate to shed new light on the songs and their performance. This was also reflected in Bono's stage personae: where the Mirrorball Man had featured in the United States – suggesting the suave television evangelist – in Europe he was replaced by Mr MacPhisto. Thus ZooTV became a kind of quasi-journalistic theatre, as well – assuming the role of news media within the medium of rock music, yet with a dramatic ambiguity rather than hectoring dogma.

It is the muscularity of U2's musical style, when set against the flamboyance of such set pieces, which seems to maintain the dynamic of their whole performance. There is a tension between the organic rock and roll of the music and the dazzling displays of its setting which works to the benefit of both; indeed, U2 are a group whose visual imagination is all the more heightened by the solidity of their music. ZooTV can be seen as an expression of the modern world as it was seen by Walter Trevis's alien visitor, Mr Newton, in his novel – subsequently a film by Nicolas Roeg starring David Bowie, *The Man who Fell to Earth*. It presents the reality of a planet encircled by the loops of communications technology, and gorged on the compensatory pleasures of capitalism. It suggests a place where virtual reality is ubiquitous – to the point of Bono's interactive duet with Lou Reed, singing 'Satellite of Love' – and where the endeavours of human enterprise must first burrow their way through the layers of digital waste and information anxiety under which they are buried. In this much, there is a comic-book graphics element to Willie Williams's vision as a designer. In both ZooTV and PopMart he stages the notion of a near-cosmic struggle – a kind of celebrity death match in which Bono becomes parodically heroic. As filmed by David Mallet, U2's entrance to the PopMart concert – scored to the gorgeous 'Pop Music' track by the oddball electropop group M – is a further ambiguous questioning of the status and power of the rock star.

Flanked by dinner-suited, headset-wearing minders (who have become to the celebrity culture of the early 21st century what the Swiss Guard were to the Vatican City), the members of U2 are ushered along the front of the crowd in the vast Mexico City arena as though they were the super-heroic stars of a Worldwide Wrestling Federation contest. Throughout this procession, Bono mimes the part of the shadow-boxing champ. Dressed in a hooded gown, he makes his way to the main stage and its elevated catwalk. The stage itself

Popmart: 'U2 used the live show as curatorial device,' a gallery of iconic pop art and images of globalisation

resembles some mutated Japanese monster mall: its single golden arch appears to be making ironic reference to the globalized identity of McDonald's, while the rotating pop logo might well be the encoded insignia on a credit card. Elswhere in the show, the backdrop projections featured the work of the veteran American Pop artist Roy Lichtenstein, whose renditions of comic-book explosions, lovers and cops became iconic pieces of American art. The influence of American Pop art on PopMart was pronounced, with Andy Warhol's pioneering representations of Mass Age culture – which might be considered the cultural equivalent of splitting the atom – being a principal informant. In this way U2 used the live show as a curatorial device, in which the whole event becomes both a gallery and a performance space.

'Playing from the heart': Remembering the victims of the 9/11 terrorist attacks. Elevation tour, Superbowl Half-time Show, Superdome, New Orleans, February 2002

But U2 have never lost sight of their origins as a passionate, raw-throated rock band. The extraordinary productions of their live performances are always, first and foremost, intended to heighten the experience of that music. With this in mind, the group's Elevation tour of 2001 might be seen as a kind of chamber piece in comparison to the grand opera of ZooTV and PopMart. The Elevation concerts returned U2 to a more direct, unmediated relationship with their audience – foregrounding the stripped-down aesthetics of rock and roll, rather than using the potential of the rock concert as a means of broader theatre.

Elevation possessed the effective device of a heart-shaped stage, painted red, at the front of the crowd, upon which the group could perform. The punning was simple and charming, providing the notion that U2 were playing from the heart. Backed by four video screens and utilizing washes of coloured light, the visual impact was both incisive and intimate – calling to mind, perhaps, the video installations of artists such as Bruce Nauman, Douglas Gordon and Bill Viola. And as U2's live performances had always touched on a secular notion of ritual or ceremony, their listing of the names of those who died in the terrorist attacks of 9/11 – notably when the group played the US Superbowl half-time show in February 2002, to one of the biggest American television audiences ever recorded – was austere and intentionally 'unstaged'. In this it resembled the memorial to the war dead of Vietnam at Washington, in which the names of the dead are simply carved on reflective black stone.

As long ago as 1976, the American critic and novelist Tom Wolfe was suggesting that the artisan workers in the pop cultural industries – industries such as retail design, advertising, graphics and commercial film-making – were perhaps more sophisticated as contemporary communicators than many of the fine artists who so often sourced ideas and images from their work. This was – and remains – a radical but plausible suggestion. Today there is a sense in which the design and production of a major pop cultural event like a U2 rock show is better able to express the speed and strangeness of the modern world than the work of many contemporary visual artists. Indeed, the visual impact of ZooTV, far from becoming a period piece of pop fashionability, now seems a prophetic vision of a world and a mass media increasingly obsessed with reality TV. Similarly, you could argue that the lighting designs for U2 shows, and their use of video walls, is more successful, as art, than the somewhat self-referential and ponderous works by many contemporary video artists.

There is an argument that says we now live in a world of too much culture – of too much of everything, in fact, moving from one form of excess to another. Under such conditions, the awkwardness and jagged edges so necessary to genuine cultural progress become blunted and dull. And the confrontation of such excess, perhaps, is the ultimate message from the visual spectacle of U2's live performances: that in a world where rebellion itself is so often commodified by multinational corporations and communications networks, then the organic power of popular culture must derive from a conversation to which anybody can contribute, as a democracy without frontiers and an art form free of the gallery.

Art, Commerce and Logistics: Designing a U2 Show by Willie Williams

There is a wonderful myth surrounding live rock shows. Through assumption or happy denial we buy into the belief that, unlike theatre, a rock show is a spontaneous event. We let ourselves believe that each element of the show – sound, lighting, video, staging – is conceived by and somehow controlled by the performers. A theatre show brings different expectations; it would be highly unusual to see the same play two nights running and notice differences in the storyline. We love to believe, however, that a rock concert is created before our eyes and that no two nights will ever be the same. This is perhaps why there are no Oscars or Tony Awards for rock shows. Somehow, the myth of spontaneity is an important part of the enjoyment. If too much of the process is revealed, the spell might be broken.

The workings of a rock concert are unlike any other staged performance. There is no director, in the traditional sense, because the 'cast' (i.e. the band) is in charge, despite the fact that the band members are the only people in the world unable to sit and watch the live show. Also, regardless of sponsorship, the band is responsible for financing the tour, technically making them the producers as well. Given that the band also has to play the songs, it is clear that on a large tour some assistance is going to be required.

The planning of a tour is a three-cornered contest, a competitive relationship between art, commerce and logistics. My brief, as the U2 show designer, is to bring triumph to the first of these while avoiding total catastrophe in the others. Creatively, a typical rock show comes together through a series of events that are the complete reverse of the creation of a theatrical production. At the beginning of the process, the only 'given' is the cast. We know who the performers will be, but that's all. Within this vacuum of knowledge, the first requirement is to design the set, closely followed by the lighting system. At some point much further down the line, the soundtrack will be provided. Then, finally, when all else is complete, the script is written (or at least a set list is handed out).

I have worked with U2 since 1983, and bear ultimate responsibility to them for the design of the giant collaboration that is a U2 show. Even though the above general principles still apply, U2 are unique among their peers in respect of their approach to performing. They are blessed with a seemingly contradictory ability to follow their instincts and yet be extremely rigorous in their intellectual analysis of the ideas. The design process is never easy, but when it is difficult it is usually difficult for the best of reasons. U2 are possessed by an endless drive to ensure that every part of the show is absolutely the best it can be, tempered by the fact that they push themselves to at least the same degree.

Much of the strength of my 20-year collaboration with U2 comes from the fact that we work intensely together but between tours we generally don't see much of each other. Consequently, our reunion at the beginning of the design process tends to be fruitful and surprising. The band will generally be buried in the studio, alive with new directions and ideas, while I show up with new thoughts, agendas and discoveries that I have gathered on my travels.

Our discussions begin about a year before the first show. Conversations initially tend to be wide-ranging, exciting and highly abstract, but will invariably contain the kernels of ideas that eventually come to fruition. I then begin to produce a range of 'napkin' sketches, as discussion documents for our future meetings. We usually pursue at least three quite different directions to see which ideas continue to spark interest and enthusiasm. Also, in terms of technology, we have to second-guess what will be available in a year's time, so it is crucial to keep options open.

My immediate concerns are not so much to do with what the stage would look like as to what kind of show this would be. Some physical parameters will be known, such as venue sizes and approximate duration of the tour, but otherwise the canvas is completely blank, even musically. The new record will be far from finished at this point. Despite these unknowns, there are plenty of other factors that can suggest the kind of show we might want to make: how the Elevation tour, for example, might relate to the PopMart or previous tours; or what else is going on in the live music industry, in art or in the world at large. We develop a sense of the often contradictory expectations of U2's audience: fans don't necessarily want U2 to change, yet neither do they want U2 to repeat itself, so it is important to thrill and to challenge the viewers in equal measure.

In tandem with the design process, Dennis Sheehan, the tour manager, is spending every waking hour on all the other preparations. As soon as the ideas are agreed with the band, designs have to be finalized and turned into engineering drawings. Bids are sought from fabrication companies and from sound, lighting and video equipment suppliers who will eventually build or supply all of the required elements. Many of these companies have a long history of collaboration and development with U2. All the while, the tour accountants require exact financial information to ensure that budgeting remains on track, always with the possibility of modifications or rationalizations to make the numbers add up. The back-line technicians will look over the stage design and let us know their practical requirements in terms of space, access and work areas. Similar discussions involve almost the whole touring team to make sure everyone starts to get a feel for what the new performance environment will be like and to raise any potential problems as early as possible. Some of these issues are real, while some simply stem from an understandable desire to make things easier to transport, so there are often battles to be fought in maintaining the integrity of the design. This is obviously not a task I can undertake alone. Since the PopMart tour, Mark Fisher has become my primary collaborator on the overall design of U2 shows. He is enigmatically credited as the show's 'Architect', though his contribution throughout the whole process is very significant. The additional energy Mark provides is invaluable, along with that of another key collaborator, Bruce Ramus, who has been my principal lighting director since ZooTV.

The crew will typically spend two to four weeks in production rehearsals to construct the show prior to the arrival of the band. All departments come prepared. I will have spent time creating an arsenal of possible lighting and video effects, moods and atmospheres, but it is only at production rehearsals that we attempt to fit all the pieces of the puzzle together for the first time. It's a Rubik's cube of monstrous proportions and doesn't come with instructions, so it can be a tense period. At this point, loss of nerve would result in a bloodbath, so a great deal of give and take is required. In this new environment we all face an extremely steep learning curve as there is an enormous amount to achieve in never enough time. Gradually, as lighting and video are programmed, as the sound system cranks up, we near completion. The images we have seen for months in drawings, renderings and CAD models come to life as large pieces of metal and piles of equipment. Confidence rises and it becomes possible to get a feel for where we are going.

Much of the performance content of the show will be established when the band arrives at production rehearsals. Nailing down some kind of initial set list becomes my first priority; usually we will agree on a beginning, middle and end, leaving plenty of room for manoeuvre in between. Songs from the new album might occupy perhaps a third of the set, leaving much open to discussion regarding what other material will work or be appropriate in this new context. A group with this much touring history develops its own traditions from tour to tour, providing opportunities for recognition or reinterpretation, both musically and visually. There will be a good deal of experimentation when the excitement of accidental discoveries is balanced with the death of promising ideas that don't quite work in reality. A year after the initial conversations, having leapt countless hurdles, held the budget together and (just) managed not to kill each other in the process, we finally make it to the delivery table and give birth to the show. Then, after all of this, when everyone has given absolutely everything they have, the tour begins.

The society of a touring production is highly feudal, broken into various departments: band, management, accounts, sound, lighting, video, back line, wardrobe, catering, drivers. Each person on tour is respon-ssible to his or her department head, who is in turn responsible to the production or tour manager, who is in turn responsible to the band. When a show is built or deconstructed on a daily basis, in the spirit of a beehive, there is no single individual who knows how everything goes together. The crew members of each department construct their part of the production from memory and the greater whole is formed in sequence. Throughout rehearsals and at the outset of a tour, the scale of the task invariably seems insurmountable, but it usually takes only a matter of days or weeks until a routine is established, then suddenly the pyramids are being built and relocated on a daily basis.

Spectacle and communication are not necessarily mutually exclusive, but in the context of a concert the relationship between the two requires judicious balance. It is wonderful to dazzle an audience, to give them something they have never seen before, never felt before, never imagined before; despite all the eye-candy that I have been delighted to impose upon the world during U2 shows over the years, I am also painfully aware that there are periods during a concert when it is crucial to get out of the way. The focus of my task is to create a space where there is contact between the members of U2, their music and their audience, an exchange of energy in real time. In the age of home cinema and on-line entertainment, the 'live' experience is becoming increasingly rare. Audiences are becoming less used to the dynamics of live performance, an observation that drove my proposal to begin U2's Elevation show with the house lights on. The individuals in the audience could see not only the band arrive but themselves, the friends they came with, the rest of the audience and tangibly understand that they were all physically in the same room. They could be fully aware that they were in the same airspace as these people whose photograph they might have seen a million times. It's not a recording. I am really here; this is happening now and it's happening only now.

U2's shows remain unpredictable, yet the relationship between the band and the audience is real. On any given night, personal events, local events and global events can steer the emotional direction of a show. If Bono is struggling, it becomes everybody's struggle. If the 'spirit is in the house' a U2 show can amaze, even if you've seen them play a hundred times before. Beyond any amount of design, planning and stagecraft, a U2 show really does have an alchemy that is greater than the sum of its parts, so I trust that documenting the process to some degree will not break the spell.

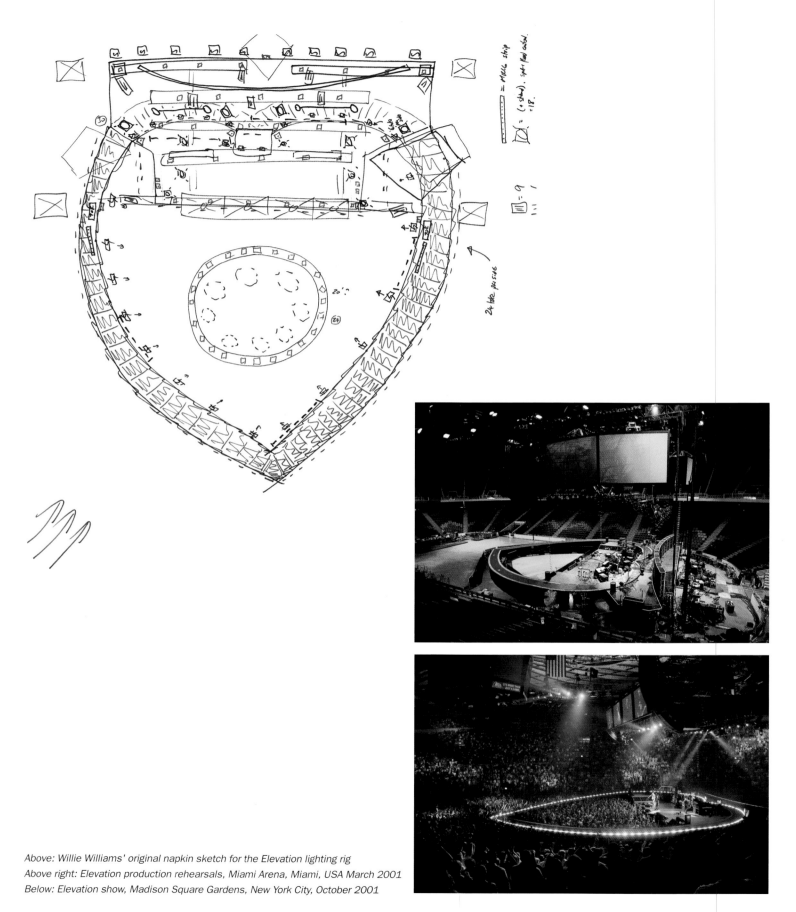

Above: Willie Williams' original napkin sketch for the Elevation lighting rig
Above right: Elevation production rehearsals, Miami Arena, Miami, USA March 2001
Below: Elevation show, Madison Square Gardens, New York City, October 2001

Interview with Paul McGuinness, Manager

When you first started, you helped to fund U2 and gave them the breathing space to develop. What did you see in them right at the very start?

Well, none of us had very much money and if I was supporting U2 there wasn't a lot of money involved. And my wife was supporting me. She was the only one who had a proper job; she was an advertising writer and I was a freelance film technician. I was an assistant director/production manager working when there was work, and sometimes for a few days at a time I was a freelance. So U2 had all left school and Edge was briefly at college, but kind of gave it up because the band was more important. Bono likewise went briefly to University College, Dublin and then was sent home because there was something wrong with his matriculation. The university discovered he hadn't passed Irish or something like that, and he had to go and resit it or something, but he never did. I came along a few months later, and I agreed to be their manager after they'd been doing gigs for a few months. I went to see them in the Project Arts Centre in Dublin in about 1978, because of Bill Graham, who was a journalist friend of mine at *Hotpress*. We went to Trinity together. He and I used to scheme and plot how we would break a band from Ireland worldwide. We'd watched this group Horslips do something like that over the previous decade and there were friends of mine in that group, including Barry Devlin, who we later worked with quite a lot in video, and their manager Michael Deeny was the elder brother of my best friend Donald Deeny. So there was that kind of contact with such Irish music business as there was, and I had dabbled in it. I'd managed a couple of other people like a folk singer called Tom Moore, and a folk/rock group called Spud who were sort of a poor man's Horslips. I got them a small record deal in England and organized touring for them in Germany, Scandinavia and England. But none of those people that I managed particularly succeeded. Horslips, on the other hand, made ten albums and had record deals with Atlantic Records and RCA – real record companies. I was a student for most of that period and I'd made up my mind that I wanted to be the manager of a big band. Or a movie producer. And my own kind of working assumption was that whichever of these two things happened first, that's what I was going to do with my life. Having said that, I had always been aware of managers, even when I was a kid. I wasn't particularly musical, but I always knew that Brian Epstein managed The Beatles. I knew that Andrew Oldham managed the Rolling Stones. I knew that Albert Grossman was Bob Dylan's manager and I kind of knew what there was to know about those sorts of people. It was definitely a clear objective of mine to be one of them.

They were your role models?

In a way, yes. I thought this must be a great, enjoyable thing to do, and I thought I'd probably be good at it. But obviously you need a great client to be a great manager. Once you've got a great client it's a cakewalk, and that's really the heart of it. Get a good client and then trust them. Trust their instincts, get them to trust you, don't be scared of the money, don't be scared of having too much or indeed too little. Use the money like fuel. You just have to have enough to get to the next place.

And that's how you felt about U2 when you met them?

When I saw them in the Project I agreed to be their manager on the spot. But after that we kind of circled each other for a few months, trying to figure out how serious we all were. And I think it was during that period that

Edge was kind of in and out of college and we gradually got more serious, started making tapes. They had won a recording session before I met them, as part of a talent contest, but it had gone very badly wrong. Whoever was producing it was incompetent and they lost Edge's guitar completely in the mix. They had not enjoyed the experience of recording and there was even a theory knocking around at one point that they were going to be a band that didn't make records at all. So the idea of being a great live attraction was there from the very beginning. The commitment to performance was there. And there was this guy called Maddox Flynn who was a kind of an actor in the Project Arts Centre which was run, at that time, by Jim Sheridan, who later became a movie director. Mannix Flynn gave the band, I think all four of them, some acting lessons and mime lessons. So you can see the beginningsof something.

What were the qualities that instantly drew you to them?

I thought they were doing badly and inexpertly all the things that they now do well. The basic ingredients haven't really changed: where they stand on stage, what they play. That's what excited people, I think. This thing with four guys on stage making big noise. A great guitar player, charismatic front man, steady bass, you know. Adam's not a flamboyant bass player, but he keeps the engine running. Larry, who was, in the early days, I think it's fair to say, not that great a drummer, became one of the world's really great drummers. And he works very, very hard at that, and, you know, was ambitious musically in a way that was most impressive in the early days. Edge is one of those natural musicians who can pick up pretty well any instrument and make music with it a minute later. Things come easily to Edge musically. Bono is a very ambitious musician, and has an enormous kind of musical imagination, but he doesn't have the technique that Edge has. Nonetheless, he's got a sort of visceral understanding of what makes rock and roll music and, obviously, he's one of the greatest front men in history. Nothing really has changed is what I suppose I'm saying. It has been a very long time, yes. But the reason they've continued for such a long time is that they continue to improve. Each of their records has been better than the previous one. I think if they started repeating themselves or treading water musically they would probably dissolve. So the future of U2 lies very much on a straight road. As long as they keep enjoying it and satisfying themselves. I mean, they are their own toughest critics. Really, no one else counts. In fact, U2 has always been determined not to allow the records, if you like, to dominate their career. U2's earliest success was purely as a live act.

They didn't have a hit album until 1983 with *War*. *The Unforgettable Fire* did better. The live album, *Under a Blood Red Sky*, was a surprising success. It was a bit of an accident. It came out of the live concert at Red Rocks, and Jimmy Iovine, who is now the head of Interscope Records, produced that in the studio. We invested all the money we made out of that tour to shoot the concert film. There was a tour profit of something like $25,000. We got in a couple of partners like Barry Fey and the record company, but we ended up controlling and owning it. Steve Lillywhite mixed the sound. (Funnily enough, he's now an executive for Universal Records, running Mercury in London. We're still in close touch with a lot of the people we started out with.) I looked at the sales figures the other day: *Under a Blood Red Sky* seems to have sold about ten million copies. It's one of our most successful records. So putting their money where their mouths were was always part of the way U2 did things. Sometimes with very disastrous results, with financially uncomfortable results. But they did that from the beginning and the character of the band as a live attraction, even when the records weren't selling, was established very early on.

What do you remember about the touring industry when you first started?

Well, our tour agents in Britain in the early days were almost more important than the record company.

We were determined to have a live career that would protect us, if you like, from any missteps with the records. We wanted to have an audience that we built up through performing live but which did not depend on record success. Ian Flooks was our agent everywhere around the world but North America. In North America, again, one of the most important alliances was with Frank Barsalona of Premiere Talent and Barbara Skydel was his kind of deputy there. She was really U2's 'responsible agent', the term they use. We'd all pay very close attention to detail and to territories, playing the right places, not overdoing it, always trying to sell out, you know? If there was a risk of not selling out in a larger venue we would err on the side of caution and play the smaller venue. It's a very important thing to leave every town, if you can, with people knowing that they could not get into that gig unless they bought a ticket early on. That was an absolutely vital and palpable part of the way we did things. I remember the great difficulty of getting any kind of recognition in a club. There'd be a band playing on a dark stage at the other end and you'd have no idea who they were. So getting the name 'U2' right visually was quite important. Our earliest attempt to do that was a construction made out of red plastic drainpipes spelling out 'U2'. We used to erect that at the back of the stage I think even before we had a record deal, and try to get people to recognize that U2 were on the stage. There's an old photograph from the Dandelion Market where we have a banner behind the band saying 'U2'. That was our earliest attempt at establishing an identity, otherwise nobody knew who it was. 'U2' is such a great graphic; it always looks bigger than anything else on a poster where there are other names and that was something we took advantage of.

Would you say that U2 were breaking new ground in those days?

I think it was very traditional, in a way. It was just applying the common-sense rules of show business to rock and roll. We also knew that there would be more excitement in a venue where people could stand up. We fought long battles over the years to try to get audiences on their feet, which was largely prohibited in arenas in America. We finally accomplished that on the Elevation tour. That was always the kind of the circle of energy that we try to achieve. And it was harder always in America, with box-office corruption and people selling on their own tickets. Inevitably we found that the people at the front in a seated audience were the people who had the most money, and they're not the most exciting people to have in the front row. So we tried to subvert that in many different ways over the years, trying to distribute tickets through the fan club, relocating people from elsewhere in the building. There were lots of things that U2 pioneered in that respect. We had some difficulties even with the Elevation tour, though, where the heart was the most kind of desirable place for a member of the audience to stand. We found that some of the audience travelled with the tour and would queue up for tickets at each venue. The same people would end up in the front row every day. That was a problem because they would sometimes sit there and watch the band and when something happened that was unexpected or different they would shake their heads and be almost put out. That's offputting for the band too. It's a constant battle to try to keep the show fresh. Obviously the freshness of the show conceals the fact that there is a script. I mean, there is a lighting script, a running order, there are things that have been rehearsed and practised. But you still try to make the show as spontaneous as it possibly can be. For this U2 rely enormously on Bono's own genuine spontaneity and his kind of candid response to the environment he's in to get that excitement. There was a great mix of scripted theatre and spontaneity in ZooTV. The first really great production I think we ever did was ZooTV. That will be remembered for ever as a groundbreaking, state-of-the-art show. There was a lot of sleight of hand there, a lot of things that appeared to be spontaneous were actually rehearsed. The idea of tuning in on a random basis to whatever was on satellite

TV: nobody would risk that going wrong on the night, so that was carefully programmed. We took on that technology at its earliest stage; those big screens had really only just been invented. And we had to pay for those screens ourselves even though they were made by Philips, who owned our record company. That was a bit of a disappointment. It also meant that the tour was pretty close to break even. If we'd had a bit of support from them it might have made a profit. The ZooTV tour, was great fun to do: it evolved from an arena show into a spectacular stadium show. And that was really the first time that Willie Williams and Mark Fisher worked on a grand scale with us.

It must have been spectacularly difficult to manage.

The tour itself was a headache to run because the band was extremely nervous of ticket-price inflation. They would not allow me and the agents and the promoters to let that ticket price go up enough to secure a profit. If we'd had just another couple of dollars, five dollars, on the ticket it would have been a different story. And I don't say that with regret, because I'm sure it was, you know, an investment in the audience that developed over the years. On the whole, U2's touring career has been pretty much successful in every territory over 20 years, with the exception of PopMart.

Why PopMart?

Well, you could say it started with the record, which wasn't really finished and wasn't as successful as we had hoped it would be. The things that we thought were sure-fire hits were not. We all believed that 'Staring at the Sun' was a solid-gold hit and all we had to do was release it and it would go to number one everywhere and it didn't. We were so wrong. We made a crap video for it. And you know you can't really argue with the public. We also had this situation where the tour had been booked before the album was finished. And putting that tour together we underestimated the difficulties of moving it around. At one point there were 90 trucks and three stages and the logistics were pretty much out of control from the beginning. We would have liked a reduced form of the show, but no acceptable design solution to that was ever produced. It was very difficult to make that enormous screen work reliably, and we'd kind of bought in to the idea on the basis of it being modular. It wasn't modular and it went wrong an awful lot: it was always slightly patchy. It was still wildly impressive, but I don't have particularly happy memories of that tour. Also, having no reduced version of it meant that we were determined – maybe too determined – to prove the point, and we took the show to South America and Japan and South Africa and Australia in its full form. That cost the earth. I'll never forget seeing those Antonovs at the airport, huge cargo planes. I hate Antonovs, I never want to see another one as long as I live. I'd get midnight phone calls from somebody loading a plane saying, 'Oh, I just discovered we need another 747 because we can't get all the steel in.' I mean, we were flying pieces of steel around the world on Antonovs and 747s! You know, you can rent steel in South America, in South Africa, but not us! We were carrying our own steel in aeroplanes! It was stupid. It was the lowest point in our logistical history and I think some of our own people were way out of their depth. A lot of lessons were learned. For the band and for myself it was this awful feeling of waking up every morning knowing that another quarter of a million dollars had been spent. It was frightening. And we never got it under control; the tour didn't make any money.

So everything changed with Elevation?

Yes. There was no great appetite to go outdoors. Not because we couldn't, but because the songs on the *All That You Can't Leave Behind* album were much more interior, more intimate, and the show reflected that. We had a great idea, which was the heart. You always need some great idea and that was it. And once that idea came through it was pretty much plain sailing and we could build on that. And that solved all our problems, that design. And once that design was fixed in everyone's mind and agreed with the safety authorities, it became a selling process. You'd see it in the trade magazines at the beginning of the Elevation tour, predictions that people were going to get hurt on the floor. In fact, Elevation was one of the safest indoor productions ever. I don't think anyone was hurt in the course of the whole tour.

How do you manage to control the budgets?

A very important part of the Elevation tour, was that we started with a budget, believe it or not, for the first time. We had never worked to a budget before. We said, 'This is what we're going to spend.' Belatedly we were imposing a discipline that we should have imposed much, much earlier. Anyway, we had a lot of fun with the other tours and didn't make much money, but we made some money this time with Elevation.

Why has U2 never accepted sponsorship for a tour?

Well, I wouldn't rule it out for ever. We've always had this view that rock and roll is one of the great images of freedom and independence. You have to be very careful with the audience who have, if you like, invested so much in that proposition and who to some extent vicariously live through a performer or a band. I think sponsorship is very hard for the audience. It's not hard for an audience in pop music, but in the sort of music that U2 write, where there's a real resonance, an emotional and political resonance, it just makes people uncomfortable. Bruce Springsteen is another case: I don't think he has ever had a corporate sponsor. We've been able to avoid it so far. I wouldn't rule it out, and we do use some sponsors in media. That's a normal thing around the world. We very often have a television station and a newspaper involved in advertising the concert. Would we ever have somebody like Microsoft? If it was somebody whose technology we were actually using in our work that would be fine. I mean, if Philips all that time ago for ZooTV had wished to sponsor the tour, it would have been entirely appropriate and it would have changed everything. We keep an open mind about it, I think. But we are always aware that the audience need to be brought along with decisions like that. *Dublin, December 2003*

Adam Clayton, The Edge, Paul McGuinness, Bono, Aislinn Evans and Larry Mullen Jr in Dublin, 1979

Boy, War, October, The Unforgettable Fire 1979–1985

Boy, War, October, The Unforgettable Fire

When a young band begins to make music, it would be a rare thing if their immediate concerns included lighting. More pressing issues are: mastery of instruments, writing great songs, finding a distinctive sound, getting gigs and generally making ends meet. Aspirations towards any kind of stage production have to remain a speck on the distant horizon for the time being. Similarly, once a band begins to perform regularly, audio requirements take priority – reliable back-line gear, a good sound system and a regular sound engineer. Most pubs and clubs have their own lighting system, or a least a few lamps to point at the stage, so until some measure of success is achieved this has to suffice in the visual department.

U2 appeared in the post-punk euphoria of the late 1970s and early 1980s, when any band worth its salt would have gagged at the notion that they were in show business. Real bands were about raw energy and 'authenticity', leaving elaborate stage productions to dinosaurs like ELO or to trivial pop acts. Even so, in tandem with their increasing mastery of musicianship, U2 were concerned about every aspect of their live show, visual presentation included. By necessity the stance was extremely simple but it was considered; the early U2 aesthetic was formed as much by their reaction against the bubblegum artifice of mainstream pop as it was by their attraction towards the primitive directness of punk rock.

My tenure with U2 was preceded by a series of lighting personnel who worked with the group to develop a distinct look for small venues. They were Jake Kennedy (who eventually became U2's production manager until PopMart), Ian England, Lin Scoffin (who to this day remains a truck driver on U2's European tours) and Angus McPhail, whose design I took over for the War tour. The elements were bold and simple: red flooring, white flags, a portrait of the boy from the *War* album cover, camouflage netting, stark lighting. The overall feel was something like the set for a Brecht play, elemental and symbolic rather than literal or narrative, and was well suited to the primary colours of the music U2 produced at the time. As the War tour progressed the show developed, with additions made to accommodate larger audiences, until the production found its natural home at the Red Rocks amphitheatre in Colorado. Nestled amongst mountainous outcrops, with bonfires burning, swirling fog and a conveniently atmospheric thunderstorm, the War tour was filmed to become *Under a Blood Red Sky* and rarely has a venue been more suited to a stage production.

At the very end of the War tour came U2's first tour of Japan. This provided the mood for much of the material for their following album, as well as its title, *The Unforgettable Fire*. When the album was released, the accompanying tour was going to have to deal with larger venues, including North American arenas (around 15,000 people indoors). There had been some arena shows on the War tour (three, to be precise), which had been more of a survival exercise than a triumph. Nonetheless, the band had come through this rite of passage relatively unscathed and the experience had served to illustrate that a change of tactics was needed in both performance and production.

Ironically, designing a production that is distinct and powerful, yet ultra-simple, can be a far greater challenge than designing a glitzy spectacle, especially when venues begin to increase in size.

There were very real growing pains as the band and production team tried to find a way in which U2 could perform to larger audiences without compromising their stance of underplayed minimalism. A number of experiments ensued: there were expressionist backdrops, rear-screen projections, unfurling white banners and an investigation of the nascent technology of computerized moving lights. Some of the ideas were admirable and worked to a degree, but it was evident that they weren't entirely appropriate. However, it also became evident that, despite the increase in venue size, there was still sufficient power in the connection between U2 and their audience to fill an arena without resorting to clever props. Many of these props were just getting in the way, so we started to remove them, giving the show some breathing space. The Unforgettable Fire tour finished its run with a clean, simple show that allowed the band to grow and to develop their stagecraft in bigger halls. More importantly, we had all come to understand how large U2's performance could be. Their power of connection, which had electrified clubs and theatres, had now grown to a scale sufficient to reach the back walls of an arena unaided. From a production point of view, this was good news indeed. *WW*

You see we built this band around a spark –
we could only play three chords when we started,
but we knew there was an excitement within the
four people, and even when playing to just ten
people we seemed to communicate that. We put
our lives on the line and just kind of went for it.
Bono

U2's music has many different elements.
If someone comes along to a concert and is
inspired to join Amnesty that's one part of it,
but someone else may feel emotionally overwhelmed by the music, and someone else again
may just come along to jump up and down and
bop. They're all relevant; they're all important.
They're intertwined, and to put emphasis on
one element is wrong. Larry Mullen Jnr

When U2 played the US Festival
I climbed to the very top of the stage,
it was like hundreds of feet up,
and I walked across the top of it
on the canvas, and the canvas ripped.
God! I can't watch that. I don't know
who the person is. I don't know who
it is, climbing up there. Cos I'm
afraid of heights anyway. Y'know,
the adrenalin is a drug and it can go
right or wrong in you, and I have to
learn to deal with it, that's all. Bono

Top: November 1984, Wembley Stadium, London. Bottom: September 1984, Australia

I don't like music unless it has a healing effect. I don't like it when people leave concerts still feeling edgy. I want people to leave our concerts feeling positive, a bit more free. Bono

To me a rock 'n' roll concert is 3-D. It's a physical thing – it's rhythm for the body. It's a mental thing in that it should be intellectually challenging. But it's also a spiritual thing, because it's a community, it's people agreeing on something even if it's only for an hour and a half. Bono

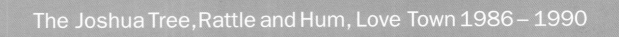

The Joshua Tree, Rattle and Hum, Love Town 1986 – 1990

The Joshua Tree, Rattle and Hum, Love Town

The Joshua Tree was U2's global coming of age; their status in North America confirmed by number-one singles, Grammy awards and the cover of *Time* magazine. The Joshua Tree tour was initially conceived for indoor arenas, of around 15,000 people. Having learned from the growing experience of The Unforgettable Fire tour, there was easy consensus on the parameters of the required design. The stage and lighting needed to be understated, with the focus drawn towards the group rather than towards the special effects. The venue capacities were to be maximized by selling seats right round the sides and back of the stage, demanding unobstructed sightlines from all directions. The stage needed to be wide and clean with all the tech areas hidden, leaving U2 alone on-stage with their amps and drum kit. Essentially it was to be minimalism on a grand scale so the new challenge was to work within this aesthetic yet produce a powerful stage design with a unique character.

Developments in lighting technology had by this time made computerized moving lights ubiquitous. I felt that rock-show design was becoming uniform as a result, though I could see the huge benefits of a lighting fixture that could move and change colour automatically. It seemed, perhaps, that we could have the best of both worlds by using follow spots; spotlights mounted above the stage, each with a human operator sitting up in the metalwork overhead. Follow spots: have a very pleasing feel because, being manually operated, they have a natural, human movement rather than looking like mechanical devices. I eventually mounted a total of 23 spotlights in the rigging, each accompanied by its own operator, leaving the trussing above the stage visibly inhabited by nearly two dozen people. These proved to be exhilarating shows, the relationship between U2 and their audience having developed into an extremely powerful source of energy. The production gestures remained simple but had finally developed a distinctive style: the stage back-lit by just three gigantic theatre lights, the band standing in pools of white light, Bono illuminating Edge's guitar solo with a handheld lamp at point-blank range. U2 finally had a show big enough fill an arena on their own terms: arresting, unique, yet apparently effortless.

As ticket demand vastly exceeded expectation, dates in stadiums (up to 70,000 people outdoors) were added to the arena shows. Being on tour there was little opportunity to reinvent the stage production, so the arena aesthetic was simply extrapolated to stadium scale. There was much debate over the use of video screens for camera close-ups. Touring video systems were just becoming available but there was concern that there would be a danger of dividing the audience's attention between the stage and the video screen. U2's Joshua Tree show was based completely on live contact between band and audience, so there was a fear that the introduction of TV cameras might unbalance this dynamic. The whole thing might fall apart. Clearly, though, in such vast buildings some visual enhancement would be necessary for the furthest seats, so a compromise was reached for the North American stadium shows. A video screen was mounted behind the mixer tower so that viewers far away would see close-ups, but the audience nearer the stage would not be distracted.

In terms of performance, the shows were very successful, with U2 finding the required personal resources to face such enormous numbers of people; but in terms of production it was here that the minimalist aesthetic probably came unravelled to some degree. I recall playing Wembley Stadium without even a backdrop, never mind video, because of high winds. The only saving grace may have been that production expectations were much lower at that time, but it is a little toe-curling to think of it now. As ever, we learned as a team and took the experience on board for the next time around.

The Joshua Tree tour was recorded for posterity in the film *Rattle and Hum* by Phil Joanou. Phil's great achievement was to capture on film what the Joshua Tree shows felt like live, collaborating with directors of photography Jordan Cronenweth (creator of the *Bladerunner* aesthetic) for the colour sequences and Phil's long-time colleague Robert Brinkmann for the black-and-white. *Rattle and Hum* was shot on film, not video, so required almost totally relighting. Once again, making this happen while on tour was a monumental task, but it was completed in only two film shoots. There was a pleasing symmetry in that the black-and-white footage was shot at McNichols Arena in Denver, only a few miles from Red Rocks. This was followed with a Ben Hur-scale colour shoot at two specially added outdoor shows in Tempe, Arizona, next door to the arena where the tour had commenced. Truck upon truck of additional lighting and camera equipment was brought in. Days of rehearsal and long nights of lighting exposure tests were required.

Predictably, once the show started the entire plan went out of the window almost within minutes. The band made a spontaneous change to the set list, throwing in 'Out of Control', which livened up proceedings while completely baffling the film crews. Carefully prepared light levels and exposures went to the four winds as soon as Bono jumped off the stage; and, best of all, some audience members decided that the additional lighting posts amongst the seats were nothing more than a vibe-crusher and dismantled them. The meticulously prepared film shoot turned into a stadium-sized busk, but Phil kept his nerve. The camera crews got a crash course in spontaneity and the result was to get on film a real sense of what it felt like on the night.

Following the release of the *Rattle and Hum* film, the three-month Love Town tour took U2 on two tangents. Musically, U2 were experimenting with roots music and had invited B.B. King and his band to join them for the whole tour. Visually, Bono wanted to move on from the tried and trusted stark monochrome to reflect the colour and feeling associated with his time in El Salvador, which had spawned some of the material on the *Joshua Tree* album. The staging was given a make-over by Chilean artist Rene Castro. A colourful backdrop design revealed different images under different lighting conditions: a snake, a guitar, a hawkmoon, a dollar sign, the Amnesty International candle. Similarly, the lighting itself also began to introduce colour and shadowplay. Most significantly, another experiment was that U2 were playing multiple nights in each city, up to nine shows in some cases. This allowed the group to experiment both musically and with their performance. It gave the production team time to try out new ideas too. By the end of the tour we were in the rare position of having more new ideas in the bag than when we had started. On New Year's Eve 1989 Bono announced from the stage in Dublin, live to the world via radio broadcast, that U2 were 'going to go away for a while to dream it all up again'. *WW*

Being a singer is a terrible responsibility.
I sometimes get the odd twinge that I wouldn't
mind playing lead guitar, just like a couple of
notes, but that's about as near as I would
want to get to the front. It looks so frightening
being the singer. Especially from where I am.
You know, Bono disappears into the audience
and you don't know what is happening. You just
have to play on and hope for the best, but it's
very worrying. But I trust his judgement,
I really do, he has an instinct for these things . . .
but it doesn't stop you worrying. I don't always
understand it, but I trust it. Larry Mullen Jnr

64 / July 1987, Hippodrome de Vincennes, Paris, France

66 / May 1988, *Rattle and Hum* film shoot, The Point, Dublin, Ireland

68 / Filming *Rattle and Hum* during Joshua Tree tour, 1987

Overleaf: film stills from *Rattle and Hum*. Above: filming *Rattle and Hum* during Joshua Tree tour, 1987 / **69**

With U2, it's the music that makes the atmosphere. There's no laser show, no special effects. And we always make sure that the sound is as good at the back end as it is down in front. If we succeed or fail, it's definitely down to our own ability to communicate the music. The Edge

The spirit that we found that was always in our music is stronger now. It's exciting for a rock and roll band to strip itself right down, to take off all recognizable signs and just bash away and say, 'This is still us.' Bono

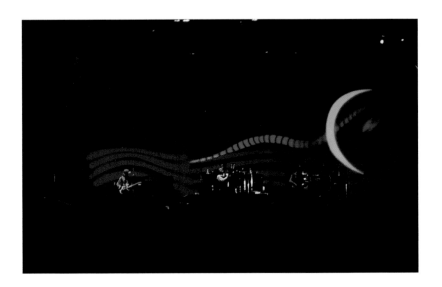

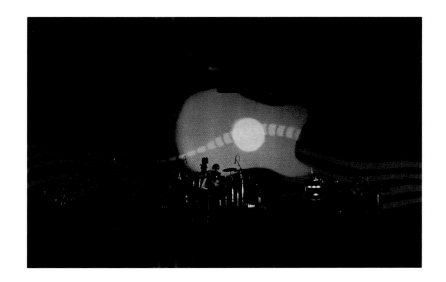

ZooTV 1991–1993

ZooTV

In the spring of 1991, having just got home from U2's self-imposed exile in Berlin, Bono telephoned asking me to join him in Tenerife where he and the band were going to explore the carnival. He told me they were making the most exciting album of their career and that it would demand a live show unlike any they had done before. He had a phrase in his head, 'Zoo TV', which he felt was a key to something, and he had an absurd pair of oversized sunglasses, which he felt were important too.

In Tenerife we had plenty of time to talk, as Anton Corbijn photographed the band on various beaches, in bars, dressing up in women's clothing and so forth. They had also air-freighted a small German car (a Trabant) to the island, so I knew something was up. Initial ideas included a stage resembling a massive record player, a giant clock and, inexplicably, the sound system being suspended inside a giant paper bag. Evidently, it was time to loosen the leash on our collective imagination.

As ever, I had brought my own agenda to the reunion. Touring video systems were still in their early days, mainly consisting of off-stage screens showing camera close-ups. It was very clear to me that there was potential to take rock show video to a level as yet undreamed of, and my goal was to create a giant video installation that was part of the physical staging; to use cameras as props, to use television images, static interference, video wallpaper. The following day it was Bono who came back with the final piece of the puzzle. He said we should issue a press release saying that U2 were taking a TV station on tour. We should not only bring live satellite images into the stage screens but also send out live broadcasts from every show – to individual homes, to space stations, TV channels, you name it. This immediately became the only idea that anyone was taking seriously and there was no further mention of giant paper bags from that point onwards. Meetings continued in Dublin over the following months. As a counterpoint to video screens, I was keen to introduce some interesting physical elements into the staging. So I proposed the pleasantly surreal notion of constructing a lighting system out of Trabants. They could be hollowed out, painted up and suspended from the ceiling with a big bright light source inside them. Once everyone had picked themselves up off the floor and stopped laughing, this too was given the go-ahead.

During the design process, ZooTV gained much strength from having the group so committed to the idea, as well as their occasional refusal to take no for an answer. A case in point was another important physical element, which became known as the 'B-stage'. For years Bono had wanted some kind of runway from the stage into the audience, but traditional issues of public safety had always been cited to kill this idea. This time there was to be no compromise and eventually we overcame the logistical hurdles with a runway disguised as a camera platform, so as not to spoil the surprise for the audience. Within a couple of years this idea of a second stage out in the crowd became an industry standard.

A great deal of video material was going to be needed for the screens, so initially we produced a 'starter kit' of footage made by myself, Mark Pellington (the godfather of hyperactive television) and Brian Eno (the godfather of ambient video wallpaper). This gave us sufficient variety to get the show on its feet, after which new additions were made almost daily.

It only took a couple of shows to establish ZooTV as the new identity of U2, and as the tour gained momentum the ideas simply ran away with us. With joy and amazement we discovered that ZooTV was a show that could be everything at once – big, small, serious, stupid, profound, crass, simple, complex, fun, frightening – and nothing needed justification. It was an infectiously creative atmosphere as ideas came in from all quarters. The touring technical team embraced the challenge of turning the ideas into reality on a moment-by-moment basis.

Help was enlisted from an ever-growing list of collaborators. It seemed that ZooTV was a concept so broad and user-friendly that almost anyone with a good idea could join in. Production manager Jake Kennedy, entirely of his own volition, hired the services of a belly dancer who had been hanging around at the stage door during rehearsals. Designers Mark Fisher and Jonathan Park were engaged to reinvent the physical staging of the show to the proportions required to fill a stadium. Artist Catherine Owens, who had initially been recruited to paint the Trabant designs, researched video makers to broaden the material available. New pieces were made by Kevin Godley, Mark Neale and the extraordinary E.B.N. (Emergency Broadcast Network), who assembled a new intro sequence featuring George Bush Senior rapping to the Queen anthem 'We Will Rock You'.

The show continued to grow and expand beyond the confines of the venue. Bono flicked through satellite TV channels with his own remote control to show world news, soft porn or home shopping. We communicated by email with a Russian cosmonaut stuck in space. There were live TV links to MTV, phone calls from the stage to the White House or to the local pizza delivery service. The male half of Abba joined U2 on stage in Stockholm playing 'Dancing Queen' beneath a mirrorball Trabant as the show was broadcast live to a single home in Nottingham. Even audience members could appear in the show via the Video Confessional, where confessions were videotaped in the afternoon and broadcast from the stage that same night. It was all real: from the Trabants to the phone calls to the TV pictures. We let luck play a part and took our chances as to what might appear from night to night. Nothing was faked – well, nothing except the bank notes fired into the audience at the end of the gig.

As new technology became available it was incorporated into the show. When ZooTV entered stadiums to become the ZooTV Outside Broadcast, giant projection screens were added. Trabants appeared on cranes, radio masts filled the horizon and gigantic message boards ran news and share prices. The projection screens became video walls as the Outside Broadcast went to Europe and became Zooropa. Bono's silver-suited preacher mutated into Mr MacPhisto, a demented thespian in gold platform soles who gave European politicians a hard time on the phone.

The riggers took control of the party calendar, mounting impressive after-show spectacles of their own. A crew soccer tournament produced no fewer than five 11-a-side teams, including one women's team. Press reporters joined the tour from publications as diverse as *Vogue*, *Scientific American* and *Auto Week*. The band decided they were having such a good time that they'd record another album right there and then, and we set up daily live link-ups to the war in Sarajevo.

We were giddy with the success and excitement of it all and, in the most glorious way, ZooTV spiralled beyond the control of any of the individuals involved. Expecting anything and surprised by nothing, all we could do was keep running until the tour finally came to an end in Tokyo almost two full years later, in the presence of Madonna and Deep Purple.

I can say with absolute confidence that there will never be another rock tour like it. *WW*

For quite a while, we sort of defined ourselves in contrast to all those early eighties British groups who only had irony, who hid behind a wink. That whole thing of clever-clever lyrics at the expense of soul. I've always preferred Van Morrison or Bob Marley, to be quite honest. But, in retrospect, I think we followed that idea through to the end, and now it's time for a new attitude. I guess the big difference is now we've discovered that irony is not necessarily the enemy of the soul. The Edge

94 / August 1992, Hersheypark Stadium, Hershey, USA

August 1992, Giants Stadium, New Jersey, USA

96 / Above: August 1992, New York, USA

Above and left: November 1992, Palacio de Los Deportes, Mexico City, Mexico / ZooTV / **97**

This is our reward for ten years' of restraint. The Edge

100 / Top and bottom right: August 1992, Hersheypark Stadium, Hershey, USA. Bottom left: September 1992, Veterans' Stadium, Philadelphia, USA

Top: August 1992, Hersheypark Stadium, Hershey, USA. Bottom: August 1992, Foxboro Stadium, Foxboro, USA / ZooTV / **101**

There is a lot of soul – I think it shines even brighter amidst the trash and the junk. Sam Shepard said, 'Right in the centre of contradiction, that's the place to be.' And rock and roll has more contradictions than any art form. U2 spent the eighties trying to resolve some of them. Now we've started the nineties celebrating them. Rock and roll is ridiculous. It's absurd. In the past U2 was trying to duck that. Now we're wrapping our arms around it and giving it a great big kiss. It's like I say onstage: 'Some of this bullshit is pretty cool.' Bono

Above and left: August 1992, Foxboro Stadium, Foxboro, USA / ZooTV / **107**

The media has rock and roll by the balls. They draw cartoons, and it's indelible ink. It's an attempt to reduce you, your humanity, your sense of humour. The only way to deal with it is to create a cartoon even bigger. Which is where this show comes in. Bono

112 / Left and centre: November 1992, Palacio de Los Deportes, Mexico City, Mexico. Right: August 1992, Hersheypark Stadium, Hershey, USA

/ May 1993, Feyenoord Stadium, Rotterdam, Holland

May 1992, Palau Sant Jordi, Barcelona, Spain

116 / Top: August 1992, Foxboro Stadium, Foxboro, USA. Bottom: August 1992, Hersheypark Stadium, Hershey, USA

*If you thought we were
over the top in the past,
check this out.* Bono

Humour and laughter, to me, are the proof of
the presence of freedom. The Berlin Dadaists,
for example, were powerful in their time because
they had the ability to unzip the pants of the
starched trousers of these fascists and mock
them. And they were outlawed because of that.
And I really feel there is a lot to be learned from
that. I've certainly learned a lot from that,
philosophically and in terms of expressing myself
through our art. The potential for subversion in
humour is something new to U2. Bono

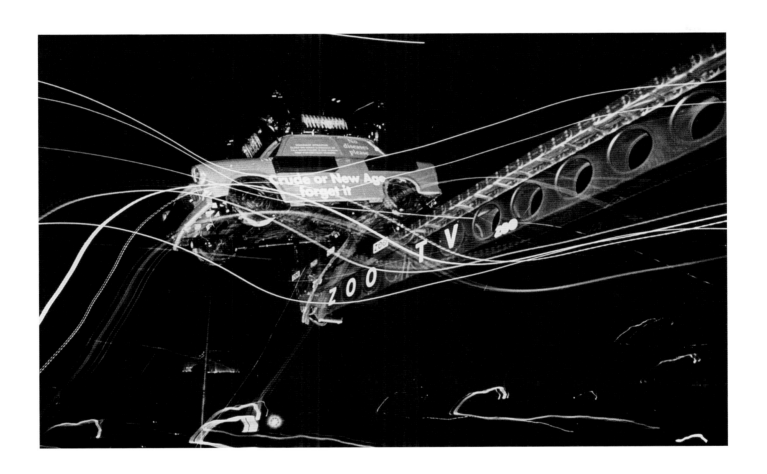

PopMart 1996–1998

PopMart

The circumstances surrounding what became the PopMart tour were unique for U2 in several ways, none less significant than the fact that this would be their first all-outdoor tour, playing stadiums from day one. There was also a very direct (and very rare) brief to me that this tour would be 'design-led', rather than being intimidated by scale or logistics. Having proved to themselves and to the world with ZooTV that, in terms of what can be toured, 'anything is possible', U2 were of a mind that the only limits to be placed on the creative ambitions of this tour were to be financial ones.

Following ZooTV, I wasn't interested in producing another video-based show for U2 unless it was going to be entirely different and a significant step forward from its predecessor. Consequently, my initial proposals to U2 in early 1996 were very physical designs, including a centre-stadium production with a racetrack surrounding the field area to be colonized by trucks, motorbikes and mobile staging.

From the beginning of the design process I had asked Mark Fisher to collaborate with me on the entire design. I wanted this to be a complete, unified design incorporating all the required technical elements, so Mark's architectural background and his enthusiasm for the oversized, exaggerated simplicity of designs by architects such as Morris Lapidus and Oscar Niemeyer seemed right on the money. As ever, we followed many avenues simultaneously, sometimes chasing the band's suggested album title possibilities. There was one show concept based around the end of the millennium ('U2000'), another involving a huge mobile disco ('discotheque'), another was a huge crashing wave and yet another a vast concrete bunker. Ultimately, though, designs inspired by colourful streamlined façades of American post-war suburban shopping outlets seemed most promising. Mark and I constructed a fantasy 'entertainment outlet' which, when the *Pop* title was confirmed, I christened the PopMart. To sell the point, Mark drew a version of the stage transformed into a supermarket, complete with shoppers' trolleys, an image of which was eventually incorporated into the *Pop* album artwork.

One of the longest-running debates surrounded the use of video, there being an agreement that this was an avenue only worth following if we could reinvent the wheel to the same degree as we had with ZooTV. Some way into the design process, returning from a trip to Japan, Mark brought news of a significant advance in LED (light-emitting diode) technology which might allow us to do just that. It seemed that it might now be possible to create video pixels (the elements that make up a video screen), which could be deployed independently of a traditional support structure. The pixels might be attached to fabric to make a huge video curtain draped around the stage, or perhaps the pixels could be spread apart, exploding the screen.

I had observed for years that video screens intended for outdoor use in daylight were vastly too bright for indoor or evening concerts, when most screens would be used at about 10 per cent of their brightness. If the pixels of a video screen are spread apart, the image will become significantly dimmer and softer. It seemed clear that there was sufficient headroom to be able to spread the pixels a long way and still retain an acceptable video image, particularly if viewed from any kind of distance. Doing this, however, also results in the screen becoming bigger exponentially in both directions. Once Mark and I began to believe that we might be able to build the largest video screen ever seen on our planet, the idea of a second video-based show gained much appeal.

After several months of experiments and demonstrations, U2 confirmed that they were prepared to take the risk of building the show around this unproven and enormously expensive theory. A video screen would be made that was ten times the size of all the ZooTV screens put together; approximately 52 metres wide and 15 metres tall, or about the size of a five-storey office building. A Canadian company, SACO, would custom-build the LED video pixels, while a Belgian company, System Technologies, would engineer and build the folding 'picket fence' supporting the pixels. For the screen alone, this would require an investment from U2 of around $7 million. The final, vital decision was exactly how far apart to spread the pixels. Playing safe and putting them closer together would greatly reduce the size of the screen, while spreading the pixels too far apart would render the images illegible. I was left to make the final decision on this myself, only a matter of weeks before the beginning of the tour, so it was an extraordinarily stressful period until I was finally able to phone the U2 studio from a field in Belgium to confirm that the screen images were clear, bright and beautiful.

Having decided to base the staging around the largest video screen ever constructed, it was clear that a very major consideration would be the material to be shown on it. The two main characteristics of the LED screen were its low resolution and its ability to produce colours of more intense and saturated hues than regular television. Both of these factors led us towards using animated imagery, with its links to Pop Art. Catherine Owens, who had worked with U2 on ZooTV, undertook a major research project to source new and interesting directions for material. She dug through countless college showreels and degree shows, and her relationship with the New York art world was to prove very fruitful. Eventually Catherine proposed that in addition to commissioning new work from individuals, we should also try teaming up young animators with veteran artists of the art world. Catherine oversaw material made by professional film-makers and college students and arranged some unique collaborations. A London animator called Run Wrake worked with Roy Lichtenstein to animate his iconic aeroplane crash images. Similarly, Keith Haring's cartoon images were brought to life, along with a 'melting' animation of Warhol's Marilyn Monroe.

In a live show, video content needs to be balanced with physical elements to break the passivity of watching a screen. The staging itself would provide some of the required relief but a few more physical gags were also required. Mark Fisher's frustration with years of stage design constrained by traditional loudspeaker stacks led him to propose that we should keep the huge video screen free from clutter by placing the entire sound system in one central ball. Most sound engineers would have resigned on the spot, but Joe O'Herlihy rose to the challenge of mixing a live show through what would essentially be a mono PA. Rationalizing the requirements of supporting such a speaker cluster reminded me of an unexplained comment Bono had made during a particularly unhinged period of the ZooTV tour, which was that he had always harboured a secret fantasy to play a show underneath a set of gigantic golden arches. Thus the PopMart arch came into being. Mark Fisher was adamant that the proportions and spatial relationships of the staging elements needed to be exactly right and spent a great deal of time polishing the design. As a result the PopMart stage, though vast, appeared remarkably simple and elegant: just an arch and a sloping line.

It is a well-documented 'rule' of show business that any performance worth talking about has to include the use of at least one mirrorball. Previous U2 shows had done so and I had always tried to put a new spin on the idea, so to speak. The Joshua Tree tour had a huge globe mirrorball. ZooTV had its mirrorball Trabant, not to mention a mirrorball singer. On a particularly whacked afternoon in the studio, Bono proposed that at some point in this new show the whole band should travel into the crowd inside some kind of vehicle. Making reference to the Parliament Funkadelic spaceship, he suggested that an oversized mirrorball should descend from the roof of the stage, move out over the audience and spew them onto the B-stage. It is extraordinary to imagine that this was taken seriously, but indeed it was. I went on to propose that the mirrorball should be lemon-shaped, suggesting that the recycling of a U2 song title ('Lemon') would be sufficient justification for this object's existence. Mark Fisher set about turning this deranged fantasy into engineering reality: the world's first (and last) 40-foot-tall self-propelled mirrorball. After this, the addition of a giant cocktail stick and stuffed olive barely raised an eyebrow.

Production rehearsals took place in Las Vegas, which is possibly the only place in the world where building a 40-foot lemon might be considered vaguely normal behaviour. The schedule ran extremely late, with the LED screen being constructed right up to (and possibly even during) the first show. The down-side of being the first to use new technology is that you are permanently in a situation of working with prototypes, so things don't always work first time. From the front, the LED screen was a magnificent, ground-breaking, hi-tech achievement; but from behind it would often look more like an explosion in an electronic components warehouse, with teams of Belgians hanging on ropes, wielding hairdryers to dry out damp connections.

The lemon too had its moments of misbehaviour, most spectacularly in Oslo after having made its journey into the crowd with customary pomp and circumstance. Coming to a standstill, it opened just 2 feet before jamming solid. All the audience could see were four pairs of rock-star shoes and ankles, feet tapping, patiently waiting for something to happen.

Such moments were rare though and, as ever, after a few weeks the production was moving from place to place without a hitch. The vast scale of the props and video images gave enormous physical power to the visual content of the show. This wasn't a cerebral exercise in the same way that ZooTV had been, images of this scale producing a far more visceral and emotional response. Even untreated footage from the on-stage video cameras could be transformed into gigantic abstractions, like Bono's eyes 150 feet wide, or lips kissing the camera lens.

Whereas ZooTV had been a sprawling mass of energy and ideas, the design of PopMart was a highly disciplined, complete concept integrating all the elements of the show: performance, music, staging, sound, lighting, video, wardrobe. Above all, though, the ideas, vast and absurd as they might have been, were very simple. In some ways, perhaps, we had inadvertently answered the conundrum of the Joshua Tree tour, of how to remain true to a minimal design aesthetic when working on such a massive scale. *WW*

We decided to eat the monster before the monster ate us. Bono

Top left: June 1997, Oakland Stadium, Oakland, USA

Bottom left: April 1997, Sam Boyd Stadium, Las Vegas, USA

Top right: June 1997 Memorial Coliseum, Los Angeles, California

Bottom right: June 1997, Oakland Stadium, Oakland, USA

If you're gonna ask people to come to a stadium you want to have it together, you want to be doing something no one's seen or heard before. So we've put together an extraordinary set. It's fun and it's funky and it can kick your ass at the back of the stadium. Bono

Overleaf: June 1997, Memorial Coliseum, Los Angeles, USA. Above: April 1997, Sam Boyd Stadium, Las Vegas / PopMart / **139**

If you can't be fanciful about your art, then you're really betraying the people who have given you your freedom in the first place. Be true to who you are and what you do and run with it, and run amuck with it, and I think we've always done that. As annoying as we can be. At least we're not dull. Bono

Right: June 1997, Memorial Coliseum, Los Angeles, USA

It's funny but even within the space of one song, you can feel the audience come and go. The only thing to do is kick into a heavier gear and go for it. Some of our best gigs have been ones that start off badly and then become manic and unpredictable. Heavy but cool is the key. The Edge

Top: April 1997, Jack Murphy Stadium, San Diego, USA. Bottom: May 1997, Arrowhead Stadium, Kansas City, USA / PopMart / **147**

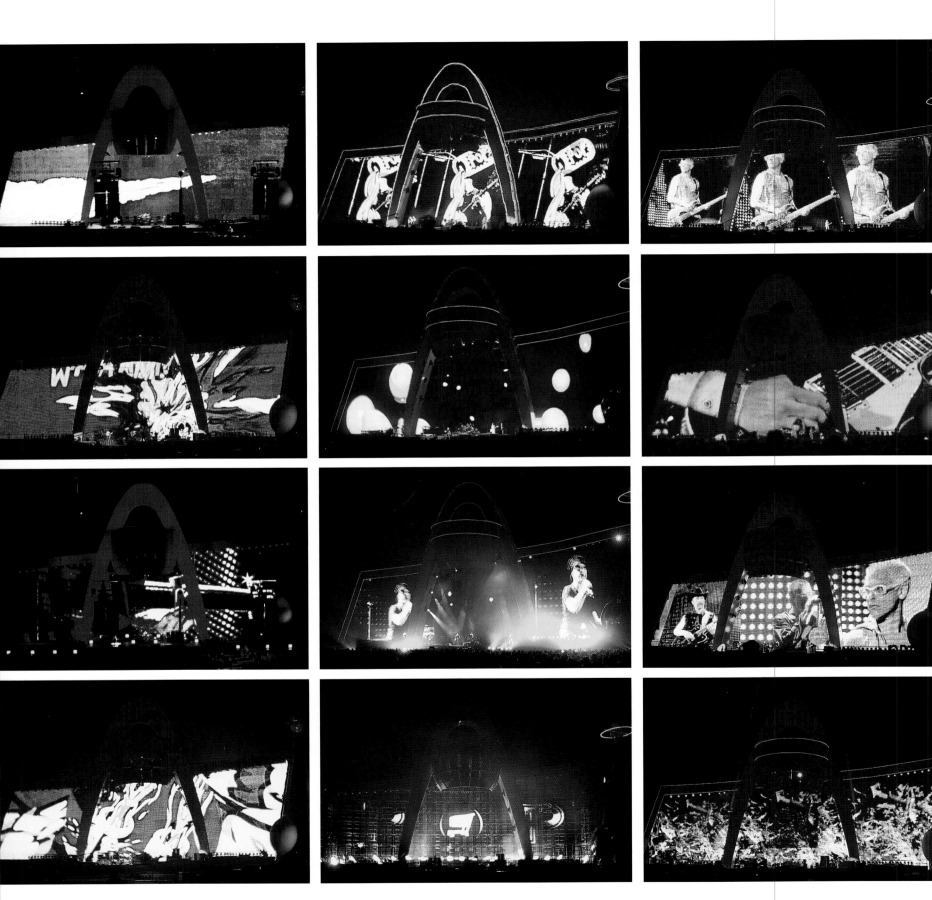

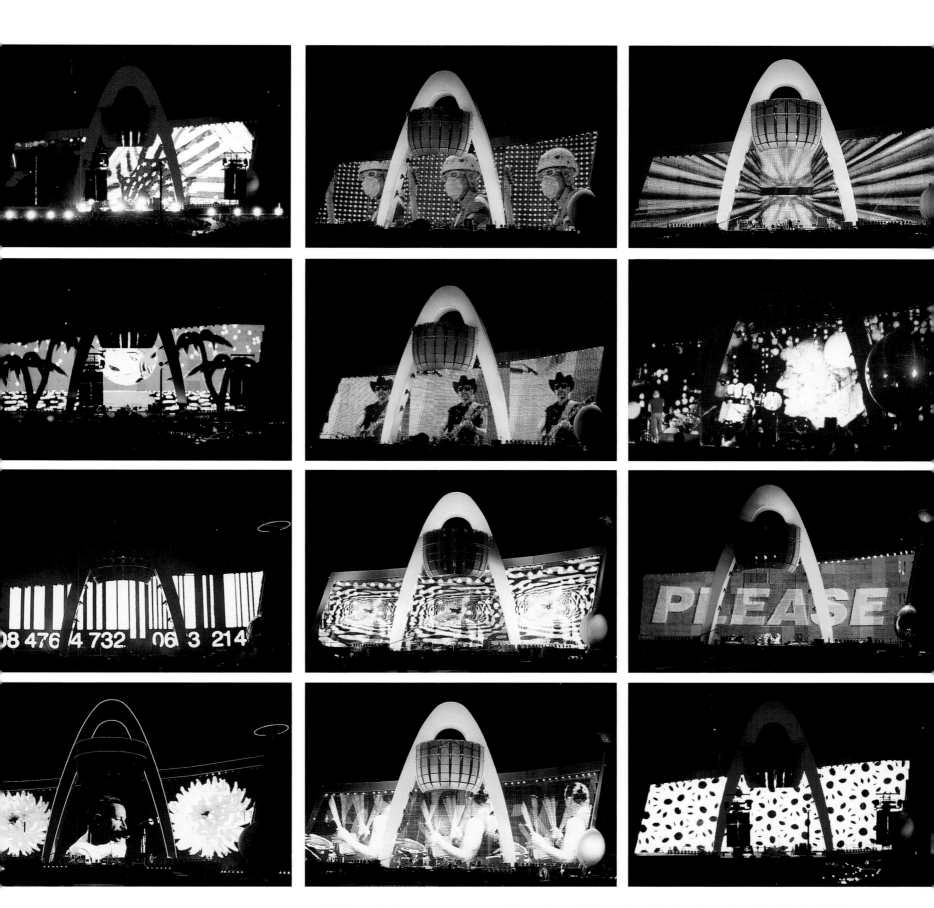

June 1997, Memorial Coliseum, Los Angeles, USA, and April 1997, Sam Boyd Stadium, Las Vegas, USA / PopMart / **151**

V

Elevation, Superbowl 2000–2002

Elevation, Superbowl

For several reasons, I approached the design of what became the Elevation tour with great anticipation. This was to be the first all-indoor U2 tour for ten years and the first U2 show in history to be physically smaller than its predecessor. I was keenly aware of a major secret weapon, which was that after years of spectacle, a large portion of the potential audience would only have seen the band play in a stadium and so perhaps be unaware of the power of U2 'raw'.

Even though the approach to the show was clearly going to be closer to the Joshua Tree than to PopMart, we were all absolutely clear that this was not a retreat in any sense. The new show had to encompass all of the above, essentially to be a distillation of everything U2 had done to date.

Getting the band out into the audience had always been a priority, so I began by thinking about a long stage that would run the length of the arena. This would allow the arena floor area to be standing room while also producing a great number of seats very close to the performance area. U2's wide demographic by now encompassed a young element keen to jump up and down as well as a more mature element wanting to sit.

I sketched up a proposal in which I laid the PopMart arch on the floor of the arena with the centre filled in. It was only a joke, but something about the space it used was appealing. What followed was typical of the U2 collaborative process. Bono looked at the shape and added two lumps at the wide end, turning the arch into a heart shape. Discussion followed about the fact that if the band were to move forward to fill the space, Larry would be left stranded at the back of the stage (given that the concept of a moving drum kit belongs solely to the world of heavy metal – and for good reason). For a solution, Adam suggested taking the centre out of the arch again and filling it with the audience. We were on our way.

It was a major logistical task for Mark Fisher to rationalize the heart into a functioning stage that would satisfy the needs of performers, technicians, health and safety officials and the production staff charged with touring this object. However, the appeal of the idea was sufficient to get us there. Particularly appealing was the reinvention of the B-stage. Since ZooTV, having a satellite stage in the centre of the hall has become an industry standard to the point of verging on cliché. However, the proposed heart ramp would allow the band to get out into the audience and then return to the stage without having to stop and turn around – a small but psychologically crucial factor for the performers. The simple act of walking on the stage would create drama, making the stage itself the key to the whole show.

My next task was how to deal with video, in particular the screens carrying camera close-ups of the performers for the benefit of those far away (known in the trade as 'I-Mag' for 'image magnification'). Video is not something that can simply be added to a show, a fact that is the downfall of many otherwise potentially interesting stage productions. We are so conditioned to look at television that moving camera pictures automatically become the focus of attention. (As evidenced by the experience of sitting in a bar with a television set on. You may be with friends, you may have no interest in what's on the box, but somehow your eyes keep drifting back to the TV.) In the context of a rock show, there is an assumption that whatever image is on the video screen must be the most important event taking place at that moment. In reality, the touring video director makes this decision, which can be little more than a random choice, or at the very least a choice entirely divorced from the overall stage picture. It is perhaps not surprising how often the stage and the video screens can appear to be producing two competing shows.

I floated the idea of doing a show with no video whatsoever, but knew the expectations of a twenty-first-century audience make it essential to allow a close-up view of the performers, even from the furthest seats. An arrangement was needed that would provide camera close-ups in a way that would not distract the audience or hog their attention. I proposed that we should have four cameras and four screens. One camera would be dedicated to each band member, whose image would be conveyed continuously to one of the screens for the entire show. There would be no cuts, no effects, no video switching, not even a video director in the traditional sense, just a continuous feed. If The Edge was to turn around to his amp rack, then we'd just see the back of his head. If Bono ducked down he might go out of frame altogether, but the four screens together would always make some kind of sense.

I called this approach 'unmediated' I-Mag, as I felt it was a way of letting the audience observe the camera pictures in the same way that they would watch the live performers on-stage – making their own decisions about who exactly to watch at each point. Also, the images were presented in black and white. For some reason, this proved less distracting than colour footage (another of my bar TV research discoveries). The video screens could now fulfil their brief while allowing the audience to look away from them and at the stage without a fear of missing something vital.

Another major visual element was the use of large-scale projection, but in an abstract way. As the show was set in the contained 'intimacy' of an arena, I wanted to see if we could completely fill the room with image or texture. Using very powerful 'PiGi' projectors we made a series of images that could gently scroll across the crowd, the band, the roof and the walls. Bono suggested that we add some fine gauze screens for him to interact with during the song 'New York' and provide more surfaces to add to the confusion of projected images. Again, black-and-white projections seemed to work most effectively in the form of star fields, moiré patterns, girders and finally song lyrics.

Visually, the show followed a disciplined progression. The house lights opening was followed by a period illuminated initially with large homemade lighting fixtures that put out unfussy blocks of brownish white light. The brighter blue-white light of follow-spots would then be added to this, followed by the introduction of bright hi-tech fixtures. The last 'act' introduced the further technology of a wide, low LED video wall across the back of the stage. In one sense, the look of the show became more complex as it progressed.

There was only going to be a small portion of the show that would use video as an effect, so we could be very precise in its execution. Once again Catherine Owens collaborated with us in sourcing a variety of material to provide colour, texture and atmosphere. During rehearsals, though, Bono was keen to use the LED wall to make more direct statements. Catherine eventually created several new video sequences that were used to introduce 'Bullet the Blue Sky', a veteran U2 song but now entirely reinvented in the context of gun control. Bono stalked the stage, scanning the audience with a hand-held lamp, though not the comforting warm light of the War tour – this was a sharp beam from a unit that even looked like a handgun.

The final leg of the Elevation tour returned to North America shortly after September 11th 2001. Playing to a nation in shock and mourning, U2 wanted to find a way to respectfully acknowledge what had happened. Echoing the scrolling song lyrics used in 'Walk On', Catherine made a video sequence for the LED wall that displayed the names of those killed in the 9/11 attacks. It was extremely moving, so this is what U2 decided to present to the entire US when they were invited to play during the half-time break at Superbowl in February 2002, watched annually by XXX million television viewers worldwide.

Non-Americans might find it difficult to imagine the nation-wide significance of Superbowl and the magnitude of the live event. Mark Fisher had designed the Superbowl half-time show on previous occasions, so he was well placed to redesign the Elevation heart stage into a format that could be rolled out on to the football field and erected in 6 minutes flat. Needless to say this was an extraordinary feat of logistics, but on the day it all went without a hitch. The instant that the first half of the game had finished, teams of stage hands raced out onto the field wheeling giant portions of the staging, which were then connected together with all the cooperative skill of an ant colony. Lighting trusses descended, projectors moved into place, back-line equipment was checked and U2 were announced. The band played 'Beautiful Day', and then 'MLK' as a tribute to the 9/11 victims. The names scrolled all over the building and up a gigantic white banner behind the stage and it felt as if the entire nation was holding its breath. The song ended and an audio sequence began, as the banner and walls bled into saturated red to announce the introduction of 'Where the Streets Have No Name'. Five minutes later it was all over, the staging was torn apart and wheeled away and the football game recommenced.

So finished the show and so finished the Elevation tour. It was perhaps a little ironic that a U2 show originally designed as a more intimate affair, would finish with such a huge, high-risk, adrenalin-fuelled live broadcast to a vast audience; or perhaps it was just another testament to the fact that when working with a group capable of such powerful performance and communication, there really isn't a limit to the kind of production that can be designed around it. *WW*

March 2001, Elevation Production Rehearsals, Miami Arena, Miami, USA / **157**

October 2001, Madison Square Garden, New York City, USA; and March 2001, National Car Rental Centre, Miami, USA / Elevation / **159**

We're really going to rock the house.
We're going in for lift-off, and our band
in full flight is something to see. Bono

Things get out of hand up there. I experience everything in slow motion. The crowd, the group, everything seems slowed down. Like a dream. It's only when I come off I realise it was me that was fired up, speeding on it all. Takes me hours to come back down. Bono

November 2001, Thomas & Mack Arena, Las Vegas, USA

164 / Top and centre: November 2001, Thomas & Mack Arena, Las Vegas. Bottom: August 2001, Earls Court, London and September 2001, Slane Castle, Dublin

Top: November 2001, Oakland Stadium, Oakland. Centre: October 2001, Madison Square Garden, New York City. Bottom: Earls Court and Slane Castle / Elevation / **165**

170 / Left: March 2001, Nation Car Rental Center, Fort Lauderdale, USA. Right: November 2001, Oakland Stadium, Oakland, USA

Left: November 2001, Oakland Stadium, Oakland, USA. Right: March 2001, National Car Rental Center, Fort Lauderdale, USA / Elevation / **171**

176 / Top and centre: October 2001, Madison Square Garden, New York City, USA. Bottom: August 2001, SEC, Glasgow, Scotland

It's all about imagination, nothing else is important.
It's not about scale – big, small, independent, alternative,
anything. Whether you earn a million dollars or lose a
million dollars. None of it really matters. What matters
is the work and the imagination of the work. Bono

186 / Top: March, Nation Car Rental Center, Fort Lauderdale, USA. Centre: August, SEC, Glasgow, Scotland. Bottom: March, National Car Rental Center, Fort Lauderdale, USA

The position of any band talking about the topics of their day is always a very delicate one. The only justification I can give is that we are expressing our convictions. I can see how it can appear patronising, but it depends on one's motivations. There are a lot of things we could get pulled up on. If people don't like it, then that is understandable, but we will be standing by what we've done. The Edge

192 / Above and right: February 2002, Superbowl Half-time Show, Superdome, New Orleans, USA

A Short History of Rock Touring

Mark Cunningham

Founding editor of live event design and technology industry publication Total Production International.

The journey that has taken U2 from the pub circuit to the world's biggest stadiums has been punctuated with landmark design and technology achievements which in themselves tell the story of the development of concert touring as an art form.

Touring artists of the highest calibre demand, and are blessed with, the most dedicated crews and the best services and technology that the live event production industry can muster – how else could they consistently push the boundaries of audience expectation every time they venture out on the road?

The immense sophistication of their touring practices, however, has a history of its own and draws upon decades of experience and experimentation – invention, mistakes and lessons learned.

Over the years, concert touring has evolved into an art that requires the kind of precision organization and logistical savvy encountered in military campaigns. On the road, the decisions made and actions taken by production or tour managers are only one step removed from those of army generals. It's sometimes hard to remember that the end result of their effort is high entertainment.

In the early days of rock and roll touring, it was all so different. The first generation of American teen idols saw the likes of Elvis Presley and Buddy Holly building their live following through tours of country fairs or jamborees, often on the backs of trailers, with little amplification. They were fan-gathering exercises on a primitive scale.

David Bowie during his Ziggy Stardust tour – one of the first to visit London's Rainbow Theatre, during 1972

Meanwhile, their British counterparts – Cliff Richard and the Shadows, Adam Faith *et al.* – made their way out of the coffee bars and on to the circuit of ABC cinemas and provincial dance halls, with just a Commer van to transport their tiny guitar amps and drum kit.

It was not until the mid-1960s that the rock concert in its current sense took shape. The seeds of what became the theatrically produced rock show were sown by American promoter Bill Graham – widely acknowledged as the man who brought a new professionalism to live rock 'n' roll at a time when anarchy and chaos were the hallmarks of the new San Francisco hippie movement.

In 1966, he transformed the run-down West Coast Fillmore venue into a tightly organized concert hall which acts including Jefferson Airplane, the Grateful Dead and Big Brother and the Holding Company used as a launch pad for not only their own careers, but the live music scene as we know it today. As well as repeating the formula with the opening of Fillmore East, a former New York City vaudeville house, Graham took over the management of San Francisco's Winterland Arena in 1968 and

set about inventing the modern approach to tour promotion.

Prior to Graham's rise to prominence, promoters were generally unsympathetic to the new beat generation's tastes and aspirations, and this would normally be reflected in an 'old school' variety package.

In the UK, even though rock music became regarded more as a serious art by 1967, promoters still clung to the same formula until the early 1970s, when bands of the calibre of Yes, The Who and Deep Purple embarked on their own tours, taking with them just a pair of well-matched opening support acts.

Although London was not without its trend-setting music clubs and cinema venues, it had to wait until 1971 before it had its first major purpose-designed rock concert venue. It was the Fillmore's team, headed by John Morris and featuring Richard Hartman and Michael Ahern, who transformed the 40-year-old Finsbury Park Astoria (which had formerly hosted The Beatles' 1964 Christmas shows) into the Rainbow Theatre.

Launched with a trio of shows by The Who in November 1971, in its first year of business, the Rainbow hosted Pink Floyd's Dark Side of the Moon concerts and David Bowie's Ziggy Stardust shows – both of which were revolutionary for the time in terms of Bowie's theatrical extravagance and the Floyd's use of avant-garde film sequences.

Outdoor festivals and one-off events took shape in the 1960s with the USA's Newport Folk and Jazz, Monterey Pop and Woodstock, while in Europe, the Montreux Jazz Festival, the Isle of Wight and the Marquee Group's jazz and blues festivals (the forerunners of the Reading Festival) held their own. Promoters were not slow to appreciate how lucrative a summer gathering could be, and the 1970s witnessed an explosion of annual events, including Glastonbury, the Knebworth Fairs, the Crystal Palace Garden Parties, Pink Pop in the Netherlands and the twinned Torhout/Werchter sites in Belgium.

These events presented a multitude of benefits to artists who structured their itineraries around a late spring album release, followed by a summer tour of the festival circuit where the production (i.e. the PA, lighting and staging) was already in place.

After The Beatles pioneered the concept of stadium concerts, the late 1960s and 1970s saw many of the world's top artists, such as the Rolling Stones, Crosby, Stills and Nash, Led Zeppelin, Pink Floyd and The Who, include stadium dates as part of their touring campaigns.

The festivals of the 1960s showed that it was possible for artists to earn considerable sums of money by attracting huge audiences to one event. Attracting these audiences to large stadiums on a more regular basis was therefore a highly attractive prospect. Soon, performing in 70,000-capacity venues on 30-date tours became the norm.

Among the earliest successful stadium rock events were the Rock 'n' Roll Revival Concert at Toronto's Varsity Stadium in September 1969, featuring John Lennon's Plastic Ono Band and a full bill of 1950s legends, including Little Richard, Chuck Berry, Gene Vincent and Bo Diddley.

In August 1972, the UK hosted its first major stadium concert – the London Rock 'n' Roll Show, also starring Richard, Berry and Diddley, plus Jerry Lee Lewis and Bill Haley and His Comets – the first to be held at Wembley Stadium. Wembley soon became as famous for music as for sporting events, and served as the premier British stadium venue until it closed in 2000.

The first tour to be acknowledged as a full-length stadium campaign was The Rolling Stones' Still Life tour of 1981–82, which was notable for a number of logistical innovations, such as the devising of separate stage productions for stadium and arena shows. This experience was drawn upon two decades later when the Stones embarked on their 2002–03 Licks tour of arenas, stadiums and theatres.

Live sound has evolved in leaps and bounds since the days of the variety packages. At first, vocalists were reinforced by column speakers while instrumentalists were projected to the audience solely by means of their own personal back-line amplifiers. What the fans heard was the result of the musicians balancing their own on-stage sound with the vocal PA and drum kit.

One of the first companies to look seriously at live rock sound reinforcement was one that has enjoyed a long and fruitful association with U2. Founded by Roy and Gene Clair in Pennsylvania in the mid-1960s, Clair Brothers Audio was the first to make Elvis Presley heard in arenas, and entered the industry at a time when the first stadium rock shows began to evolve, notably The Beatles' concerts at Shea Stadium in New York.

It was not surprising that the hysteria generated by 55,000 screaming fans overwhelmed the sound of The Beatles' back-line amplifiers and the minuscule house Tannoy system. The Shea experience was a turning point. It encouraged the evolution of larger, more powerful PA systems designed to deliver faithful, controlled sound to larger audiences, while a new generation of professionals, such as the Clairs, Hanley Audio, Showco and the UK's Tasco and Electrosound, set to work on devising new methods.

The Grateful Dead's sound engineers devised a PA system – dubbed the Wall of Sound – for a concert at the Hollywood Bowl in July 1974. It was unusual in that all the loudspeaker cabinets were lined up in 'wall' fashion behind the musicians. The system was a combination of six individual elements, responsible for delivering vocals, lead guitar, rhythm guitar, keyboards, bass and drums. Each band member had individual control over his instrument. Although an interesting approach, it failed to take into account the quality of sound and the mix experienced by the audience at the rear of the arena, and therefore did not become a technical standard.

The Dead were one of many leading bands who operated and maintained their own touring sound (and/or lighting) system. Several artists, or their heads of crew, gravitated towards forming their own production companies during the 1970s, when it was realized that additional incomes could be earned by renting sys-

tems during downtime between tours. Examples include the formation of Britannia Row Productions by Pink Floyd, M.L. Executives (The Who), Nocturne (Santana/Journey) and Delicate Productions (Supertramp).

As sound reinforcement grew in sophistication, so did the tendency for systems to become more compact and efficient. The latest generation is the Line Array. Flown above the stage, the Line Array appears like a 'claw' of loudspeakers, with each cabinet radiating hi-fi sound to the audience at precise degree increments throughout the concert venue.

Whereas bands of the 1950s and 1960s had no need for a dedicated sound engineer, employing one became standard practice as systems grew and equalization/control became an issue. Mixing desks have developed from simple four-channel creations through to today's fully automated, digital consoles that memorize and instantly recall various parameters of mix settings. The latest models also feature internal processing, enabling the front-of-house engineer to access any number of effects (reverb, echo delay, distortion, phasing) for specific vocal or instrument channels.

The Who's long-serving technician, Bob Pridden, who joined the band in 1966, is widely regarded as the first dedicated monitor engineer – a job borne out of the band's need to hear themselves more clearly on stage. Until then, Townshend and co. had relied on the forward-facing PA speakers and their back line. With the rise in volume levels and the complications of acoustic reflections off the walls of larger venues, on-stage sound had become virtually unintelligible.

Pridden, and later other engineers, added monitor 'wedge' speakers at the front of the stage, and sidefill speaker stacks, pointing at the performers, to give them a more faithful delivery of their sound (according to what the audience heard), and a second console was positioned in the stage wings to control the band's own mix.

By the early 1990s, several artists, including Tears for Fears, and Stevie Wonder, had taken on board wireless in-ear monitoring as a means of further improving the fidelity of their personal stage mixes. Using earpieces like those worn with a Walkman, artists could now be fed hi-fi mixes of their performances, minus any unwanted additional stage ambience. Compared to what The Beatles' audiences (and The Beatles themselves) heard, we now live in an age of aural luxury.

Music fans and road crews alike cannot fail to have been amused by the 1984 spoof 'rockumentary' *This Is Spinal Tap* – a movie based on real-life incidents. Although TV shows often went the extra mile for top artists, set design for tours simply did not exist until the mid-1970s, by which time the multi-platinum-selling artists of the day could afford to fuel their egos by realizing their wildest scenic dreams.

At the forefront of rock set design early on were the Fisher Park team (Mark Fisher and Jonathan Park, collaborators on ZooTV's set), who furnished Pink Floyd with the architecture for their legendary tours for *Animals* (a.k.a. In the Flesh, 1977) and *The Wall* (1980–81) – the latter sporting an exploding Stuka bomber, life-size Gerald Scarfe puppets, Floyd's trademark inflatable pig, and a polystyrene wall.

Little Richard was one of the headlining stars at the 1972 London Rock and Roll Show, Wembley Stadium's debut concert event

In 1974, The Grateful Dead's Wall of Sound briefly revolutionized PA system design

Syd Barrett of Pink Floyd awash with the liquid light effects that helped to define the psychedelic mood of 1967

The live re... show was now occupying ... no ...
even the pro...cers of big-budget Broadway ...
such as Th...'s tour and the appearance of ... ...
shift of ge... oughout the 1980s and 1990s, as ...
became ... ...phisticated. When ... arrive...
ed a ... ... ase opportunity ... ... re in ... ...
... ...

Cli... such as Adam ... and the ... ...
Duran's 'The Wild ...', with ... ...
Hollywood blockbu...s ... et ... ...
their touring shows had to catch up. Th... ... ...
live concerts began to so..., which ... ...
the set desig... as well as significant cont... ... ...
...nstruct... ...companies, including Stag... ...
Brilliant S... ...

Simil... ... reos ... ...ed in the list
artists w... ... b...various permu... ...s ...
lanterns, ...floage lighting in ... to ... ...
tively soph...ate...d, the scene ...e ...r ...ght ...g ...
was minimal ...til the psycho...ele ... ...e ...

The peri... cre...ted as be... ... ...
designer wa... ... ...che...d n...de ... ...e ...
known as Chip Monck. Th... ...
was respons...le in ...han ... ...mich ... ...ar
lighting by introd...ing bo... ...s, ...
...fle...ator) and Super... uper follows...
washes of colour across the Fillmore ...
became ...f such ...un...n ... ...n ... ...
atmosphere.

The Rolling Stones hired Monck for ... ...
band's 1971 ... ...t was a visual turning point, b... ... ...
include a painted fibreglass set, follow-sp... s an...
truss that wa... rai...ed by hydraulics. Th...ks to M... ... ...t wa...
possible crea...te and maintain a consistent 'look' ... ...
Monck's UK counterpart was ...n Croft, a th... ...e ...
expert who worked on several Stones tours with Monc... ...ith ...
Brown. Croft founded ESP Lighting in 1973 and thro... ... ...
of the decade was the premier UK light... supplie... ...f ...
production manager) to legendary tours by Tho... ... ...vi...
Elton John, Queen and many more.

One of the lighting techniques of the psychedelic mus... ...
the 'liquid light show', as popularized in San Francisco ...
Swinging London by influential bands such as The Gratef... ...
and Pink Floyd. The Floyd's Peter Wynne-Willson and Mike ...eonard,
in particular, were masters of liquid light – a technique th...
involved mixing coloured oils and heating them to produ... ... ...le
effects, which created a mysterious ambience when pro... ... ...
to the stage and over the band's faces.

For higher-ranking bands, laser shows were added to the lighting designer's palette during the 1970s, with The Who leading the
way. However, the most significant development came in 1981
when Texan production company Showco created the Vari*Lite –
the world's first 'intelligent' moving light – and debuted it on a
European tour with Genesis, the band who co-funded the product's
R&D and manufacturing. The 'nodding bucket', as the moving light

... ...
... ...
... ...
... ...
... ...
... ...
... ...
... ...
... ...
... ...
... ...

... some ...anged with ...ching ... ... and ... ...e fo...
one ... ...n ...i...to ... ...
a concert hall ...ven in mid-air.

Touring has now matured as an ind...try ... ...ed by a ...te
...ck of one ...mate pro...ssionals, ...cognised as
a busin...ss w...ch survi...es and pro...per... ... ...s sh...s of its prime
m...ers. The ... m 'roadie' over...ns a... ... ...e ...d...d an for
someone who ...ses such a diver... ...y of ...e... ... technical
skill... ...ot to mention the social attribu... ... usa... ...urvive
several months as part of a crew.

Until the Fillmore venues spread their influence, road crews, as
we know them today, simply did not exist. Even the biggest hit-
m...kers of the early to mid-1960s employ...d just a driver and at
the most two 'roadies', who would share the tasks of liaising with
venue managers, box-office staff and hotel receptionists, as well

Large screen projection played a major role at Led Zepplin's Knebworth shows

Pink Floyd's Dark Side Of The Moon tour of 1972–73 became legendary for their use of quadrophonic sound and cinematic backdrops

[text illegible] with [...]

[several faded paragraphs, largely illegible]

tour manager [...] Roger Waters [...]

[...] movie [...]

[...] try [...] seemed to the [...] economic influence [...] tour and [...] design of smaller monitors [...] less truck space and [...]

[...] brought to [...] lucrative [...]

[...] existence of equipment and communications systems such as the mobile phone, SMS text [...] and the Internet [...] rendered [...] obsolete. The production manager of [...] faced with organizing a major event today without [...] these modern tools. And yet not even the fax was [...] the crew of [...] at Wembley Stadium in 1985 — the most logistically demanding show ever staged at that point. Even more bizarre is the notion that even in the late 1970s, the production office at Wembley Arena was still without a telephone — touring staff would resort to contacting supply companies from a public call box along the corridor.

But for all these shifts in creative design, technical expertise and the greater efficiency of the backstage infrastructure, it's always the music that matters most. The smoke and mirrors can provide a magical distraction but, just as in the days of Elvis and The Beatles, it's ultimately the performing artist's responsibility to seduce the audience.

Management

Ellen Darst
Principle Management, US, 1983–93

At the time the *War* record came out in February 1983 I was working for Island Records. Commercially speaking, I think *War* really put U2 on the map, at least in America. They were starting to have real success on radio, outside of college stations and progressive rock stations. The *War* record earned the band much broader commercial acceptance and *Under a Blood Red Sky* really put the icing on the cake. So by the time *Unforgettable Fire* came out, people were ready for it.

In this territory, and I believe this was true around the world, the *Boy* record caught a small group of influential people's interest, but the *October* record kind of left people scratching their heads. The *October* record really showed all of U2's own ambivalence about what was happening to them. There was a lot of conflict in their circle about whether you could be in a rock band, with all that implied, and still be a person of faith, which was extremely important to them. There was a lot of conflict about that, a lot of pressure on them to choose between the secular and the spiritual worlds. So in some ways the *October* record reflects all that. It was a pivotal time for them, and having gotten through that and moved on, the next record, *War*, was a real affirmation. 'Okay. We are here to stay.'

I loved them. The level of commitment was staggering. At that time Warner Brothers had made a really unusual commitment to artist development. Basically we used touring (often in lieu of airplay) for press and marketing opportunities, to build a fan base and sell records. I was Warner's northeast person – and the first U2 dates were in the northeast. Boston was one of the places that U2 was first played on a major radio station, WBCN.

The United States is a different market place now than it was then, but it was and is a huge market. In England and Ireland there are radio stations that cover the entire country. Here there are thousands of radio stations, and hundreds of rock 'n' roll stations. Nearly every decent-sized town has its own rock 'n' roll station; the big cities have several. This also pre-dated the big broadcast chains so individual stations had autonomy, so it took a tremendous commitment on the part of an artist and on the part of whoever was paying the bill – the record company, generally – to keep a band out there long enough to make an impact. You had to go out, talk to the press, play in front of people, go to radio stations, visit record shops. It really was grassroots campaigning. Well, in a place as big as this, that's a huge commitment. And a lot of artists didn't want to work that hard. Some of them kind of resented the idea that they would be called upon to promote themselves. It was, 'Well, I'm a musician, I play music. Don't bother me with the rest of this stuff.'

There were many things that set U2 apart from the rest, but maybe the most important thing was their sheer ambition. They wanted it so badly, they were ready to do as much work as it took. They were also very clear about the parameters within which they would promote themselves. There were a lot of things that they wouldn't do, like radio station IDs. 'Hi, this is Bono and you're listening to WXYZ in Passaic.' All the bands were out doing that, but U2 wouldn't. From the very beginning they wanted to be in control of how they were perceived, how they were marketed; it was really personal for them. I helped fashion ways in which they could do the self-promotion, but still be true to themselves. But really, those things came from them. U2 had the instinct and I had the knowledge of the market, to be able to help them get across without cheapening them in the process. They were so willing and ready to meet everyone. They couldn't do enough. I really appreciated that, because I was ready to work really hard and I wanted to work with people who were ready to work just as hard. I just saw how much they wanted it. Musically the level of commitment and the risk-taking were really exciting. For me, their energy and their almost naked ambition were, irresistible. I really appreciated the work ethic, and the willingness to just go for it. I went to work for them directly in 1983.

The Amnesty International Conspiracy of Hope Tour was basically organized by Bill Graham, me and Anne-Louise Kelly. It was the most difficult tour I've ever done (and, thankfully, the shortest). By the time it was over we were pretty well wrung out. Finally, after Live Aid, Self Aid and then the Amnesty tour, the band realized it was time to get back to their own thing. All of those events required making your own needs subservient to the larger goal. That meant giving up control and compromising in all sorts of ways. I think everybody, by the end of it, was a bit burned out. It was gruelling. It was a point of exhaustion.

Live Aid, especially, had a huge unanticipated impact on the band, commercially speaking. The Amnesty tour had a big impact in the States, but Live Aid was huge, high-profile, international, a once-in-a-lifetime kind of event. And although that wasn't their motivation it ended being hugely beneficial to their career. It also ratcheted up the pressure. It was a big turning point. The stakes suddenly got even bigger. It had always been very much a team effort, but what we saw over time is that you can't maintain that small personal family feeling when you've got 200 people on the road. It's gone. The Joshua Tree was a wonderfully exciting tour. It really was a lot of fun. In my mind this was sort of a watershed. The production was still pretty simple, but it was so effective. These were the first big U2 stadium shows and they were mighty. The record was huge. It was certainly a high point for them artistically and commercially.

I did feel sometimes that they were working too hard. Some of the tours went on too long. They didn't know how to stop doing what they'd had to do at the beginning, which was go at it non-stop. They had trouble learning to pace themselves. And, of course, managers tend to want bands to work. I think Paul sometimes overbooked them. Bands don't often have this kind of longevity, so one never knows how long you'll remain artistically and commercially viable. So there's a tendency to say, 'Okay, let's go for it, go for it, go for it.' And because U2 are as ambitious artistically as they are, they want to keep trying things, and be out doing it. Testing the limits of how far it can go. There are a lot of good reasons for it, but sometimes it felt like it was time to stop, time to regenerate creatively, and time to give the public a rest too. How can they miss you if you won't go away?

I think *Achtung Baby* is some of U2's very best work to date. It marked a change in the way they related to the audience. It moved away from that earnest, self-revelatory thing, to the shades, the whole Fly thing, Bono with the glasses. People were really bothered by the glasses. Gone was the forthright persona, and in its place was irony, the last thing their audience expected from U2. The audience perceived a change in their accessibility and some resented it. I also think it marked a change in Bono. Probably it was just self-preservation, a decision to not give quite so much of himself away. Of course, it was partly parodying the whole celebrity thing, but I think it was also his way of acknowledging that he needed some cover. *The Joshua Tree* was just heart on your sleeve, right out there, giving it all away, all the time. This was different. We'd go into interview situations, and people would want him to take his glasses off, which he would refuse to do. It was a schtick. But I also think he started to need the distance they created. It was just too much to be out there all the time. I think their audience loved their openness, but you can just end up with nothing left for yourself. Bono's one of these people who's just in 'go' mode all the time. He has more energy than 5000 people put together. He's never been very good at pacing himself or holding back, and in a way I thought that was his way of saying, 'I need a little more for myself.' Bono is just like this force. Intellectually and spiritually and on every other level. He's also probably one of the funniest people I've ever known, one of the most driven people I've ever known. I know a lot of musicians and artists, but I can't really remember ever meeting anybody with as much life force as this guy has. There's a dark side to that too, but mostly he's used it for the good.

Thinking back to those early days, Red Rocks was pretty wild. The weather conditions were horrible and the gig, complete with filming and recording, should have been called off. It was scary. It was very tense. Financially, everything they had was riding on the filming and recording of that gig. To have pulled the plug on it would have been a disaster for them. Instead they managed to make magic from all the adversity. It really was magic. The tougher the going got, the better they got. Always.
Gloucester, MA, May 2003

Anne-Louise Kelly
Principle Management, Dublin 1983–97

I was just out of college when I started working with Paul in September 1983. There was only Paul and myself. It was the time of *Under a Blood Red Sky*. I was very much based in the office. It was only later that I started to do more travelling. Ellen Darst was already working for them in America and she was in charge of all the touring side of things. Everything to do with recording was based from here. The record company was in England and the band mainly recorded here in Dublin. Part of my job was to coordinate all aspects of the recording process and the promotion of the records. That would involve going into a venue, for example Hansa for *Achtung Baby* or Slane for *Unforgettable Fire*, or going to Los Angeles. I would work out the time schedule, the budget and liaise with the record company. We always had a fair idea when the album was going to finish. Now, it may not have ever finished at the time it was supposed to finish, but we would know in which season it was supposed to finish!

I was in charge of everything you could think of outside of the studio relating to the album. I liaised closely with the record company, and on the artistic side with Steve Averill, because as soon as we were a quarter of the way into the album we would start to consider photography and artwork. That side was always taken extremely seriously and the process took a long time. The band have always been involved with every aspect of their work from the very beginning. It's their work, it's their image, and it's their direction. My role was to make sure that it all happened, that the right people got together and that the production schedules and budget were adhered to. Quality control on all U2 recordings since *Rattle and Hum* has been done very capably and competently by Cheryl Engels, who is a complete technical wizard. Scarily so! She has the band's complete trust and she's fantastic. Cheryl was working for A&M Records in Los Angeles at the time when we were recording the album. That's where we met her.

Bono initiated it and Ellen and I really pulled the Amnesty Conspiracy of Hope tour together. The band were working on the beginning of the *Joshua Tree* album. Ellen and I would do our regular work during the day and then go on to make calls at night to ask other acts if would they participate in the tour. We worked round the clock. Looking back, you could say that it was a kind of watershed. At the time, all we really did was work. Bono worked extremely hard and I think people around them worked very hard. But, yes, the Conspiracy of Hope tour was certainly an eye-opener. Paul couldn't be there because Kathy, his wife, was pregnant at that time, so Ellen and I were there on our own. And we had no tour manager: it was just us and the band. It was, like, 'Come on, on the bus. Off the bus. On the plane.' And it was pretty stressful. But the plane was fun, the hotels were very basic, and we had a ball! Peter Gabriel was wonderful. The remarkable thing about Peter was he was the first person we asked and he just said 'Yes' without any hesitation. And all of the artists who participated were incredibly supportive … because it wasn't easy. I remember a night in the hotel where a lot of guys got up to jam after dinner.

Bill Graham was the roadie! And that's a lasting memory …

[...]n Castle, Dub[...] during the recording of The Unforgettable Fire [...]

[...] a shoot [...] in [...] there [...] stuff going on [...] work. But it was always great fun [...] certainly for me. It was hard work but, in the end, I did enjoy being in Berlin from a politica[...] artistic point of view, whatever you want to call it. You hav[...] remember that previously we had always been geared around America. So I enjoyed being in Europe [...] working with Steve Averill and Anton Corbijn, particularly on *Achtung Baby* ... looking for cows with big horns. True gentlemen.'

Dublin, October [...]

The Ritz Ballroom.
From left:
Goldstein.
McGuinness.

The Unforgettable Fire tour,
Radio City Music Hall, New
York City, December 1984

played for bigger crowds. That's the key. They built an audience. The reviews were terrific. I remember a funny thing that happened at one U2 performance early on. When U2 played the Academy of Music (the Palladium) for the first time and I was looking at the stage, I saw that Bono was wearing plaid trousers. They were so awful that I called Paul and said, 'Lose those pants!' My eyes were falling out of my head! I said, 'If you want, I'll tell him. Lose the pants!' Normally we would never say anything like that. Only when it's a disaster.

FB: Was that the last time?

BS: That he wore those pants? I believe so. Here's a summary of the 1983 tour: the single for 'New Year's Day' shipped 24 January, 23 February we shipped the album; $7500 a night, sound and lights between $1500 and $2000 dollars, five days maximum in a row. Days off near Los Angeles, San Francisco, Phoenix, Denver and probably New York. That tour started in Chapel Hill, North Carolina. They were playing 3000-seaters and colleges, such as Brown University. They played Red Rocks on Sunday the 5th, then they were in theatres in Kansas City and Tulsa, where Old Lady of Brady must have held 2000 people. Then they played Meadows in Austin, the Bronco Bowl in Dallas, the Musical in Houston. In LA they played the Sports Arena.

FB: So basically they broke with the major cities. But look: they were breaking everywhere. After those dates with J. Geils in Florida, they came back to headline in 1983, at the Jai Alai in Orlando in Tampa, in Miami. You see, at the very beginning it wasn't like market-to-market or anything. When the record came out, if that record started happening I mean, the band played for the same amount of money all over the country. When you break an act live it all depends on how good they were at the last gig there. And U2 did it incredibly well.

BS: But let's say that you played a 1500-seater and you only got 1000 people in the place. Well when you go back you're gonna play that same 1500-seater again and hope you sell out the show and create your demand and your market. It's the way you build a band, and we were always very careful in not overplaying our hand, not putting an act in a 10,000-seater prematurely where they only get 6000 people. That's what created excitement, and that's what creates an illusion that a band could be even bigger than they really are. It's about perception v. reality. It was an expression that Frank and I hated. At a certain point in Los Angeles there were people who used to tell us we were all wrong because we believed in reality. 'It's not reality, it's perception,' they'd say. We like to deal in reality. We have much better results dealing in reality.

FB: Before I set up Premier Talent, agents would wait for a band to have a record and then they'd all go after it playing the act in the same places. I, on the other hand, broke bands live, even if they didn't have a record. We created new places for the acts to play and those places have become the best places to perform.

BS: That approach is perfect for bands who can have a career working, playing live, because you can't depend upon every record being a hit. Or *any* record being a hit. So that's the important thing.

FB: I remember when Chris Blackwell told me that they were dropping Island and going with Columbia. This was after *Joshua Tree,* after Chris had done such a wonderful job for them. It was so unfair

I decided I just had to speak to them about that. And it wasn't Paul McGuinness – I spoke to the group. They felt that they could go to Columbia and get a lot more money and that sort of thing. And they probably could have. Of course, Columbia could give them more money, but they had nothing to do with breaking them. Island did. And U2 were doing very well with Island. They didn't really need that much more money. So basically that's what I talked to them about. I talked to them about how unfair I thought it was after all that work. Here's an Irish band that had no record or anything, and Chris worked very hard, and so did I. They broke and now Columbia and everyone else was after them even though they hadn't been initially. It would have been terribly unfair. And that's what I told them. And thank God eventually they ended up staying with Chris. U2 broke live, that's what people thought about them: they're live performers. And if they bought the records, fine. That added to it. But if U2 didn't even have any records, they'd still keep getting bigger.

BS: When you were a great live band and toured and toured and then you got a hit record, then that was all icing on the cake.

FB: The touring business in the 1980s – that was the culmination. In the 1990s the down turn started and a lot of that had to do with MTV.

BS: A lot of bands were created via a hit single on MTV, so you had a lot of turnover. But if you look at who does today's business, it's still the older acts. Those are the acts that are playing the stadiums, that are playing multiple dates and arenas, that have a long history of incredible live touring that wasn't based on hit records. Their success was really based on getting out on the road and doing great shows. Now you have bands that have one hit single playing arenas. Artists today don't really have touring experience, or know about creating a great live show. You can't compare them with U2, with The Who, with Springsteen.

FB: Even the old acts that did have hit albums are still considered live bands. And that's why they would be doing just as well now, with or without a new album to promote. That's what people know of them, and that's how people saw them for the first time. It had nothing to do with the albums. And that's the problem with many acts today. The business today is a throwback to what it was like before I started Premier. That's how the business was then. Back then, everyone kept saying that this rock stuff would be over in a year, a year and a half.

BS: It's like being back at square one.

FB: Maybe it's because we got out of the business! We started seeing that happening, and this wasn't the business that we created.

BS: We didn't sign a lot of those new acts because we would go to shows and expect to see something credible. Some great bands came out of it, such as Pearl Jam, Nine-Inch Nails too. But the majority of what we heard was just … Maybe we were jaded.

FB: We weren't jaded.

BS: Maybe we were spoiled by great music, by great performances.

FB: If we were wrong, and if the act was great, it would be happening for them. And it's not. Nowadays, the record is the most important thing. The successful bands make it because of the record, not on their live performance.

New York City, May 2003

Ian Flooks

Agent, world outside US, 1982–1997

The agent is a kind of sub-manager for an artist's performance career. The general idea is that you try to build up their performance career and make them more famous to support what's happening in their recording career. Usually, you get the band you represent into clubs, to begin with, and then perhaps you get them to support other people. I deal with promoters and club owners. One of the things I did early for U2 was to arrange for them to support Talking Heads at the Hammersmith Palais in London. I was also the agent for Talking Heads, who were at the time very, very big. That was considered an important career move for U2. As bands get bigger, you become responsible for deciding where they play. In other words, are U2 going to play the Hammersmith Palais or the Forum or Brixton Academy? What exactly is the show, what's the ticket price? Then you negotiate the deal with the promoter and make sure the band gets paid. You do that with a series of people around the world.

I remember hearing U2's first album, *Boy*, on a demo tape. I was driving to north London to see a stadium we were using for someone else we represented. I put it in my car cassette player and was completely blown away. I couldn't believe how good it was. I'd undoubtedly heard them before – '11 O'Clock Tick Tock' had been released by then – but I hadn't heard this album. I stopped the car and listened to the album the whole way through. It's something I remember very, very well. It was 1978–9, the year before we started Wasted Talent. It was a whole new thing. There weren't really any independent agencies at the time, so U2 came with us, as did Ian Wilson – U2 came with Ian, effectively. Wasted Talent's first six bands would have been The Clash, Talking Heads, B-52s, The Police, REM and U2. That was the whole roster. Our biggest around 1979/80 was The Clash.

Agents then weren't doing what we were doing, which was trying to develop the bands. They just booked bands and took commission. Paul McGuinness was one of the first managers to involve an agent closely in the decision-making process for the band, in the strategizing. He was one of a small group of very, very strong managers. He was always in our office when he was in London, so we got to know each other. He worked with Ian planning the club tours. I was aware of what they were doing, but not closely involved. My involvement really only started in a big way when the band were recording *The Unforgettable Fire*. That's when Ian suddenly decided that he was going to leave and manage The Alarm. U2 were getting to be big then. We knew that this new album could do big things for them. They spent a lot of time in America and were becoming bigger there than they were here. Paul always felt that America was an important market to break. Most people here don't have a clue how to do it. But Paul worked on that very early, with Frank Barsalona as U2's agent there. Frank, at that time, was pretty much god in America. He's a very moral and loyal person. There weren't many people like him around, that's for sure.

My perception of touring in America was that it was much more about organization, about getting the sound right, doing deals with sound companies and trucking companies, booking travel and flights properly. The whole thing in America was just so different to Europe because America was, and probably still is, dominated by radio. You have one main language, one record label, one culture. A marketer's dream. When you are touring in the same month to Sweden, Belgium, Italy, Portugal, Spain and Yugoslavia, the marketing techniques are completely different. In terms of the touring, one of the things I really appreciated about U2 was that they trusted my judgement. I would put the tour together and say, 'This is the tour.' And they would pretty much say, 'Great. That's great.' There weren't huge debates. There might have been questions and things, but that was the way it worked out. Paul is very good at asking the right questions, at delegating. That made my life, my job, much easier.

Of all the shows that I did with them, I can think of one in the whole of that time, maybe 16 years, which didn't completely sell out. U2 are the only band I can say that of. That was always Paul's strategy – not to book too large a venue and risk leaving seats empty. I think it took seven or eight years before they played Wembley Arena. I remember having conversations with Bono, where he didn't want to play Wembley Arena. He wanted to continue doing Brixton Academy. I think I had to explain to him that he would have to play Brixton Academy probably for a month and a half to satisfy even half of the demand. It was more sensible to play Wembley Arena for a few nights. Bono felt that he wanted to maintain an intimacy with his fans. He felt that putting them in a huge hall, where he was a long way away from them, was not what U2 was about. But then, of course, they played arenas and got used to it. They had the ability to make arenas feel like they were little clubs anyway.

I remember arranging the first stadium tour for *Joshua Tree*. Everybody had agreed we were going to do it. I'd booked it, set it all up and gone off to Australia to be with the Eurythmics, who were having a huge tour down there. Tickets for the U2 tour were going on sale the next day. I got to Australia and because the jet lag is horrible, sort of day for night, I took half a sleeping tablet at about two o'clock in the morning. Around three o'clock I got a phone call from Paul McGuinness saying, 'You have to talk to Bono. You have to talk to him personally because we're not going on sale tomorrow.' And this show wasn't just a couple of days at Wembley Stadium; this was a whole two- or three-month European

Support band 'MacNas' at Zooropa show, Wembley Stadium, London 1993

Top: Joshua Tree show, Wembley Stadium, June 198
Bottom: [...] Joshua [...]

...Prior to that I had worked until 1979 with Led Zeppelin and from 1967 with groups managed by Peter Grant, Led Zeppelin's manager. With Led Zeppelin, I was the assistant to Richard Cole who was their tour manager and the hours were deadly. I was looking after all the group members and also Peter Grant, and near the end, I was trying to take care of Richard as well. I would say, without exaggeration, that I was awake and on call about 20 hours of each day. Luckily I had never gotten into drink or drugs so was able to cope with...

We were expanding too on tour and it wasn't very long before we had the full complement of backline technicians. The same had happened with previous groups and adding specialists and technicians was an ongoing process. A tour accountant was added, Bob Koch, and a security chief, Ron Mcﾠﾠﾠrey (he was so essential to our first big shows but sadly died a few years ago), who had worked on the Led Zeppelin tours and was an ex-cop from Boston. He knew all the venues in the USA and the security staff which was extremely important as to how we played those venues and what we wanted from the staff working our gigs. Most of the security staff then were just bouncers and had little respect for the audience. If you got out of line, they just threw you out. We had decided they should understand that the only reason they were there was because U2 were playing and since all the expenses were set by the group they should understand that they were indi...

The crew almost always does the get-out after a show and travel to the next city by buses (these are specifically made for touring crews and have all the comforts that you would need to spend a day in them). They also do on more gruelling runs. As far as the group goes, I generally charter a large jet for...

Paul McGuinness and Dennis Sheehan, mid-1980s

The U2 touring experience is quite wonderful. It's a home away from home. The group members and families were great friends when I met them and they are now even greater friends. They have worked really hard at their vocation and this has shown through the great and hard and tough times. We have been blessed with a group that redefines the boundaries of their music album by album, keeping them exciting. A lot of fans would say that the songs mean everything to them, the music and the words. I feel that Christianity is the basis of all that they do. I don't mean that in respect of religion. I mean in all that they do, say and act. We even had Father Jack with us on the Elevation tour. He expected to stay for just a month at the beginning but ended up with us for the whole tour. He has been a lifelong friend to the group and has always blessed our touring, but he is more than the proverbial Bible-carrying mentor. His presence is calming. His words are short but well chosen and totally appropriate on each and every occasion.

The group are very honourable people. When they start building, they are building on something that's already quite big. They build with Everest in mind but when they get to the top they still feel the need to go higher. I don't think there is any high point for U2: they have continually gone higher and higher with their music and have reached pinnacles of achievement with all that they have embarked upon. Our tours are like that as well: we have always strived to go one better, and we've felt that has been achieved. U2 have proved that you can be great achievers and still lead fairly normal lives and respect those around you and those you come into contact with. After all, we are only here on this earth for a short period of time. What else would I have done?!
Ireland, February 2004

most places are quiet after midnight when we arrive. The transition is smooth and we always have a hospitality suite at the hotel so that we can relax for about an hour after we finish our work for the day. It also serves as a time-out while our baggage is taken to our rooms and suites. We have to use the hotels as our offices so communication with the management and staff of the hotels is very important and they have to understand how we do our jobs. Sometimes we set up an office within the hotel and we all generally go there and work. We are a seven-day-week working group while on tour and as much as we know that there are concerts on certain nights there is also the running of their business every day. We make most of the single videos while we are on tour so two-day breaks are looked at for filming. We also record a lot of the new singles while on tour so studios have to be looked at or mobile recording vehicles are booked and ready when we arrive at a certain location. The group has meetings almost on a daily basis about all aspects of their business and this helps keep them on top of it.

Shows are always great. I believe that for me the greatest experience is when the group is ready to go on and they walk out onto their stage. I generally do a countdown as we use music intros and timing is essential to them being on stage just at the right time. Then I walk out into the audience and look at people's faces. They light up. This is a big part of why I enjoy doing what I do for a living. That jubilation and happiness for those two and a half hours while the group is on stage are totally worthwhile and priceless.

After each show the group usually has a review of the show. This sometimes takes a few hours but usually a little less time. Sometimes we listen to the tapes from Joe's sound desk or view the videotapes of the show. This way, if there are small problems they are dealt with and the show remains at 100 per cent. Every night they play, U2 always give more than seems possible, and it will always be like that. Their perception is that you should come away from a U2 show remembering everything you've seen and heard. The show is different every night, and fans that go to numerous shows will tell you so and explain the differences in fine detail.

Above: A security guard distributes water at Love Town show, November 1989, New Zealand. Bottom right: Bono signing autographs after the Elevation show, 18th November 2001, Las Vegas, USA

Bob Koch

Tour business manager, 1984–Present

I first came to U2 as a staff tour accountant for a firm known as Phoenix Management. U2 was just breaking in the States and their management felt it would be advantageous to have a business guy with arena and stadium experience in North America. The timing was perfect, as I was just coming off the Jacksons' Victory tour.

I first met with Frank Barsalona, Barbara Skydel and Principle Management's Ellen Darst just as the Unforgettable Fire tour was about to switch into full gear. The people felt right, I loved U2's writing, and before I knew it I was settling my first U2 show at the Brixton Academy. Tour manager Dennis Sheehan had been handling the business duties up until my arrival, in addition to everything else that he was responsible for. At the time, it was common for a tour manager to also handle petty cash and show settlements. As the band's popularity was exploding, Dennis was quickly becoming overloaded, thus was quite happy to pass the money baton to me.

In the early days, we had a variety of agents to negotiate our performance deals, with different agents in the various territories. In North America it was Premier Talent, Frank Barsalona, who had a staff of agents communicating with each local promoter. Each venue required a separate deal. As the deals were being created, I would sit down with our responsible agent, Barbara Skydel, and review the individual budgets. She would act as our mouthpiece with each promoter, as we argued the expected costs for that particular show. The resulting 'flight plan' was directly related to what earnings we could expect for each stop on the tour.

We were part of a rolling snowball, getting bigger and bigger, known as the Joshua Tree tour, which was a combination of arenas and stadiums. Fans were fighting for tickets to every show. I can remember realizing how quickly the entourage had grown. Three sound guys became seven. Four lighting techs became eight. Five trucks became twelve. In catering, instead of being at dinner with thirty people and a few locals in a cafeteria, it was suddenly seventy people and a separate circus tent to handle the multitude. Today many rock and roll tours gross hundreds of millions of dollars, putting food on the tables of a thousand families in each city. While there cannot be a U2 show without Bono, Edge, Adam and Larry, there also must be thousands of local personnel, handling security, ushering, advertising, stagehands, loaders, etc., etc. In many ways, we are a travelling team that hooks up with a local team to deliver history each and every night.

It is necessary to highlight the importance that U2 places on fair ticketing and to understand how the mechanics of ticket distribution have changed since I began with the band. Especially in Europe, tickets were printed by a bonded printer then driven to all the outlets for sale. In the late 1980s, electronic ticket distribution (Ticketron and eventually Ticketmaster) changed the way our ticket inventory was managed. Thanks to computerized ticketing, the entire inventory can be available at every outlet at once. As a result, shows sell out in hours or minutes, rather than months or weeks. U2 watches these trends and insists on policies that put tickets into the hands of the true fans at fair prices. To this day,

we still conduct regular surveys of our audiences to gather information relative to ticket purchase experiences. On the Elevation tour, U2 were keen to develop a ticket-scaling plan that had both reserved and general admission tickets. We were able to offer general admission tickets on the floor, right in front of the band on a first-come, first-served basis at the lowest price, while reserved seats were available on the sides at higher prices. This way the show could deliver a commercially prudent gross, but still be fair to the ardent fan on a budget.

This might be some boring accounting trivia, but I want to mention an interesting audit policy that we employ at our bigger gigs. While many bands have people to click the number of punters that enter each gate, we use a different approach. We have special U2 ticket stub bags that we hand out to our truck drivers. They oversee the collection of torn ticket stubs into those bags. They each count out 1000 stubs so we can get an accurate sample weight of 1000 tickets. We then weigh the entire pile of tickets and determine the quantity of stubs, based on the weight of the sample. It's amazingly accurate. At the very least, we determine whether it's necessary to hire interns to count the stubs at all.

U2 now works with a global tour promoter, who in turn engages local promoters in each city. This centralizes our tour advance communications, as we only need to address the key issues and concepts once. The global promoter becomes the band's agent *per se,* which further streamlines the effort. It is clearly the most efficient way to tour.

Live performance is so essential to the soul. It's a combination of camaraderie, a validation of what you've grown to love, and verification that it's really that good, whereas I think with U2 what happens is that you verify that it's even better than the real thing.
Chesapeake, MD, January 2004

The Elevation support fleet

... to get to where we thought would be ... what was always further ... further away. In the ...

... in this respect ... is a word that ... your reach should always exceed your grasp. I think it's absolutely true of U2. I've learned that every single day we should learn something new. It's always an education process. The way technology has developed in the music industry is beyond belief. I've been doing this as a professional for 30-odd years and I'm still excited at the prospect of learning what's next, what's new, and what's coming around the next corner.

Roy Ginir has always been a champion of the U2 cause. At the US Festival in May 1983, when Bono decided he was going ...

... should be ... part of the biggest band in the world.

The new ... of shows required a ... ... had experimented with on ... new ... songs that we had done. Designer Jeremy Thom ... started from his ideas and the thoughts of above he plus the band and Willie came up with the 200ft or so wide ... stage ... huge. It was enormous. It became apparent that we would need a vast amount of PA for our new challenge. We designed a bigger and better sound system for that outdoor leg of the tour as we were now dealing with huge audiences from 50,000 to 90,000 and we designed a three-tier flowing configuration ... a total speaker configuration of 144 ... and ... speakers with 16 k4

... ... the show ...

Joe O'Herlihy briefing band and crew on ZooTV sound issues, August 1992, Foxboro Stadium, Foxboro, USA.
Left to right: Stuart Morgan, Robbie Adams, Joe O'Herlihy, Bono, Larry Mullen Jr, Adam Clayton, The Edge, Dave Skaff, Dennis Sheehan

front-fill speakers. We needed a lot more sound crew. Steve McCale, Chris Fulton, Jim Bang 'Boomer', Scott Appleton were recruited as each show now required a set-up day prior to the show day. All the shows were completely sold out. We finished this leg of the tour in Cork, my home town. It was Edge's birthday – what a party!

Back to the USA for the third leg of the tour during which the band wanted to make a concert road movie and album, starting with the indoor show and finishing with the stadium show. We would use the remote recording services Black Truck with Dave Hewitt and his crew to record all the audio for the movie soundtrack with Thom Panunzio at the controls and Jimmy Iovine as producer. This project was to become *Rattle and Hum*.

The first time we met up with B.B. King and his band was at a show in Texas where he played support. Bono wrote a song for B.B., which we rehearsed at sound check and played that night when B.B. and his band joined the band on stage. The whole thing was filmed and recorded. It was one of those magic moments on the tour that made it to the movie and album. We would see a lot of B.B. King and his band in the years to come.

When we finished the indoor shows in Hampton, Virginia, on 12 December we had to travel across America to Sun Devil Stadium, Tempe, Arizona, where we filmed both shows on 19 and 20 December for the outdoor show segment of the movie. But before that I had an appointment in Dublin on 16 December, as my wife Marian was due to have a baby – our fourth. The band arranged for me to fly on Concorde back home to Dublin to be present at the birth, and hopefully be back in time for the shows on the 19th and 20th. In the Concorde lounge at JFK I called home to see how Marian was getting on, and she told me that I had better hurry up. We had three children, but I was never present at any of their births as I was always away working. I got to London and called home, and when Marian's sister Clare answered the phone I knew I was in trouble; she told me that Marian had gone into the hospital and that they were expecting the baby to be born very soon. I felt sick with the fear that, having travelled halfway around the world, I was that close and yet so far away and there was nothing I could do about it. I flew to Dublin and got in at 9.30. I reached the hospital at about 10.05 and our beautiful daughter Louise was born into my arms at 26 minutes past 10. I had made it to the hospital with 20 minutes' grace. I have had some incredible experiences in my career working with this band but that night was to me the highlight of my life so far. Concorde whisked me back to New York and I flew on to Phoenix just in time for the big film shoot of the last stadium shows of the Joshua Tree tour, and thus ended a fantastic year: 1987. We started the preparation for the upcoming Love Town tour with band rehearsals in Dublin in the summer of 1989. B.B. King and his band joined us on this tour.

The next period in the band's career was *Achtung Baby*. It was time to put the love affair with America on hold and re-establish their roots in Europe. In November 1989, the Berlin Wall came down and this made a lasting impression on the band. It was decided that Berlin would be the city for the band to record the next album in, at the legendary Hansa Ton Studios. We arrived in

Berlin on the first anniversary of the Wall coming down and it was such an incredible place. It was an inspired move from a creative perspective, because you were going to a city that was buzzing with excitement, with millions of people everywhere hoping for a new beginning.

The band went from having this great rock 'n' roll stadium sound to this fantastic new grunge-like industrial sound. They really redefined themselves, and that sound was to establish what the 1990s was going to be all about. *Achtung Baby* and *Zooropa* were masterpieces. This whole period was like a vortex fraught with danger because there were so many different avenues being explored, a serious amount of sonic frontier was being breached, crossed and extended. Dan Lanois with Brian Eno and Flood established directives and areas to experiment. Bono would basically keep changing things around and turn everything on its head. He would drive everybody nuts, but inevitably get the best possible results. To develop creatively you have to absorb what's going on around you, and that's what ZooTV was all about. It was in keeping with the fantastic musical changes that the new album *Achtung Baby* had achieved.

The ZooTV production ideas were the direct result of the influence received while working in Berlin. When you get to the stage of tour pre-production, the audio department is always looked upon as the poor relation. It wasn't particularly pleasing, because I felt that the band had gained their reputation and credibility for great live sound quality in the previous ten years. That was something I took pride in. It was obvious that I had to fight for my space now. The ZooTV tour stage-set design must surely be the best multi-media rock show ever and is something to be very proud of. The way the ZooTV tour was constructed went hand in hand with the approach to the sound design for the tour. We had to do things differently to achieve the best possible results because of the vast difference in audio quality achieved in the transition from the album sound to the band's live performance of the new songs from an audio perspective. To replicate the new sound was probably the hardest step we had ever undertaken.

Everybody was involved in the process: the band, the production team, Brian, Danny, Steve, Flood, Robbie Adams the studio album engineer and myself. At the time we didn't have the technology from an automation point of view to deal with the volume of treatments and effects needing to be changed during the performance of each song during the live show. Three sound engineers were required to do the show every night. The sound was split across three consoles; I would mix the show and Robbie would do all the effects and treatments.

The sound department started the ZooTV tour in the passenger seat of the Trabant; now we ended up in the trunk. Few people realize or understand the enormous difficulties that the stage-set design for the ZooTV Outside Broadcast tour created for the sound department. I don't honestly think there was ever a conscious thought about trying to kill the sound department on this part of the tour, but it felt like that at times.

It was a new departure for the band. Willie, Jonathan Park and Mark Fisher were selected to come up with a design that would make the transition from the indoor show to the scale required for the outdoor show. We never did it like that in the past. On previous stadium shows our approach was always very straightforward and quite conventional.

When we got to Hershey Stadium for production rehearsals the fun and games began. Each department co-operated with the others and overlapped on various different technical inventions to make it all work. The stage monitor position was now under the stage and the only visual contact with the band for the monitor engineers Dave Skaff and Don Garber was via CCTV monitor screens. It was very difficult at first. As the sound department was my responsibility, I was totally determined we would succeed. The 45 stadium shows on this leg of the tour are testament to that fact and we did succeed quite magnificently.

The PopMart set and stage design once again threatened the integrity of the sound department. After we had achieved the impossible on ZooTV, I thought that the lessons learned would be brought to the table for PopMart. Not so. With PopMart, I had huge difficulty because I was handed the sound design as a done deal, and I had to find ways to supplement the design. I sat down with Roy and Troy Clair and Greg Hall of Clair Brothers Audio and said: 'Right, this is the set design we have to deal with (affectionately known as the Orange Pumpkin) and as I will be mixing the show in a mono configuration I need more speakers. I want to develop a smart and clever way of supplementing this system.' Clair Brothers embraced the whole concept idea and were not negative in any way.

I think we got the best possible result in horrific circumstances. The worst sound in the entire stadium was right where Bono's microphone stand was, underneath the pumpkin. In my 20-odd-year relationship with Bono, he has spent all of his time in front of my sound system, but on PopMart he would have to run out to one of the wings just to get away from that hot spot of sound, and then it became, 'Oh, this is a good visual out here on the wing, plus I can hear and sing much better than over there.' It was a huge challenge. I rose to that challenge and made it work as well as possible but it wasn't ideal in any way. When you tour a large show, production becomes departmentalized, and you have to home in on your department's responsibilities. I strive for strong discipline and efficiency within the sound crew, along with my system engineer and crew chief, Jo Ravitch from Clair Brothers, who has been working with me on U2 tours for 20 years.

All That You Can't Leave Behind was the essence of U2 in the sense that every single song is listenable and pleasurable and has something incredibly special going on. You find yourself going back to it time and time again. I wasn't around the studio for the making of this record as much as I normally would be because of commitments with REM and The Cranberries. The band decided that they were going to work sporadically on the record and take as much time as necessary. They'd never approached a record like that before and I think it worked out well. It was brilliant to see Edge take the guitar out of the case again – a great guitar record, you know?

The music gave me great inspiration in knowing that the

Elevation tour would redefine things again, drawing a line pretty much back to basics. The record and the material was a huge indication as to which way the tour was going to go. We would be back playing concerts indoors for the first time in ten years. I was happy because I felt that we were getting back to the original vision, the emotional communication and contact with the U2 audience was going to be re-established. From the very first day in rehearsals I felt so strong and positive that this was the correct avenue to explore. This is basically Bono on stage touching hands with the audience that's a foot and a half away from him. That is what this band is all about. This band established that method and form of contact with their audience way back, so now it's like back to the future.

The Elevation tour was probably the most vital ingredient in changing the philosophy of sound companies the world over. As a direct result of the lessons learned on the PopMart tour, Clair Brothers Audio went back to the drawing board to dream it all up again, much as U2 had at the beginning of the 1990s. In the music industry, production values were changing at a very rapid pace; we were streamlining in every single aspect – staging, set design, sound, lights – everything was getting smaller and more efficient. The world of sound had a lot of catching up to do. History was being made right before my eyes. Clair Brothers Audio had designed and developed the new i4/i4B Line Array technology which I had used on the REM Up tour. This system sounded quite magnificent. I felt that the Elevation tour was the ideal tour for this quite perfect sound system.

U2 have always wanted to create and generate something quite different in the live context. We've always said you can go and put the record on in your front room and jump around and that's great but when you go to a show there has to be that special something that adds another dimension, that makes it quite exceptional. I think U2 have done an extraordinary job from that point of view.

When we start a new campaign it usually begins with the recording of the new album. Making a record nowadays can take up to the best part of two years and it is during this time that I get to know what the new songs are all about, particularly what they will sound like when we go into rehearsals and make the transition from the album version of the songs to the way the songs will be played live on stage. This is a very important point in the preparation required because I get a complete understanding of what the new songs are all about. This involves understanding what the band are trying to achieve from every song and what the different arrangements and mixes do in relation to the character of each song. I get to know every aspect of the new songs intimately, in particular which effects and treatments are used on the various songs, because these will have to be replicated for the live show.

The release of the album usually includes a short promo tour to promote the new record. This will usually include the band performing at selected cities and venues around the world. Preparation for this segment of the campaign will include some band rehearsals just to get the six or eight new songs up to speed for performing them live on the promo tour.

Top, left to right: Des Broadberry (Edge's backline keyboard tech) and Tony Woodoff (keyboard programmer for tour rehearsals) in understage 'keyboard world', ZooTV production rehearsals, February 1992, Lakeland, Florida. Bottom, Monitor engineers Dave Skaff and Don Garber in understage 'monitor world'. Elevation production rehearsals, March 2001, Miami Arena, Miami, USA

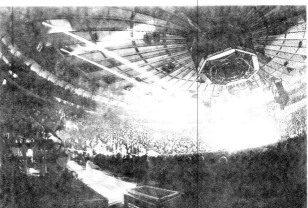

Cabling putting the power into
Pop Mart, Memorial Coliseum,
Los Angeles, June 1997

The PopMart set before completion of the arch-cladding, Memorial Coliseum, Los Angeles, June 1997

'Jeez, I hope he doesn't fall.' You know, there goes the end of this whole incredible thing.

In the mid-1980s, as a company we grew quickly, expanded our audio inventory and capabilities, always pushing new boundaries. Joe O'Herlihy wanted an active part in the evolution of the Clair S4 speaker system, which was always being redeveloped and refined. And Joe always took an active interest in making sure that not only was he with the best, but he was contributing to the best, too. Pushing the envelope and advancing the art form ...

RC: Joe was willing to try any new ideas. Other people were always saying, 'Let someone else try it first.' He would come over and listen and do the tests and go, 'Okay, that'll work, let's give it a go.'

GH: Before the current Line Array systems everyone used the same cabinet to do everything necessary in a given venue. And what happened was that the sound would make it halfway to the back, but the cabinets – which were designed for a certain distance – never made it the whole way to the back with full frequency sound. So Clair Brothers were one of the first companies to design a different cabinet for longer distances. And Joe O'Herlihy and Clair Brothers worked that out together so that when U2 went out, the people in the higher and further sections would hear the sound the same as the people down front. That was accomplished by using these different types of long-throw cabinets integrated into the overall system design.

RC: For its time it was totally unique. And Joe was willing to come here to take it out and try it. And obviously it translated into a better sound for the people in the audience. Joe was good at using new equipment. U2 depended on Joe entirely to make the sound as perfect as possible, given any challenge or any concert location...

GH: U2 and Springsteen were the leaders in giving a great deal of attention and concern to make sure that the guy that bought the ticket up there was having the same experience as the guy who was sitting in the third row. It was a good time for getting good sound. Joe always wanted to have the latest toy, widget, gizmo, he wanted to make sure that he could go to the band with confidence and conviction. He has always done his audio homework diligently, and is fiercely proud of that part of his job.

RC: And his group backed him. That was the important thing. Rather than saying, 'Look, can't we cut back on this?' they backed him. That was the difference. Some bands would say, 'That's another 100,000 for the tour – sorry, we're not doing that.' Joe never had that problem. Joe always got total co-operation.

GH: Joe always kept us on our toes. And we appreciated that because you're only as good as your last show in this business. You can get fired over a bad mike cable, you can have $2 million of PA that works well for 99 shows, but on the 100th show your mike cable might go bad. So, you're only as good as your mike cable in that case – the weakest link of the system, the $30 link could ruin you in the eyes of that band. And that's always been the strength of this company: worrying about the small details – how the case lids fit on, how the systems pack and travel ...

In my mind, *The Unforgettable Fire* was pretty much the launch-pad for them, especially in America. They had 'Bad' and of course 'Pride' which was the absolute breakthrough song here. If the listeners weren't won over by 'Sunday Bloody Sunday' and the *War* album, then 'Pride' put the icing on the cake. It was the first anthem; you can't get it out of your head. It was a great message, and universally connected to everyone. *The Unforgettable Fire* was the first album that you listened to every track with headphones.

RC: I see it from a different point of view. I think that 'Sunday Bloody Sunday' was different. It was the first time a drummer was playing a military beat. To me that was 'Whoa! I love that!' Here's a drummer who set the mood. It was the first time that the drums sent chills down my back. Not only the vocals and the guitar riffs, but the drums on this cut. As a sound engineer I'd never heard that before and it was a thrill.

After his movie career the Colonel needed to reinvent Elvis so they had this TV show, and invited 200 kids just sitting down on the floor. He and his small band were on in the middle of the audience. He was kidding around with them, having fun. Bono, many times said: 'I love that Elvis in the round show when he wore the leather.' That stayed in Bono's head and left a lasting impression on him. And almost every artist wanted a B-stage set-up in their shows after that, funny ...

GH: It's where MTV and VH-1 got 'Unplugged' from. It's the root, the father of the concept. On ZooTV they came out into the centre of a stadium with 70,000 people around them. In the centre, open to the elements, brought the acoustic instruments, just sat around and picked. I loved ZooTV because it was totally over the top. PopMart was just too big for its own soul and aspirations. Joe and I still joke about this. This has always been a band that doesn't need any props: a drum riser, a black curtain, a couple of spotlights and a searchlight. With PopMart I think everybody was glad when it was over. Joe was challenged with the design daily and had some totally miserable times. The main PA design was centred on a big orange ball centre-stage in front of the arches, and we redesigned a special trapezoidal S4 just for that tour so we could mould the speakers into what we called the 'orange pumpkin'. The bottom row of S4s were these special trapezoidal S4s so that the whole thing could come together into a spherical cluster shape – and the whole main system was painted orange per the show design. It was the first time we worked hand in hand with designer Richard Hartman to do that. So, you take the good times, you take the bad times. And hopefully you have a lot more good times than bad times.

All touring disciplines met halfway on Elevation. It was a huge artistic success, from a design standpoint and in execution. And Joe had his renaissance – and won industry awards and accolades from peers. The PA was restored as an important concept in the entire scheme of things. That show worked so well from every angle and every aspect including the most important one: emotional. It morphed between pre- and post-9/11 with inspiring results. We were very, very happy for Joe and the outcome of the tour – it was a brilliant achievement. Fair play to him, as they say in Ireland!

RC: And someone must have started catching on because some of the props that were there in the beginning became less of an issue towards the middle of the tour. The video walls that went up and down – they spent a lot of money to get those to go up and down, sequenced, the whole nine yards. Bono started saying, 'Do we really need this?' And all of a sudden things started getting a lot simpler. 'Let's cut that out …' And they start connecting it back to their roots. The stage worked well and connected right with the audience. Artist–audience interaction at its best, and always a key element to the best U2 live shows.

U2 has probably been our longest-standing rock and roll account, other than Elton John. Clair Brothers were always there for U2's tours, and the equipment was created for the U2 tours so that they could be the best. There were always new things and new dimensions, and they were always treated with priority. When the latest U2 project details first came to our desks in the office I can guarantee you that we stopped and made sure that they had the newest and the best. And Joe was always here to make sure that it was the newest and the best.

GH: For the most part, it's been a labour of love. The Elevation tour gave me the same feeling as the first time I saw them. And that's a hard thing to do, when sometimes in this business you feel like you've seen it all. There are just not too many of those bands left out there.

Lititz, PA, May 2003

PopMart – the bigger picture, Memorial Coliseum, Los Angeles, June 1997

Production

Steve Iredale
Back line and stage, October, War; production manager, Unforgettable Fire–Present

War tour crew, clockwise from top: Tom Mullaly, CJ Patterson, Willie Williams, Steve Rainford, Joe O'Herlihy, Steve Iredale, Japan 1983

I can remember the day I went for the interview. Tim Nicholson, U2's first tour manager, rang me and said, 'Can you come down? We want to talk to you about a U2 thing. Paul McGuinness and Barry Devlin have been speaking and Barry suggested to Paul that you would be the ideal person for U2.' The interview went well. We didn't really talk too much about what the job entailed. Tim showed me all the equipment that was stored in a back room, which consisted of Larry's drum kit, a Vox AC30, a really odd amp that Edge had bought somewhere in America on the Boy tour, and a couple of Harbinger cabinets that Larry was using for monitors, which Adam ended up using years later for a bass rig. That really was the extent of all their equipment. They wanted me to start on back line: they were planning to tour more and I'd had back-line experience, having worked with Horslips.

One of the first jobs I did with U2 was to pick up Joe O'Herlihy at the station. He was coming up from Cork. Joe got in and the first thing he says is 'Welcome aboard. This is not your normal band.' Those were his exact words and it's so true. Joe made the point that these guys don't do anything the way you think they should. Initially I found the individuals in the band quite odd and quite difficult to deal with. Different backgrounds, different ideas. I came from a more traditional type of set-up, and they, from day one, had their own ideas about how they wanted to go about things. Bono and Edge were the most assured individuals that I've ever come across; they knew exactly where they were going. They were very demanding in their approach and the expectation was very high.

They had this old white Volkswagen LT28 converted minibus. It had a compartment for equipment in the back and it had a row of seats for the band. I ended up driving it around Dublin, moving whatever needed moving from A to B. They were rehearsing in the room that Jack Heaslip had made available to them in Mount Temple School. For some reason this stopped being available, probably because school was back after the summer break. We became nomads, and eventually started rehearsing in an old warehouse belonging to Windmill Lane Studios in Creighton Street. I would get a call saying, 'We want to rehearse' and I would have to go and turn the gear on, and make sure it was working. Leave them to it for six or seven hours, return later to turn off the gear, and check to see if Edge had left a note saying what needed to be done for the following day. I was making an awful lot less money working with U2 than I was with Horslips – sometimes we didn't get paid for weeks on end – but I consciously made the decision to devote myself to U2 as there was the prospect of doing dates in America and in Europe, and that appealed to me.

My first show with U2 was on 16 August 1981 at Slane Castle, with Thin Lizzy. Production was limited to a couple of risers for the CP 70 piano and the drum kit, and it stayed that way for the whole of the October tour. During the US leg of the War tour in 1983 we cemented our relationship with Clair Brothers, our sound supply company. Dave Natale and C.J. Patterson came with the system, and helped us on our way. The shows again were of a mixed variety, but late in the US leg we did two arenas, LA Sports Arena and Worchester Centrum. The LA show was our first attempt at flying a PA, and putting together an arena-style lighting system. I think we learned more that day than any other day we have toured.

In February of 1984 I was invited over to work with Nocturne, a well-established video and lighting company in San Francisco, to find out whatever I could about touring. Nocturne was set up by Journey as their own production company to service their tours. In San Francisco there were venues like the Cow Palace, Oakland Arena, the Civic Auditorium and the Waldorf Theater where I would see the shows from load-ins to load-outs on a daily basis; watching Bill Graham's people putting on shows, understanding the union labour system first hand. While I was doing that and being localized in the Bay area, Willie was going to shows all around the States. We looked at the various companies in the industry to see who the key players were in lighting, PA and staging. We looked at set design, and who manufactured the sets. We looked at various rigging techniques, and the best approach to take. One thing that was very obvious was that Journey had a very smart method for touring: their 360-degree show was unique, and it was obvious that this was generating a serious amount of additional income. It was also interesting because it changed the whole dynamic for an audience. There were thousands of people who wanted to be behind the stage. It's like the crowd that goes to watch football, and wants to be behind the goals. You see what the band are seeing and you're right on top of it. Paul liked this idea when he saw it, and it was decided we were going to tour this way. That, in itself, dictated how spartan U2's productions were at that time. The stage positions have basically stayed the same – we have always kept the performance area the same – and the only thing that got moved around over the years was the piano. It's a simple set-up but it's not that pretty from the back – it never has been because they all have their little quirky bits of equipment everywhere. It's exactly the same when they are in the studio.

Pat Morrow at Nocturne was very helpful. He gave me a tremendous opportunity. Pat Morrow really was the guy who developed the video industry, as we know it today, and all the Nocturne people were trained with a very good work ethic. One thing Pat and my time at Nocturne instilled in me very early on was to have a deep respect at all times for the union people we were dealing with and to build a relationship with promoters. Pat and Benny Collins were

In discussion during rehearsals for ZooTV Outside Broadcast, Hersheypark Stadium, USA, August 1992. From left: Steve Iredale, Bono, The Edge, Paul McGuinness and Tim Buckley

particularly good about that. A lot of people from Europe went over to America with reluctance, and fear of what they were going to encounter when dealing with the unions. We decided to kill them with kindness. We gave them T-shirts, sweatshirts – we gave them bundles of stuff. We might have been naive about it, but we certainly believed in what we were doing. We wanted to tour in a way that we enjoyed, not in the way people told us we should be doing it. If Bono said, 'Why can't we put the PA at the back, behind the band?' we'd do it, and we would say to people: 'Give us ten reasons why we can't do that.' We played with the PA behind the band's front mike-line for years, which made Joe's life difficult at times, but also proved the point that you could do it.

We came back from America with a full package of people: Clair Brothers for sound, Tait Towers and Michael Tait for lighting and staging. Those were the sort of people who impressed us with their enthusiasm and their thinking. They knew an awful lot more than we did and could help us big-time. If we want to do crazy things, these are the people who can do it. There was a report generated and sent to Paul about how we should approach the next level of touring for U2. We decided we wanted to do 360 and since then we've never done a one-end 270-degree show in an arena when a 360-degree show was possible.

For Bono the contact was very important – getting close was the thing. One of the boundaries that Bono was pushing the whole time was to close the gap between the band and the audience. Larry has quite a good view of what's going on during the show and how well the audience is treated. He's very aware of that whole dynamic. The entire band are concerned about the audience and how well they're looked after, and it's a primary concern for all of us. The audience is the first rung of the ladder. If we don't have an audience, we don't have a job. We have a great safety record within our organization. It did take a long time to persuade Bono that we needed a barricade, and when the barricade became a mainstay of our touring it certainly didn't appeal to him, but it created a comfort and a safety zone for him that we could actually control. We were the first band to tour a barricade in Europe. We used our own folding barricade designed by Michael Tait, who also designed the first major modular roofing system for outdoor staging. I remember we fought with the GLC about using it in Wembley Arena.

With Bono, whatever is going on about the music, the feel has to be right for him. I remember very early on in the Dublin clubs he

would stop the show and make them rehearse songs because they weren't getting it right. He's done that all through his career from day one. You look back on the live transmission from PopMart in Las Vegas and it has happened again 20 years later, during 'Staring at the Sun': 'No, this isn't right. Stop, stop, stop!' On TV! One of the great things about them is they don't believe in boundaries whatsoever. They would perceive that as being negative thinking. With Bono in particular, the unpredictable is what makes it so exciting.

Gregg Carroll joined us in 1984 when we were in New Zealand on the Under Australian Skies tour. Willie and I were walking down the street with our U2 jackets, very nice and very hip, and this kid comes up and says, 'Give us that, would you?' It was Gregg Carroll. He was in the local crew there and he started paging Bono's cable and everyone was saying, 'God, this guy is good, let's bring him with us.' So he joined us for the rest of the tour in Australia and Europe and then came back and lived in Dublin. He was a lovely guy, a very genuine individual. He got very close to everybody. He was tour manager for the band on the Amnesty Conspiracy of Hope tour. Then there was the terrible motorbike accident in Dublin. Joe and I travelled with Gregg's body from Dublin to New Zealand. And we never once had to check up on where that coffin was. We used to see it passing us by all the time, always going where we had to go. The band followed on a couple of days later. It was a major event for all of us – it was a real growing-up process. You run around in a happy-go-lucky way … just doing whatever you want to do, and suddenly, bang! It brings you back to reality. It grounds you very quickly.

The first stadium-size show that that we did was 21 June 1985 at Milton Keynes, the Longest Day, promoted by Tim Parsons of MCP. It was a huge event. Edwin Shirley did the staging, and there were a whole bunch of Clair's people there as Joe decided that we needed a minimum of 120 S4s to make this happen. We were naive about steel and scaffolding and stuff, but we learned quickly. We had a very eventful day, and we didn't make any mistake twice. Then on the 29th of the same month we did Croke Park in Dublin for the first time ever and that was the monster for us. That was the introduction to stadiums for U2 on their own turf, on their own terms, and for the band and all the crew it was great. They had a strong bill of support acts for both these shows, and Paul and the band always ensured that was the case from that day onwards.

The Joshua Tree tour was that much bigger. Joshua Tree was

All packed up and ready to roll. Elevation tour flight cases, Earls Court, London, August 2001

The band and crew with their fleet behind them on the Unforgettable Fire tour, USA 1985

a very simple yet slick presentation. It was a big stage for its time: about 200 feet across and 80 feet deep. The Love Town tour was very hard work because we had the B.B. King thing on there. I don't think anyone knows what Love Town was about, to tell you the truth. It just sort of happened. It was an endless saga of events that were taking their toll. There was a lot of soul-searching going on – and we were burned out as well. Very burned out as individuals. We probably expelled any sort of tolerance of each other at that stage as well. It was a long tour and every time we went to do something, something happened. Like a plane broke down, our equipment was late, or Bono's voice went. I had to evacuate the venue in Sydney for a bomb scare … it was endless. The shows were quite interesting at that stage; there were some really good shows.

With ZooTV we moved on to a different level. We started by just doing indoor shows. We had a huge amount of new elements, and had to design something that we didn't know anything about, so we were inventing a whole concept at that stage. Nobody had done any interactive-type shows like that with loads of media playback. Pat Morrow was involved in providing and suggesting personnel. For ZooTV Outside Broadcast, Fisher Park designed this most outrageous and elaborate set. They had a model of it and a meeting was convened in Dublin, which everybody imaginable was brought into because Bono wanted to bounce as many ideas as possible. I was very fearful of what I was seeing because this thing was a monster and there was no way it was going to tour. It was probably 300 feet wide, like a big sail, and I was just thinking about wind and the potential for something horrible to go wrong. We broke for lunch, and as Jonathan Park was putting it away, he'd taken down all the elaborate sail and screen systems, and was left with this raw steel when Brian Eno said, 'Isn't that wonderful?' and Bono said, 'What do you mean?' So we were just left with a skeletal scaffolding system, and that's what we toured with. That was the most amazing tour ever, in my opinion. We toured the world with one universal system, and two staging systems; from an efficiency point of view there was nothing ever to match that. The show had everything you could ever want. The crew loved it as much as the audience.

ZooTV had a very localized element which developed on a daily basis: 'Television: the drug of a nation.' There was a lot going on and the cost in generating it was considerable. Also we were taking out elements that had never been toured before: Barco rear projection screens modules – which made up the main body of the show had never been toured before. The off-the-shelf unit had to be rebuilt and made tour-friendly. It was a massive learning process. The fact that these units don't like being in the rain was a good starting point. Richard Hartman helped us considerably with the whole mechanism, packaging and design to allow these pieces to tour. He broke the Belgian crews' hearts, driving them on to make something that would work on a daily basis. The belgians were vital to all the video development from ZooTV onwards and you won't find many tours on the road today carrying video without a Belgian in the ranks.

I think taking PopMart to Sarajevo in the end was one of the greatest things I've ever been involved in with. The Austrian promoter Wolfgang Klinger, the Croatian promoter Marijan Crnaric, Paul, John Giddings and myself travelled to Sarajevo to see what the reality of putting on a show was. Some people were suspicious of why U2 were doing this. They wanted to know what the Bosnians, and the people of Sarajevo, would get out of it. It was just that they had no trust in a lot of people, and they had every right to be like that. They had spent four or five years under siege: 18,000 people had been killed; snipers had shot 1800 children; everywhere you looked there was devastation. When we arrived there was no electricity, there was a limited supply of running water, there were bomb craters everywhere. There were bullet holes above my bed in the Holiday Inn. I found it depressing and it frightened me, because I'd never seen the effect of war that close. I must admit, when I left there a couple of days later I was determined that if we went anywhere on that tour we were going there. I made a couple of further visits to Sarajevo to organize what we would need to make the show happen. I felt that we couldn't do any stripped-down show; we had to do the show that was touring.

Below: Building Elevation from load-in to showtime, Oakland Stadium, Oakland, USA, November 2001.

7 a.m.

9 a.m.

11 a.m.

It was important that we didn't go there to do them a favour, or patronize them. This was a U2 show, so we were going to need to charge money for the people to get in there. One thing we had to achieve with this show was to say to the world that Sarajevo is back as a normal city. So we treated it like anywhere else in the world. That was the way we had to approach it and that's the way I talked to the crew about doing it. Everything we were doing there was very difficult. There was a huge element of danger. There were unexploded shells all around Sarajevo; the surrounding fields still contained live mines. The stadium would need sweeping on a regular basis to ensure its safety.

The cemeteries of people who died during the siege surrounded the stadium. Marijan went down there and worked on ensuring the organizing went well. He had difficulty at times because he was a Croatian. We had a Muslim choir as one of our support acts. We had people from Serbia at the show. You had to negotiate your way through many levels of bureaucracy, and we used local people. The tickets had to sell through the post office and from the boots of cars because there was no distribution and no telephone system. We generated an income there, and we ended up leaving money behind. The money that was generated for the rental of the stadium, and the arena facilities – they put that straight back in. They painted it, they fixed the plumbing, they put toilets in – I get sent photographs every couple of weeks showing the new developments. The response from those kids and everybody involved that night was absolutely phenomenal. We had kids there from Serbia and from Croatia, Slovenia, Austria, Italy. There are so many great things that happened around that night that the people in Bosnia deserve all the credit for – it was something special.

On many levels the band have a whole group of people they like to get involved: Bono's friends from the early days, particularly Gavin Friday. Paul always takes notes, he's a very involved manager, probably one of the few managers that's seen virtually every show the band has managed to perform in 20 odd years. He can be very objective and very conscious of what's going on. He pays great attention to what's happening in rehearsal and he'll still make comments about it. Every night when we do a show we have the first encore break where the band come off stage to take a breather, Paul's always in the quick-change dressing room. I'm there because I do the next lot of cues, and need to relay any changes. Paul always comes in and talks to Bono and the band about how the show's going or what he thinks of it. Every show without fail. The Edge is the mechanical hard nut, so he would always look at the new technology. Bono would see it in a totally different way. It's not the technology; it's what he can do with it. It's a tool, it's a plaything, it's a big toy. Edge is very much the musician. Larry, I think, likes to keep it simple, which he does with his drumming. Very simple, but very solid. Adam is the same. Adam is like the conscience of the group in a lot of respects. Bono has always said that about him. He's just sort of a person making sure we don't do something really stupid. Adam's also the person who's been responsible for picking and suggesting the opening acts that play with U2 over the years. Larry has always taken care of the merchandising side of U2, making sure it's good quality and not too expensive. They all have their roles.

In the planning stages of a tour Joe will come back to me about the PA and about the monitors and I will try to get that integrated in what Willie and Mark are dreaming up. At times we're at opposite ends of the scale. We will firmly butt heads on things: all of us have very strong opinions on what should happen. But it ends up being very good common ground on what we've all tried to set out to do. All of us have very strong opinions on what should happen but we have a very professional attitude to what we do, and we only approach things that are achievable and realistic. I think that's one of the main things that we've given to the industry: a sensible approach to how it works. But also, what we do we've always done very well. The reason we all hang together? We know each other. We know the good points and we know the bad points. The band has sort of got a good ear. It's a bit like a marriage as well: you know that if your wife's having a bad day, you stand back. We're going to fight with each other, but if anything ever went wrong we'd always be the first to step in there for each other. That's something that's always happened.
Dublin, March 2003

1 p.m.

3 p.m.

Showtime. Madison Square Garden, New York, October 2001

Jake Kennedy

Lighting designer, Boy, October; deputy production manager,
Joshua Tree, ZooTV; director, PopMart

From left: Jake Kennedy,
Willie Williams, Sam O'Sullivan,
Love Town tour, Australia 1989

U2 were noisy, they were intense. We all travelled in a small VW van – including the equipment. It wasn't any bigger or better than that. We picked up lights locally. Joe O'Herlihy had a PA system. He ran a PA company, of sorts. He would drive ahead; sometimes I would go with him. Sometimes we would just meet at venues and how we all got there was a bit of a mystery. Even in those days I believe the band knew they were going to do what they have done. It was never said, never talked about, but there was always this colossal work ethic on their side, which is what impressed me most about them. Joe and I were in our early twenties then, 24, 25. Larry was 16, the other three were maybe a year and a half older. But they had this massive energy that you knew was going somewhere. It was, of course, the logical steps of conquering Ireland, conquering the UK, conquering Europe, conquering America. Between the time I joined, when we were playing small clubs, and the time I first stopped working for them at the end of 1981, we had gone from clubs to the Santa Monica Civic Hall – a fairly serious size. We skipped the entire American college circuit, which would have been the norm.

We went from tiny clubs in the States to 2000-seat venues. I think the *Boy* album was just so good it attracted attention in America ahead of all the other competing punk things. The Americans I don't think really understood the punk thing as it was understood on this side of the Atlantic, so they didn't have the same respect for the hierarchy of punk bands that were coming out of England – and in the middle of all that noise coming out of the UK, Ireland and Europe was the *Boy* album. And it just struck a chord with American kids and American radio. Add to that the hard work the four guys in U2 did.

At the end of 1980 we were travelling with a lighting system, which consisted only of 24 lamps hung on a scaffolding arrangement. Their first set, which I designed for them, I dragged in and out of clubs and it was supposed to fit almost anywhere. Every club we went into we used the house lights, and the house sound system for most of that first tour. Joe and I spent all our days off ringing ahead to venues to get specs on lighting systems and sound systems; even so, 80–90 per cent of the time you never knew what you were going to get until you actually walked in. It was quite scary, but it was part of the adventure really. I remember in one place up in Albany in New York where some guy had built the entire lighting system himself, all home made.

The Boy show certainly wasn't choreographed, very often there was no set list. Bono spent an awful lot of his time in the audience, and in long guitar breaks he would just take off. That little scaffolding frame that I had around them as a device to hang lights on wasn't built or designed for somebody to be climbing on it, but he climbed on it every night. I think on some level in Bono's head he was thinking, 'Well, I know my space; now I'm going to get out of it.' And there were no radio mikes then, so it was miles of mike lead and people running along behind him. He would get stuck up on top of PA stacks and poor old Edge very

often would have to keep playing the solo till he came back. So it was very free form, it was very intense.

When the Boy tour finished I think we all knew that there was a bit of history being made here, that this was not a short journey. The effect that had on me was to question my ability as an LD to go all the way on that journey with them. I realised I hadn't, so I stopped. This was the end of 1982. At the end of 1986 Steve Iredale started talking to me about coming back to work with him on the Joshua Tree, which I did. The Joshua Tree tour felt like real rock and roll. It was big, it was loud, it created a stir. That moment when the band meet the audience – nothing will ever replace that. They used to start that show with 'Streets' and there would be that long keyboard intro in the background and then as it hit the full-on band thing and the lights went up and the audience were there ... I don't think in my life that there's anything that equals that. And while Bono still did a bit of running around and climbing he was very close to the point where, at that first meeting of the band and the audience, just a look in Giants Stadium would do it. He had conquered and destroyed the fourth wall. That's what he developed into as a performer – being able to keep 70,000–80,000 people in the palm of his hand without running around the stage, without climbing up on the roof. What they have as four people, playing the music they play, is what it's all about. I think that's unique.

We finished Joshua Tree with a collective sense of: 'We know what we're doing and we do it very well.' That was a hugely important thing for a small band of Irish people coming out of the shadows of the rock and roll industry to the centre of it. So there was a swagger about the whole operation and we really felt maybe nothing was impossible. There was a certain foolhardiness in there, but that was part and parcel, I think, of the swagger. Love Town grew out of *Rattle and Hum* and was sort of the touring version of the movie. As an organization it was a confused time. The band were uncomfortable with where they were going and we were all disjointed. We came off the Joshua Tree tour with this great world-conquering energy. The tour had been a collective effort in its design and concept. With Love Town, at the design level and at the operational level, the whole creative philosophy had gone adrift. Bono had lost his voice, we had to reschedule shows, it just never seemed to end. It was messy. For the first time the energy wasn't there and there was a sense that the thing lacked cohesion. By the end of that tour everyone was ready for a break.

In 1991 Steve and myself and Willie knew there was a tour coming, and we were actually researching in a lame sort of a way. We sort of had permission from the band to work up an expense account, fly and see shows that we thought were worth seeing. Pat Morrow from Nocturne, Terry Lee and John Lobel, from LSD, were advising us on this. Willie was talking to the band on all our behalf and he got the vaguest of briefs that whatever we did next had to do with television. That's what we got and that's where we started. The three of us were at a café in Rotterdam at a Gloria Estefan show. We went for lunch and between twelve and six we effectively and literally designed ZooTV on table napkins. Willie took all the napkins away and that was it. It was very early days. Nobody knew whether it was to be an indoor show, an outdoor show, what way the campaign was going to go. The album wasn't finished, there was a lot of head-scratching and worrying going on at all levels. But we kept plugging away at the TV thing, and really the three of us became the sort of basic drivers of that design. Without discussing it, we took on different aspects of it and bit by bit broadened out the sort of panel of experts, if you like, who were involved. Steve has a fantastic engineering brain. He knew what would hang, he knew what loads stages could carry, he knew what would fit in trucks; Willie's creative imagination was going in a different direction; and I sort of straddled the two. That was the sort of loose design team that we came up with. One thing we got the band to agree with was not to do an indoor/outdoor tour. They could do the indoor bit, and then do the outdoor bit, but not mix the two, which is what we had done on the Joshua Tree tour. Any production person will tell you that doing an outdoor show one week and then an indoor show is a complete nightmare. So we knew whatever we came up with for the indoor part had to be transferable outdoors and had to be modular enough to become huge.

Willie Williams was moving into that sort of creative spokesman role by this stage. Steve would have been the antithesis, if you like, of Willie: the hard-nosed engineering, mathematical side. Willie was more free-form. Spike attended a lot of the meetings from Upfront Staging. So the group broadened out from the three of us to quite a large group, which included the band, Fisher and Park, Spike. Ned was brought in because Ned was actually making videos and, again, we got to sa point where, okay, we've got the system, we know it's going to hang up, etc., but what can we put on it? We can't just put the band on it – that's really boring. So who do we get? Ned. He may remember it differently, but my memory of it was we were in the office one day and I said to Ned, 'You better come to this because you're the only one who actually knows anything about video.' He came in and the rest is history. The sheer scale of it was mind-numbing. I invited a friend of mine, a professional cameraman, who was used to looking through the lens of a movie camera and taking in and reading stuff, to come to the show. And he said, 'It's just too intense for me. I can't take it all in. My brain will not take in all the information that's coming at me.' That stuck in my mind as an interesting comment, and that's the sort of show it was. We dished it out full-on. It was an astonishing tightrope walk between losing the band, losing the audience, losing the technology, losing everything. Every night was high-risk, high-octane. From beginning to end it went from being quite loose to being quite choreographed. It was a learning curve. What we had to learn was when to turn the technology off. The answer, to a certain degree, is animation. It took that long to figure out how to downplay it, or how to use it.

The Belgians were key to PopMart as well as ZooTV. We had decided we were going to get the biggest screen in the world – we were going to build the shaggin' thing if we had to – and that's what we did. The technology didn't exist when we made that decision and its legacy is huge. In one of the buildings in Times Square in New York there's a circular screen, an LED screen. That screen would not be on that building if we hadn't done PopMart. I know that there's a direct line between that screen and the PopMart screen, because the same people built it. I see stadiums all over the world with LED screens – they would not be there if Pop Mart hadn't happened.

To take that entire PopMart show into Sarajevo at the end of a war period was astonishing. It was a one-off in the middle of the tour, and it was very special. Steve was responsible almost single-handedly for getting us in and out of Sarajevo.

I think their live shows have always been honest. We took a lot of criticism about that on into ZooTV and PopMart, about whether it was honest, or whether it was cynical or 'What the hell are they doing now?' sort of questions. But I think there's always been an honesty there that the fans have latched on to. U2 have always been consistent in a number of things: the quality of the music, the quality of the live show and their commitment to human rights. I think that as long as the message is consistent, people will listen. And the honesty with which it's delivered is important. I think there's always been a fearlessness there. You know, nothing was ever impossible to them or to any of us around the band. I think we all felt, from the very early days, that if we were going to do something then it had to be done right. It was as simple as that. People may have demurred, or people may have hiccuped, or people may have blinked, but at the end of the day whatever we set about doing was going to be done. Simple as that. Had to happen.
Dublin, February 2004

PopMart stage, Memorial Coliseum, Los Angeles, June 1997

Rocko Reedy

Assistant stage manager, ZooTV, PopMart; stage manager, Elevation

I started with U2 at the beginning of the stadium portion of the ZooTV tour. Tim Lamb, their stage manager at the time, needed somebody to help, so they brought me in as a second stage manager. I got along great with the band, we work really well together, so I did the outdoor stuff on ZooTV and then again on PopMart. It's very much a family vibe, these shows. Steve Iredale, he's one of my heroes. He's a great guy, very knowledgeable, considering he started out with them in clubs and then they exploded: they went from arenas to stadiums, literally overnight.

My responsibilities involve stage management. I have to interact with the local unions. They know me, so we've got it to a point now where we dump the trucks, climb out of the trucks, and everybody gets their own little piece of real estate. After everything is dumped they go into production. It's pretty much the same each time, the 88-foot-wide and 210-foot-deep hockey arena, so everybody has their bit of space where stuff goes. For me, just walking around I know enough to gauge how far along we are, before I can do a cut of local labour. If pieces aren't in place then we can't bring the rest of it in on top. Also if someone's got a problem, I want to give them enough time to sort it out before it cascades down to the next thing.

The concept I give my crew at the beginning of each tour is that we put together a chair for the band to sit in. The principle I present to them is: this is the chair, the band tells us what they want the chair to look like; Willie tells us, 'This is the design', the band approves it; that's our chair. This chair needs to be identical, not an extra piece of duct tape hanging there, not one leg shorter than the other. I want all the stuff in exactly the same place unless it's not physically possible,' so the band never has to think twice about it. Even if the dressing rooms are off-stage left, they always enter stage on the right because then it's exactly the same every time.

When I'm doing my job they never talk to me. They speak to me more at the beginning of the tour where they're feeling it out and they're a bit nervous. There's a line of communication that starts with Steve and Jake. I'm the next step down from that, but most of the time, especially because you have that family vibe, you can anticipate it. There are certain people on the crew who have a better vibe of what's going on, what's bothering the security guys, because they're with them all the time, and I can get tips from them, just little things, so they don't have to think about something. There are also the arrows that I draw to the dressing room every day. I do that on every tour. Any time you walk in the building, look for the arrows, follow them backwards to the dressing room and forwards to the stage. So the band know. I was a consultant for the movie *Spinal Tap* from when I did a tour with Styx, years ago, in 1978. Styx were huge in America. I started with them in 1974; they were a multi-platinum five-sell-out-nights-in-a-row band in America. Many of the stories in that movie were actual things with Styx, including the one where the band goes down into the catacombs of a venue and gets lost. From that day forward I've done arrows on the ground. The other thing I do is my arrows in little shopping lanes for trucks outside. I'll use spray glue so that it stays down because it won't stick to concrete otherwise. I mist the ground with it like hairspray. Between the glue on the tape and the glue on the ground, it sticks. It takes for ever getting it off. I am the original tape Nazi.

On ZooTV and PopMart our riggers, English, Irish, New Zealanders, were very flamboyant and very hard working. Everybody was truly busting their ass 24 hours a day. In the stadium tours they had to bust their ass first so that everybody else could get their stuff up on stage but then they'd be done so they had time during the day, while everybody else was still putting their stuff up, to create mischief. They decided to take that creative mischief energy and divert it into a party, which we called the Riggers Arms. We'd decide on a specific day and have a Riggers Arms party. These guys would go out to the local theatre company and bring in all

Right: Riggers on Zooropa tour 1993. Clockwise from top: Warren Jones, Mark Kohorn, Pete 'The Greek' Kalopsidiotis, T.J. Thompson. Far right: Rocko Reedy's duct tape 'shopping lanes' for Elevation load-out. Thomas & Mack Arena, Las Vegas, USA, November 2001

these goofy props: we used extra lights, made it real vibey, put shit all over the place which made it look like a total monkey house, and we'd have this great party. It became a tradition. Because they were doing multiple dates in some cities, sometimes as many as four or five dates, the band would stay in the town and were able to hang with the crew a bit more. They would come to these parties and from time to time would tend the bar for the crew, you know. They'd pour the Guinness, and that was a nice vibe, because you could sit and talk a bit. But it was kind of an unsaid rule that it wasn't anything to do with work, so we'd talk about family. It was very nice, because as our employers and as pop stars, they live in their world.

I liaise a lot with security. Scott Nicholls and I have done a number of tours together and we work together to figure things out. There's a good team effort going on there and Scotty's great. He's got the right temperament for it and a good grip on his crew. He knows how to address the situation to get people to calm down, as opposed to letting it escalate into, 'Who do you think you are, mister?'

Jake Berry and I have known each other for 20 years but we never toured together. He always set the bar for the best in the business and the rest of us tried to keep up, and when I told people that I was doing Elevation with Jake they said, 'Oh, you guys will never get along. You've both got huge egos and you're both assholes.' We got along great, but there were tensions at first, there was the competition factor that we had for so long.

On Elevation we had the core touring crew with us, with some changes. Truly in this organization, much more than others, even the guys who don't talk that much had a perspective on the vibe or the family core. The thing I say to all of them from day one: 'Two things matter in life: your health and your family. The stuff here, we're very good at, it happens to be what we do for a living, but a big rock show doesn't matter if you don't have your health and you don't have your family.'
Las Vegas, November 2001

Rocko Reedy (far left) oversees load-in, Elevation tour, Oakland Arena, Oakland, USA, November 2001

Jake Berry
Production manager, Elevation

I don't think the production manager role has varied too much. Back in the early 1980s the production and stage manager were one job. We didn't have email; we were lucky to get a telephone line. I remember advancing AC/DC from a payphone! So it's come a long way, but the job hasn't changed. You still have to keep abreast of all the rules of fire codes and safety codes. It's definitely more corporate now. For big shows, production managers get involved in the design a little bit, and the movement of gear from A to B. Working with the designers we all have a sense of our needs. We modulize the gear and staging so that we can take it round the world. The first people to modulize were probably Michael Tait and Clair Brothers Audio in Lititz. They'd make something that was 45 inches by 33, which means you can pack it in a truck two across or three across. They, and a lot of production managers in America, started to realize that packaging was an essential part of a tour. In the early days, loading a lighting truck was like having a bad game of Tetris.

The role of a production manager is to get a great team of people together and keep a tour on budget. It's pointless having a great tour if the crew are crap. I'm lucky, I have a great crew and we've groomed a bunch of good people to move on to bigger jobs. You become a mediator and a problem-solver, whether it's about the gig or personal things. We fend off all the crap that another hundred people don't want to hear. Everybody has to know in two minutes what they're doing. We're the bridge between the band, accounts, set designers, business managers, tour promoters and everybody else on the road.

I'd met Paul McGuinness and Steve Iredale before. I ended up going out with U2 on PopMart as the Concert Productions International rep. I was asked to work as a consultant for both sides, for Clear Channel and for U2, although I was paid by U2, so that made me a U2 person. I was probably the highest-paid 'chair organizer' there ever was. That was a standing joke, but it was my first insight into the U2 camp. The first time I was there they gave me a pass to get into the production office and I got thrown out of catering. We got to know a few people and it calmed down a bit. PopMart was a great show. It was put together fast and the band were under-rehearsed. They came out with an album which people criticized because it was different, too far removed for the regular U2 fans. That became a heavy weight to carry around. As far as the show was concerned, though, from a production point of view, it was pretty ground-breaking.

When Elevation came along, I wanted to do it. U2 wanted to keep Steve Iredale, so Steve and I sat down and talked about how we would approach it. I think I managed to bring in some change, at the very least. It was a great tour. Every tour is great when it's successful. Especially when it's successful on the back of something that was a bit of a disaster. Elevation was a bit of a U2 rebirth. You were out there as part of the band being reborn again, the band playing to sell-out crowds, the band getting the critical acclaim that they deserve.
London, July 2003

Top: Jake Berry (right) assisting load-out, Elevation tour production rehearsals, Miami Arena, Miami, USA, March 2001.
Bottom: Jake and Steve Iredale 'sit down and discuss' how they would approach the Elevation tour production. Miami Arena, Miami, USA, March 2001

Design and Staging

Jeremy Thom
Set designer, Live Aid, Joshua Tree

On the Joshua Tree tour the 'monitor underworld' was introduced to ensure the band and crew had total communication without distracting the audience

I'd been on the road with the Boomtown Rats for 18 months or thereabouts, back in 1979–80. I toured as their designer because Bob Geldof and the band wanted to have a different look every day. Thereafter Bob and I both lived in Chelsea. He had just finished with the Band Aid Christmas song and came up with this daft idea for a show to raise money for Ethiopia. He talked to Harvey Goldsmith and I got a phone call asking me to design the stage and set for Live Aid at Wembley. Philadelphia came up a while after that.

Live Aid was a landmark. It was the first point in time when rock and roll (and the audiences who supported it) did something on a global scale and got politicians to sit up and take notice. It was quite clearly the first point in history where anyone had taken rock and roll seriously on a political and financial level.

We used a similar layout to the Live Aid stage – the revolve with a three-wall split and viewing platforms buried in the side scaffolding – for the Self Aid show in Dublin the following year. Then Steve Iredale got me involved in the Joshua Tree tour, initially for the indoor set. They were having some issues with how to lay the band out. Bono wanted to do a 360 show in arenas. You couldn't do 360 with the set-up that they had, because of the monitor walls and all the sort of cack that The Edge had: just piles of stuff that surrounded the stage. So they needed a solution, and they had some ideas about how they wanted to tidy it all up. The answer seemed to be that what you needed to do if the band wanted to be 360 was hide everything other than the band themselves. So it made sense to stick the band on top of the crew and equipment and put the crew below and to the sides. It seemed like a new way of solving an old problem and improve the sightlines for an arena show with low seating at each side of the stage. But there was no art or artifice about it. The crew need to see the band; the band need to see the crew. But they need not to be seen by the audience, so you hide them. This was just for the indoor. The outdoor was planned primarily for stadiums with the stage at one end, though we also needed to make it work in open spaces like the show on the docks at Gothenburg harbour with ships and the city in the background. The staging for the indoor and the outdoor was entirely different, but it was all planned at the same time. So there were two different things running in parallel. We would discuss both set-ups at meetings with the band and production in Dublin.

On Joshua Tree there were two different tours with two totally different looks. The indoor had an entirely technical look: all greys, and metal and the mesh between the band and the crew. It was always a given: band and crew need to see each other.

And there was a lot of persuading: 'You'll be able to see each other, because what we're going to do is light the crew, behind the mesh, as well as lighting the band.' The business of the indoor stage became a fantastically technical exercise, and finessing how it was built to minimize truck packs and to minimize time and minimize labour. In those days of drawing by hand, doing 3D renderings was complicated and time-consuming, and it was actually much simpler to build a scale model. We did this all the time: it was the standard method of presenting to the band. We would build very accurate models since the same model, once it was approved by the client, then became a briefing tool for the workshops. Even below the surface these models were accurate. All the structure was in there. So you could go in to see the band and say, 'Okay, this is it,' and then take the stage floor off and say to the production, 'This is the underworld and this is how it all works.'

Everything the band did they did together. The four of them were around for every meeting that had anything to do with either of the stages. Larry tended to be the guy who discussed the details of the set. He was the one who tended to have the most comments about the look, and to get into the nitty-gritty of it rather that just the big picture. Paul and Jake Kennedy were usually around, Tim Buckley and Steve were always there. These meetings were fairly informal, chaotic even. Lots of things going on at the same time. It was never like: 'Okay, present to the band. Start now.' It was sort of like, 'Ah, is everyone together?' Then the model would sit there and they'd all come in and out and I'd spend a day in Dublin going through every aspect of it with all the various departments individually and together.

There were two versions for the outdoor set, with one look for the support band which transformed with a drape exchange into another one for U2. This was the first complication, because removing drapes reliably and safely in a wind is really hard, without having massive amounts of mechanics and things – which we weren't going to tour with – but we sorted that out in the end. We used kabuki drops rigged so that they slid down slightly sloping, tensioned wires when released; that way the drop was controlled even when the wind was gusting. The cloths were built and painted by a workshop in London called Kimpton-Walker. They had been my workshop of choice for a while at that point because they were small, young, willing to do wacky things. They were a skilled theatre workshop but it took me about three years to train them into how to do things rock and roll-wise. Building a theatre set and building a rock and roll set are two entirely and completely different trades. There's nothing other than painting that are shared skills. Having been on the road, having toured, having had to fix things on the fly, was the best apprenticeship I could ever have had to enable me to do what I did then. I used to come in with finished sets the day before delivery and attack them. In the beginning the crew would get terribly upset about all the stuff that they'd built which I was trying to destroy. But I was saying, 'There's nothing that I'm doing today that isn't going to happen to this set in the next year of touring. If I can damage it now then you haven't built it well enough.' It ended up being a challenge between me and the workshop crew to see whether they could build something that I couldn't destroy. And if I could break it in the workshop, it was destined to break in Boise, Idaho, or Osaka, Japan. And that's definitely the wrong place for it to fail because you're too far away to fix it swiftly and easily. It took a couple or three years to get to the point where they really understood that this was the fundamental difference between touring with rock and roll and theatre sets – and then they built stuff better than anyone else. Sets are custom and unique, there's nothing about a set that comes off the shelf. It's not like a lighting instrument that's been designed specifically to tour. It's something you're building from scratch. So, as you build it, there are a number of things that you need to consider: how does it tour, how does it pack, how does it truck, how do you fix it, how do you break it, how many people does it take to put it up, what happens when it rains, can you do it in the snow?, anything, everything. Temperature difference. I mean, if you're doing a tour of Sweden in the winter and everything's cold, you can't get metal parts together in the same way that you can in the south of France in the summer, because they come out of the truck and they're frozen. Also, you better make sure your crew's wearing gloves, because otherwise they stick to it. And you can't get connection pins together if it's cold. Heat tends to manifest itself more in soft goods than hard stuff: it rots, it falls apart. Fabric welds go soft. There are all sorts of things. All the vicissitudes of touring. I'd been on the road for 12 years and learned as I went along. The toughest thing is making certain it works every day. It's just durability.

The outdoor stage was huge for a touring show. (Although now it would be considered quite small.) It was unfussy, uncluttered, nothing much arty about it, just very straightforward, very clean. I don't recall it being a specific part of the brief, but certainly it was part of the general vibe, which was: don't even think about being fussy, because it won't fly. It suited me just fine. I wasn't an art director. I didn't do much art and frou-frou. I was a pencil guy: draw lines, form elegant shapes, define the skeleton, here's how it's built, here's what profile it has, always try to make it look clean and classy, and then dress up the form to make it look finished and fine. Above all a stage set always had to work practically before I could begin to make it work visually.

By the time we made it to the first show we were so completely wasted. It seemed like 23-hour days every day! I remember it being 110 degrees, rushing backwards and forwards between the outdoor and the indoor sets. One was at the university football stadium, and the other was in the indoor basketball arena. Two sets being built at the same time. Putting out fires all the time – without cell phones or walkies!

The late 1970s was when it all started to turn around into a real business, and the production became the thing that steered the tours. Before then it had been management that ran tours, and they, of course, didn't really understand what it took – other than

The huge Joshua Tree outdoor stage at Sun Devil Stadium, Tempe, Arizona, 1987

huge amounts of money! So as designer you were compromising to management's view all the time – that's just how it was. U2 was really the first band other than The Stones that I'd experienced where the production team was an equal part of management in terms of how decisions were made and what was needed. So here they had management, they had the band and they had the production guys who became a very important part of the decision-making process. I would defer decisions to Steve Iredale and say 'Does this work for you?' And knowing that if he said it did, then it had the blessing of band and management because he was close enough to them to call it. Things that were technically important, doing things in a certain technical way that saved money, or saved people, or saved truck space, became an important part of the practical exercise of building the tour because management therefore saved money in the process. It was the first time where the integration between big tour management and big tour production really fitted together well – like a jigsaw puzzle of which I became a part. So this was a new experience, and bear in mind this was really the first thing I'd done with both management and production from U2. I'd done Self Aid but that was mainly a production exercise with little or no interaction with the band or the office.

They were the big fish in the relatively small pond of Dublin, and they were already formed as a unit before they left Dublin, before they went worldwide, before I worked with them. They relied on each other and leaned on each other and looked to each other before they went out into the big, wide world. They left Dublin with an attitude of invincibility: they could conquer the world. 'Hey, it doesn't matter – just another tour.' Off they went, and they did it. It is quite astonishing, this diverse selection of people thrown together and all of a sudden it's like: 'Yeah, this works.' They seem to have done the weeding-out process pretty thoroughly and everybody there was a stand-up guy who really knew what he was doing – and why.

We were dealing with a family, and a family who'd chosen themselves, chosen each, other and who had a mutual respect for one another. A bunch of people who fundamentally had their hearts in the right place and chose people who were similar, who they could work with and tour with. I never had any complaints about the politics of U2. It was very straightforward. If they said they were going to do something, that's what they did. If they said they weren't going to do something, then you might as well stop debating it. If they said they were going to send you a cheque, they sent you a cheque. There was never any messing around in terms of business or politics, or money, or any of those things. Mind you, in true Irish fashion, they could discuss and debate matters of infinitesimal detail until the sun went down (and often rose again)! They were just straightforward and it was such a relief to deal with that. They're good people and they give a shit about what they are doing. Add to that the Irish bloody-mindedness and this moral indignation about things being done that ought not to be done, which is exactly what Geldof had: 'This is fucked up, let's deal with it.' In a way, they're cut from the same cloth, those guys. People who are prepared to say, 'Well, fuck you if you won't sort this. Let's just do it.' And just be bloody-minded about it. The more people say no, the more they head butt. It was a great process and an enormous pleasure to be invited in to be a part of it all!

New York, July 2003

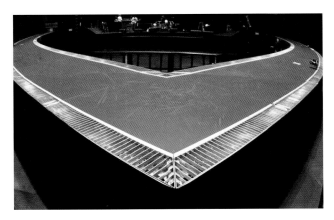

The design of the the heart-shaped B-stage for Elevation involved immense attention to the smallest detail

Michael Tait

Tait Towers, US lighting supplier, War, Unforgettable Fire; set fabrication, Unforgettable Fire, Joshua Tree, ZooTV, PopMart, Elevation

My career began in 1967 when I arrived in London from Australia. I was working at the legendary Speakeasy Club when I was asked to help out with an unknown band called Yes. I started driving the van and working on the gear. In the late 1960s, while the music industry was alive with musical talent, the technical side of the concert industry was still in its infancy. Those were primitive days. I became Yes's lighting designer and production manager.

It was never my intent to be in 'business'. For the first 12 or 15 years I only worked for Yes. I didn't think: 'I'm going to have my own lighting company.' While sound equipment was developing mainly in America, England was the home of innovative lighting gear. America had a lot more theatre and movie lighting equipment available, but there was no particular drive to develop

specific concert gear. In England we didn't really have that much, so early lighting guys like myself, Graham Fleming (Pink Floyd) and Jonathan Smeeton were forced developed our own. When I started the only portable dimmers were resistive. You could make toast on them!

In 1978 I moved to Lititz, PA. I teamed up with Roy Clair and bought an old shoe factory. We converted it into a rehearsal studio and my manufacturing facility. In 1983 U2 came up to rehearse for the War tour at Clairs' studio. I'd been off doing some Grateful Dead shows, and when I got back to the shop Willie was there looking at the new Avolights board I'd just acquired. When his rental equipment arrived it was old-fashioned stuff and he took one look at it and said, 'They're out – you're in.' So we just took over the tour on the spot and it went from there. U2 in those days of course didn't have sets, but they did want some funny little lighting bits so we built them. The band, the crew, everyone were very close. It was kind of a family thing. They were trying to use their music to get people to understand what they were doing in Ireland. There was always a message.

After that tour I flew to Dublin, where the band were making *The Unforgettable Fire*, to talk about a set. The band liked the ideas that Willie and I presented. I shipped the gear from America to rehearsals in a London theatre. I built 28-foot towers to hold up the truss which, possibly, were the most dangerous things ever designed by anyone on the planet; they were pretty lame. But we made them work. It was a very simple set which consisted of a walkway behind the band gear which Bono never went on because he was always out front climbing on stuff!

Jeremy Thom designed the Joshua Tree stage and I built it. It came to be a classic kind of U2 design. It had sloping sides and back so Bono could run up around on top. There was bar grating so the monitor guys who were underneath were able to see the stage. Of course at rehearsals Bono fell through the access hole (on almost every tour he falls off something)! I remember it was painted one colour and the band arrived and said, 'No, no. We don't want it that colour. Change it. Paint it grey,' or whatever, so we stayed up all night, painted it and, of course, the next day the band said, 'You know, the original colour was better, paint it again.' That's where I developed my 'Until they ask you three times, you don't do it' rule. When a band comes to production rehearsals for the first time, and the house lights are on, they're going to hate everything. And if they had a bad limo ride or whatever, they're going to hate it. You shouldn't let them in at the load-in end; only let them in at the punter end when the stage lights are set: 'Here's your stage,' and they always love it. Of course, after the initial thrill has worn off, it's human nature to want to change things: 'Oh, I hate that. Make it higher. Make it lower.' And if you do it, you're dead meat. You do not do it. If they ask you the next day, you say, 'Oh yeah, we'll get to it.' But if they ask you the third day, 'How come you haven't done it?' then you do it. That's because changes usually go away after one day.

When automated lighting arrived I saw that to be in the moving light business would take millions of dollars. Nocturne

Lighting was looking to expand and bought all of my lighting equipment. I then shifted exclusively into set production. Having been on the road, I have learnt a lot about the psychology of bands. When a designer comes to me with a stage design, I look at it, and I know if the band is going to be able to work with it. Can they hear each other? Can they see each other? Are the relationships right? I don't usually build verbatim from the drawing; I collaborate with the designer to edit the drawing so it works for the band without compromising the look. For instance, the position of the drums can be critical. If the drum riser is 4 feet high, the bass drum will be right in the vocalist's ear, he will not be able to hear, and he'll hate it. And it'll be there for one day and it'll be moved. The other thing that's been very important for bands, that almost doesn't change with a band once they are established, is the distance from the bass drum skin to the downstage edge. That distance can be etched in stone. Every band is different, but for a particular band it is constant because the bass drum sound, the way that radiates out, is very important. It's what holds the whole band together.

It is always exciting to work with Willie because he has great ideas. From the beginning one knew that he was off-beat. His lighting was innovative, but what really tipped me off to Willie's ability and skill was seeing his work in *Propaganda* magazine. It was fantastic, just cutting edge and everything you'd expect, nothing like a fanzine. It was just in a different league, and one knew there was someone who had an eye, who knew what it was. There's not a lot of them around, and not as many that are as multifaceted as Willie. Mark Fisher brought a sense of scale to the design, and smoothly amalgamated Willie's wild ideas along with his own. His concepts were unique yet ultimately practical. He is unusual in this business, which is really a business of misfits. We couldn't get a job elsewhere, and we didn't want to do anything else. Mark probably wouldn't want to work in the normal world of architecture, because he'd be bored out of his mind.

With the Elevation heart-shaped stage, Willie wanted lights all the way around the edge. He came up with an idea for a grille all the way around the inside and outside perimeters. So we had to figure out between us which lamps to use and where to place them. I wanted to flush-mount all the strobes, T3s and the plugs into the deck so they didn't take up any dolly space. He wanted the grille in a radial pattern. Therefore all 3000 bars were individually cut, jigged and welded. It was a huge amount of work, but you know, they're the kind of details that make the difference: painstaking but totally worthwhile.

There are certain acts that when you first see them, you know that, without any major screw-ups, they are going to be big. When I saw U2 the first time it was obvious: they had 'It'. The band's talent is skilfully accentuated by their production. U2 are one band that benefits from 'film-noir' lighting. There's a lot of back-lighting, silhouetting and shadows. The black and white video is grainy. U2 have achieved all of those looks so successfully. On Elevation, the heart, the video and the restrained use of Pani projectors created an inspiring spectacle. And they've got great songs. They've got incredible music. That doesn't hurt!
Lititz, PA, May 2003

The mural painted by Rene Castro and Placa community artists during the Joshua Tree show at Oakland, USA, November 1987

Rene Castro
Set designer, Love Town; Trabant artwork, ZooTV

We got the idea to paint something for Central America after the time Bono spray painted the statue at the outdoor concert in San Francisco, and the sculptor painted the Joshua Tree backdrop at the show the following night. I took a number of artists and while U2 were performing in the Oakland Arena we painted two huge backdrops that said, 'Peace in Central America'. During the last song of the show, 'Mothers of the Disappeared', a bunch of people came on stage holding crosses with the names of the people that had disappeared in Central America because of the war. That was really significant, especially here in San Francisco because there are so many Central American people living here.

Bono called me: 'Rene, I would like you to do a design for a small tour that we're doing with B.B. King.' They wanted to do something in relation to Amnesty International. I was really politically active then, and he was eager to know what was going on in the world. We talked constantly about the cloths and the colours. Then we came up with the idea of how to do all of this: not have the backdrop illuminated until the very end. We projected the symbols through the screens and then at the very end we threw the lights on the stage. Willie said, 'Rene, make me the drawings in black and white so we can project them.' And there are the symbols projected: the guitar, the snake, the moon. Six symbols altogether. We chose them because it was Amnesty International. It was about money. The dollar sign is money, the snake who transforms, and a guitar and a sun and a moon. The snake represented temptation. Back to the Garden of Eden. It's all symbolic. I think it was not obvious, but it was there. And that's what we wanted to do. We wanted to do something that was subtle. For that reason one of the backdrops we illuminated all the time and it was huge. It was 50 feet by 150 feet. Huge. They rented a whole warehouse for us to paint. We painted with pistols, the four of us. The snake and the moon we tried to do like the communist symbol of the hammer and sickle. This is the design that they fell in love with. This is my five minutes of glory.

I've been working with musicians all my life, but this band is different. Bono is really a political animal and probably that is what grew with us, how clever he is and the discussion never ends. U2 tread a really fine line. It's really difficult to do that. They are the mainstream. The more exposure you get, the more you are open to criticism. But, if that is affecting the music and the message, that is the fine line because I think they are one of the best rock and roll groups in the world, no question about that. Now, do they need to sacrifice that in terms of political correctness? I don't think so. People need to do what they're passionate about. I think Bono is really passionate about it. He really thinks about the foreign debt, other countries, mechanical, economical equations, and he knows why it doesn't work, so he puts that message across. Some people ask me, 'Rene, why do you do this and fight?' and I say, 'I need to do this, it's my connection. It's what I do.' And the way I do things is not formal. I am not a set designer – I know that. The situation is different, the experience is different. In the 1960s, you know, my idols were Che Guevara and Fidel Castro. Now, Che Guevara is still my idol. Fidel Castro, everyone has too many questions about the situation in Cuba, including myself, so it's different. The world becomes a commodity now and you have to be clever enough to understand all the changes. The older you get, you need to know that better. You need to have an answer. And that's a big task. Bono's taken the risk. He's a man who takes risks.
San Francisco, March 2002

Amnesty International issues informed the symbolic design of the Love Town tour set, 1989

Richard Hartman
Stage interface consultant engineer, ZooTV, PopMart

I was a very low-profile character on ZooTV. In fact, I was kind of a janitor. I would go in and fix things. That's what it was. And because ZooTV happened in the middle of summer, it was very hot. We opened in Hershey, Pennsylvania, which is like a sweat belt, almost tropical. At any rate, my trademark was that nobody actually knew who I was because I would just come in and fix things, then I'd go away. Spike Falana, of Upfront Staging, got me on board. I wound up with a blue sponge and a rubber band on my head to keep the sweat out of my eyes while I tinkered. There was an overlap between the steel set-up and when the production loader came in, so I usually left and went on to the next set-up because they were leapfrogging cities. I was sorting out stuff with lighting, video, for all sorts of departments. U2 were creating a customized show that just didn't fit into a lot of people's categories. The various companies that came to the show arrived with stock equipment, some of which had to be customized for this particular show. I became like a project manager. Any time you put together a tour, there's a period of time at the very beginning – usually just after the band has signed off on what the design looks like – when you actually have to start building this thing. The design has to go out to contractors, to engineers, to make sure this thing isn't going to fall down. My niche, now, is acting between the designer and the engineer and the fabricator – working out what their problems are, their strengths and weaknesses.

During the 1990s the technology dealing with video projection changed most. From an artist's standpoint, video screens developed also because they wanted to make this little speck at the end of the hall larger than life: screens were about projecting the star on the stage bigger than he was. Now, on ZooTV, Bono played a lot with it – I mean he danced across the cubes, he went in front of the screens, he integrated himself with the picture till eventually you didn't know who was real – the artist who was dancing or the picture. It was a very strong theatrical thing to play with. That subsequent theme was then used in PopMart, where instead of having a series of small vidi-cubes they had a single LED screen that was about 150 feet wide. With PopMart, Bono in particular played with the image of reality versus image – which one was real? And he was larger than life. There was just no way that you were going to upstage an image that was 75 feet high and 100 feet across. It wasn't going to happen. When you get involved with a video screen it can become a director's show or an artist's show – this game goes back and forth. It runs the risk that it can become a director's show and not the artist's show, which in some ways is perhaps what PopMart suffered from, because the image got larger than the artist.

I had to make that LED screen work. I was asked to stay on the tour past the initial time, to see if I could keep the screen together for this tour. That screen became a real cause célèbre. I wound up being the crew chief for the screen. And that crew slogged. They stayed there all night tweaking and preparing and trying to make this thing work. They were so dedicated. It really became a

circuit cards at Saco in Montreal, and they were put into the mechanics in Belgium. When Saco ordered up the components for all this stuff – and we don't know the how or the why or whatever – they ordered a batch of what were known to be faulty resistors that had the ability to change their resistive qualities in different levels of humidity, or something like that. When we finally got these electronic screen techs on the European gig they looked at the circuit card and identified this component which had been flagged as a rogue component. Its properties meant that sometimes this thing would accept data and sometimes it would just light up like a Christmas tree. It always seemed to happen at about seven o'clock at night, just about the time that the doors open. They used to run a signal across the wall on a very fine line, which we could see on stage but which the audience couldn't. Every time this signal hit one of these rogue resistors, that tube would just flicker randomly. Each tube, or stick, is about six feet high and about an inch and a half wide, and has in it five or six circuit cards. There were several thousand sticks in the screen. So the stage video crew was always dressed in climbing harnesses, with muffle headsets, climbing ropes, screwdrivers tucked into their pockets, on standby in case we had to change tubes during a show. The whole tube comes out. They drop a tube and you send up another. We kept a store of perhaps 20 good tubes on standby.

It wasn't until we got halfway through the European tour that we identified what was causing this. I can remember standing backstage by a soft-drink cooler full of water. We'd been up all night and we put a test battery on one of these cards and threw it into the cooler. And it worked. At that point we just looked at each other and said, 'This is not about water.' The frustration was intense. The video guys were the unsung heroes of that tour. When U2 finally did the video shoot for PopMart in Mexico we actually had a perfect screen for the show.
London, March 2003

Left: The 'unsung heroes' of PopMart – the harnessed stage video crew vigilantly maintained the massive screen throughout the tour

The PopMart video wall measured 150 x 50 feet (750 square metres) and consisted of 4500 tubes mounted on to 175 foldable panels

very intense time. It was a very bonding time. This thing blind-sided us. It often just didn't work. We subsequently found out why, but it drove us nuts. It drove the people in Belgium who made it nuts, because they couldn't figure out why this thing was misbehaving. You would get a situation where here was a picture and all of a sudden these LEDs would start to twinkle and wouldn't respond to the picture data. All of a sudden they'd go blurry and then lights on one of the tubes would go. The screen was made up of thousands of tubes and they would change colour and God knows what. But you'd lose the whole video image.

The most spectacular event happened in Washington, DC, when we got caught in the middle of a torrential thunderstorm while setting up the screen. Everything got absolutely soaked. When we turned the screen on, most of it looked like a carnival ride. There was picture interspersed with data colours and big panels would turn all green. Because it was so big and it was so dynamic, at one point I thought they were gonna make us leave it in because it was such an art form in itself. But the video crew were all horrified because this didn't look like a picture. Their reputations, their integrity, and who they were were absolutely attacked by this thing. We beat that screen to death for the next however long that tour was – which seemed like an eternity – to make it work. This screen was so far ahead of its time. On paper the idea was actually quite brilliant. It was only in its execution that it fell apart.

The mechanics for the screen were all made in Belgium. The LEDs came from Nichia, in Japan. They were assembled onto

Jonathan Park

Set designer, ZooTV Outside Broadcast

If you're going to play Giants Stadium to 70,000 people you've got to play it big. Willie Williams first approached me and Mark Fisher because he knew we had worked on a grand scale. And he had big ideas! I think I would say that he definitely wanted to make a big picture that told a story. It wasn't just a performance of individual songs. He wanted every song to be able to light up the stage and have power, to have a narrative context that made the song mean more and leave a memory. He had his own particular ideas, but liked to interact with us because we had the experience and other views about how to make the envelope of the performance bigger. How to design it, how to engineer it, and so forth. Which is what we were doing for other bands. Like doubling the size of the stage. When U2 jumped from arenas to outdoor stadiums, there'd be five or ten times the audience, which is an enormous leap. You might be going from 7000 to 70,000 or from 10,000 to 100,000.

Lighting was important and size was important. One of the things you get at a stadium rock show, which you don't at an arena or theatre show, is that you don't have to move your head at all – even if you're quite close. For U2, we wanted to make it so you had to look from side to side so that the impact on your feelings was heightened. A bit of what we now call shock and awe. Well, in those days we called it the 'Wow Factor'. It was all about enhancing the visual spectacle so that all sorts of other interesting things were happening that made you feel closer. You could see the small person singing, and you could see a bigger version of them some-

where in the Imag, but together with the scenic envelope and the way the lights were changed you actually got an impression of being involved in the action. With U2 we extended this concept by coming right out into the middle of the field with the long thrust stage.

I remember walking the infield of the Hershey Stadium with Bono. We were just chatting and he was saying, 'I don't really know how it's gonna play when we get in the open air, because I'm so used to having a roof over the songs. I'm not sure how they're going to fly without a roof over them because we've always performed indoors.' And of course they did fly. They were beautiful because the technical production of the music had improved so much over the years that it was possible for the songs to work on that scale. And he was able to go out there and project them, with the backdrop of the screens and the lighting. The whole thing came alive. So the background to making Bono's songs fly out in the open air was the enhancement of all the staging. I was gratified about this because we were all so focused on projecting a big scenic environment for the performance to take place in.

We gave U2 the platform and they did the songs. But we always developed the thing directly with them. You see, in rock and roll there aren't any directors. The directors and artistic directors are basically the stars, the performers. And we were quite unusual in this case in that we were independent consultant designers. We interpreted their desires for projection and communication in a way that they were happy with. Mark has a very good conceptual grasp of ideas, so he's great at working with clients. He has an incredible sense of 'can-do'.

Paul McGuinness was very enabling about all this. Paul said to any doubters, 'Let them get on with it.' And it was fantastic for Mark and me to be given, together with Willie, permission to get on with it without further intervention. Paul was one of those guys who obviously did deal with the details, but he knew when the detail was not important. Just get on with the big picture. Just let the guys do it. And he didn't dabble. Neither did Bono. Having said that, the great thing about working with this band was that when we were out on the road they changed things all the time, developed them, improved the show.

During the rehearsals for ZooTV at Hershey, in Pennsylvania, there were lots of meetings in the canteen and out in the field. After rehearsals, there would be a group of people there including Gavin Friday and others who would comment on the performance. Even the catering manager would be involved in these meetings because the band were extremely democratic and they would listen. They wanted people's responses. The production camp was wanting to make life simple and achievable, and the design camp was wanting to make things as artistic and as interesting as possible. Richard Hartman was in between. He used to solve the problems!

We created a catwalk because I wanted to have a bridge across the back of the stage. Mark and I were always trying to get the performance off the floor. Stack it up. To make a better picture for the audience. To activate the whole stage, not having everything on the flat. And Bono could then cross it during the performance …
He opened the show from up there; quite dramatic in silhouette.

One of the many band and crew meetings during ZooTV Outside Broadcast production rehearsals, Hersheypark Stadium, August 1992

But then how would he get off? So we installed a fireman's pole. And voices said, 'Oh, no. Bono can't do that. It's far too dangerous for him to go down a pole.' But Bono wasn't shy about any of this. If you wanted him to try out anything, he'd do it!

It was just amazing with U2 because they have such energy. They were totally enabling and proactive and really involved. So it wasn't like the dressing room would suddenly open and an entourage of people would come out surrounding the star. Bono, Edge, Larry and Adam were out there, in the field, asking questions, working it out and saying, 'Yes, you know, we can have the barrier lower than that because I really want to ...' Their overriding interest was always to communicate with the audience.
London, March 2003

Band rehearsals at Hersheypark Stadium for the ZooTV stadium tour, August 1992

Mark Fisher
Set architect, ZooTV, Popmart, Elevation

What is the biggest change in your work since you started in rock 'n' roll?
I've become more confident about what I do. Practice means that you get a better sense of what works and what doesn't. Quicker decision-making is the biggest change. I try to design a rock show in the length of time it takes to fly home from a meeting. I think that anyone looking at my work would say that every show was different and that they were all connected to the conversations that went on between the artist and myself about what the artist wanted. I take my sketchbook to the meetings and if I have a good meeting, by the time I leave it we've sort of agreed the sketch of the conversation there and then. I usually do a bit more work very quickly afterwards to lock it down in my head. Then I get on with the business of working it out in more detail. I try to steer my conversations with artists around things I know can be done, which is always a good start. And then, within that, I try to be as wild and crazy as they can afford. The biggest constraint on imagination, in the end, is money. When people have no money they always say, 'All you need is imagination.' But believe me, imagination and $150 million is a lot better than imagination and $50.

I've always felt incredibly lucky to have stumbled over these big British and Southern Irish bands at the moment in history when, for a whole set of completely random reasons, they were at the peak of their purchasing power for extravagant stage sets. I just happened to be the kid standing at the side of the road when they went by. Pink Floyd was influential because they got there before anyone else, in terms of scale. They were reinventing the stadium rock show long before I was invited to join them on the Animals tour. They were the first to deconstruct what has become the generic form of an outdoor rock concert stage. The basic form evolved out of the Concerts on the Green that Bill Graham did in San Francisco in the late 1960s and early 1970s. A flat stage roof was lifted up between scaffolding towers supporting the PA. So you had these big towers of scaffolding each side of the stage, a flat roof in the middle, and the stage hiding in the shadows underneath. The stage structure never engaged with the stadium in which it was built. By the early 1970s this form had been widely adopted in the USA and Europe, and it's still in use today. By the time the Floyd got into big outdoor shows in 1973 and 1975, they were trying to break away from this boring, boxy architecture. I'd been involved in temporary and portable architecture since the mid-1960s, so I was interested in what they were trying to do. It was a sort of collision of my culture and their culture. But it took another 10 or 11 years (through to 1989), before I got the opportunity to deconstruct a stadium stage properly, with The Rolling Stones on Steel Wheels.
When did you first get involved with U2?
If you remember the three big tours of 1988 (U2's Joshua Tree, Pink Floyd's A Momentary Lapse of Reason, and Bowie's Glass Spider), they were huge shows done in identical generic stage boxes. In the end, in spite of the best efforts of their designers, they all looked more the same than different. When U2 wanted

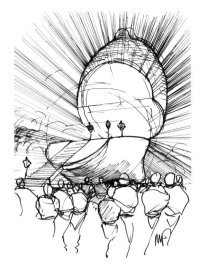

PopMart's mirrorball lemon: from Mark Fisher's original drawing to the real thing, 1997

expand their 1992 arena tour into stadia, they wanted to break out of the generic box. They called Jonathan Park and myself, and we came up with a design. I remember doing a whole lot of 'fax art' for the set, sending Bono long drawings, 10 inches high and 3 feet long, so that they went into the fax machine and came out on the roll of paper at the other end. Finally, we built a model and went to a meeting in Dublin with Brian Eno and the band. We set up this big model and the proposal was widely declared to be far too expensive. I said something like: 'Well, you just take half of it away.' There was a long pause and I remember getting up and going to the model and taking half of it away and putting it back in the box. After that, the design went through a major shift. What was to have been a large-format slide-projection show using Panni or PIGI projectors became a video tour. Originally it was going to be a giant wall of slide projection, a sort of Christo curtain wall across the stadium. It changed radically, and became a much more deconstructed thing in its second iteration. We placed what were at that time very large video screens randomly above the stage, and put vidi-cubes on the stage. If you look through the first drawings and the original model, they're completely different to what was finally built.

You have designed several shows for U2?
The fact that U2 ask me back must mean that they see some value in employing me. But exactly why, I have no idea. I wouldn't presume that it's because they think they get better design. I was not brought in at the beginning of the development of PopMart, because when he started working on it Willie solicited ideas from other designers apart from myself. Gerard Howland, an American opera designer, proposed a big Baroque theatre-type thing. I remember being at the first meeting I went to in Dublin, speaking against the practicalities of his proposal, even though I really like Gerard's work. Those situations are always a bit weird; you don't quite know what your position is in the meeting. I wonder if I am showing them my designs because they want me to be the designer, or because they want something to compare to Gerard's proposal? I don't think the band see that kind of beauty contest as something that compromises your professionalism or questions your ability; they see it as a way of opening up the field of ideas.

When PopMart was being talked about – but not as PopMart because it didn't have that name at the time – I was talking to Willie Williams and mentioned that I had seen a large panel of LED video screen. It was the first panel to arrive in America, and very few people on the planet had seen it at that point, in 1995. It was a one-off that a crazy man called Phill Scheldt had built for the Texas State Fair. Willie and I were talking about trying to do really big video to move on from ZooTV and I said to him, 'I've seen this LED video screen, and it's all in separate pixels; we could break it up. We could take panels and turn them into a blanket.' Phil brought a prototype over to Varilite in Greenford and we hung it up and looked at it. The concept, placing LED pixels about 75mm apart on a cargo net, actually worked. That was the basis for our first proposal. We were not going to have any set at all; we were just going to unroll a video screen blanket over the seats at the back of the stadium. It's still the best

idea we've had for deconstructing a stadium, to turn the whole building into a video screen. But in the end we thought, 'Well, maybe it would be more controllable if we hung it up on our own frame.'

Later we got on to the idea of kitsch in our conversations. There is such a tyranny in the architectural form of the generic stadium rock stage set, and I thought, 'What can I do to break it up?' I realized that the one thing that really forces the tyranny is the PA. So I did a sketch putting the entire PA above the middle of the stage on two giant antlers with a huge video screen behind. Willie sent the sketch back with an arch drawn on it, and off we went. This all happened very quickly, in December/January of 1996/7.

What's the main difference between working with U2 and, for example, working with The Stones?
The thing about working with U2 is that Willie leads the design process. With The Stones, Mick and Charlie lead it. If you ask me what my relationship is with Willie, I would say that I take a back seat conceptually, and eventually move forward to develop the form once I understand what Willie's trying to do. Which doesn't mean that I necessarily create the form, because in the case of PopMart the breakthroughs came from both of us. I moved the PA to the centre and put it on a pair of legs. Then Willie figured what we needed was a kind of 1950s kitsch. So I introduced the language of Morris Lapidus, one of my favourite 1950s architects, and we turned the whole thing into a kind of Flamingo Hotel. One day Willie just said to me that we needed a lemon for PopMart. He was very focused: he's always precise about these things. He mentioned it to me in the cab going from the airport to the studio in Dublin, so we stopped at a grocery store on the way to buy some lemons. We held a real lemon up to the model. And I did a sketch in the meeting, of an impossible-to-open lemon and then of a lemon mirrorball with people standing on a deck inside, everything opened. Well, if somebody asks you for a mirrorball lemon, that's what you draw.

What are you aiming for in your designs?
I remember that on ZooTV I promoted the big neon sign that went up on the top of the PA. What I'm always looking for, I think, is legibility in design, or what the artists Gilbert and George rather marvellously describe as 'colloquialism': the idea that a design is accessible, that it's easy for the audience to walk into the stadium and understand what it is that they are looking at. With PopMart it was clear that the set design was a satire on consumer culture. I don't think U2 couldn't have passed it off better. No one could have looked at the PopMart logos without thinking that they were lampooning the corporate world of McDonald's, Shell or Esso. I thought PopMart was a very good, very complete piece of work.

What about Elevation?
Elevation was another tour where U2 weren't completely sure if they wanted to get me on board at the beginning. The conversation was more sort of 'We're only doing an arena show, why do we need Mark Fisher?' They continually questioned everything, especially the question of whether or not the whole big production thing was a waste of money. The goal became the creation of a

modest show that had big production values. Willie made the first conceptual suggestions (the arch laid on its side, the heart) and then once again I came in underneath and gave structure and dimension to the whole thing, and integrated all the technical stuff. In the end it looked like what everyone had imagined, but nobody had drawn. They all said, 'Oh, yeah. Right. That's what we were thinking of. Yeah, that's great.' Which is of course why, in the end, they don't really understand why a set designer was necessary. Because if I do my job right, what they see is what they thought they were seeing all along, at which point they think: 'Well, why did we ever need a designer when we always knew what we wanted?'

I think Willie's very good at reading their minds and getting them comfortable. In Miami, before the first Elevation show, the band were getting a bit twitchy about whether or not they had enough production on stage. It can be a challenge when bands decide to go minimal: they get quite nervous when they leave their props at home. I remember being in the dressing room with Bono and Willie about five days before the first show. We were reminding Bono why we thought what was out in the arena was okay, why it was all that U2 needed to do a great show. I reviewed the design like you would write it up for a design magazine. I went on about the content of the show, why the design was consistent with what the band were doing, and how it met all of their objectives relative to what they had discarded after PopMart. At that moment they needed to feel that the minimal stage set out in the arena was underpinned by ideas they could feel secure about. It had all been said before. It just needed saying again. My side of the conversation was about what it means to commit yourself to something: namely, you actually have to be committed to a belief, otherwise it won't look like you're committed to anything and people might notice.

Any successful band has a sense of its own identity that you could characterize as its brand. You can understand this by wondering if Mick and Keith would have been happy going out on the Elevation stage. And the answer is absolutely not. They would never have gone near it. But for U2 to have a symbol that was controversial – controversial because its meaning was both so banal and so absolutely unassailably innocent – was highly provocative. Because what can you say is bad about the values of the heart? So it's banal; so what? What's banal about loving people? It takes you right back to John Lennon and the peace movement and, you know … what's your problem exactly with the idea that people should love each other? That's where U2 is coming from. For The Stones to have that amount of ideology under their feet would be highly vexatious; The Stones still want to look tough; they don't want to look like they've spent a lot of money but they definitely want something that sends out subtle signals of power.

Are we at the end of big stadium tours?
I think maybe we are. I can't see anybody being as big as The Stones again; being able to mount worldwide tours like they have done requires brand penetration on a global scale – they are the Coca-Cola of rock! U2 probably could, but I think they're wise not to try. They deliver a more honest piece of entertainment in an arena; it is much more consistent with their brand. They are more accessible to the audience, and the show delivers a far more emotional experience. The world's changed; it's more fragmented and huge world stadium tours are difficult to sustain without a worldwide market. Outside the USA it is difficult to justify the kind of production budgets that sustained the big tours of the 1990s; the audiences simply are not there. It will not be the end for big travelling shows, but perhaps it's the end for travelling shows that have a world market. That's the important distinction. If Robbie Williams could manage to crack America, then maybe, just maybe, you'd get back to that level of production once more.
London, September 2003

Stairway to lemon. Bottom: ZooTV at twilight, production rehearsals in Hersheypark Stadium, USA, August 1992

Lighting

John Lobel

Light & Sound Design, lighting suppliers, Joshua Tree–Present

The first U2 tour I worked on was the Joshua Tree. I hadn't met Willie yet and was looking at the plot for the lighting thinking: 'Well, this is different, this is goofy. There's an amazing amount of stuff that's not here. Where's the show?' Well, I found that out when the house lights went out. So many lighting designers put a system together that covers all contingencies and then concoct a show using those standard tools. Willie's approach is different: he conceptualizes what he wants it to mean, and then he figures out what he needs to make it look that way, and he doesn't put in anything else. He's the most restrained lighting designer ever! He can take a common element, something that somebody else would use as an accent, a throwaway gag, or a transitional device and turn it into an entire song by using it in a new way. Or he'll take incredibly simple things and repeat them or leave them static so they gain power. But most importantly they must fit the mood and vision of the song and the overall show. That clarity of vision helps make the shows so dramatic and powerful.

The Joshua Tree was powerful because of its simplicity. I describe that tour's lighting as 'maximum minimalism'. It had enormous amounts of pure white light and broad swaths of colour that were used really sparingly. There were 96 Nine-lights on that show. Those are big lights, so that's an enormous amount of light. The first time that we hung them they were all scattered in pairs, in a very exact but seemingly random way, in front of the PA. And not only did they block the sound, but they were also time-consuming to hang and they rattled. So Willie said, 'Okay, we'll do something else,' and we put them in straight lines around the PA wings. Most designers whose band had spent that much time and money on an effect would have used them full on for half the show, but he used them in the most restrained fashion. The first two cues they only came up to 50 per cent intensity so then when they came up to full in 'Streets' it made the audience just roar. It was one of those things that a lighting guy will never forget.

The roof that Upfront Staging built for the Joshua Tree stadium shows was so far advanced from anything else at the time. It was the best outdoor stage in the world. It had the best deck, the best weather protection, the best clear span. And I think that show sounded better than any stadium show I'd ever heard.

We started one leg of the tour at Giants Stadium in New York with an ambitious 27-hour load-in schedule because of football games, but we were delayed due to bad weather and delays in the steel load-in. Lighting got access to the stage maybe a day late; morning of the first show. We always try to get everything set up in time for the show, no matter what – we pride ourselves on that. No way was that going to happen this time! So Willie made a list

Lighting operator, ZooTV, Wembley Stadium, London, August 1993

of priorities on a piece of paper. Every so often there was a dotted line and a cut-off time. Every half-hour he would rip off another part of the list, and finally, at the time when there was virtually nothing we could do, we had a little stub of paper. We'd eliminated most of the lighting system. It was a great show anyway, but there wasn't much lighting! We were working throughout the show to get stuff working and I was completely frustrated. I remember at one point we said: 'They're not on the list, but fuck it we need a victory here,' so we put the three 16Ks (custom-built, huge lights) on flight cases, made them work and rolled them on-stage just in time for the cue where they should have flown in from the roof. That cue was our victory against time and the elements. Years later one of my mentors, Allen Branton, said 'A good idea that isn't ready by show time isn't such a good idea after all.' That's one of my favourite sayings, and every time I use it I think of that day.

Zoo was the sensory overload of all time. It was a show that got better the more times you saw it because there was so much content in it that you could not possibly appreciate it and get all the subtleties on even a dozen viewings. It was so big and wide and so spread out and there were so many things going on in all directions. And it kept going and it kept changing as it went around the world. Even if they could do the exact same show every night it was impossible to watch the same way twice. I remember a moment from the third or fourth show of the US stadium leg when I was wandering through the audience watching the crowd watch the show and at one point there was this line-up of a dozen people, each of whom was looking in a different direction and totally mesmerized. One woman was staring at Bono, one guy was staring at The Edge, one guy was staring at the video screen, another guy was reading words on video monitors on stage, a woman was entranced by Adam, another guy was looking over at the video message boards watching phoney stock quotations run by … And then a guy at the end of the row was the only one looking up at a full-size orange car with blinking lights all over it, hanging over his head on a crane a hundred feet up in the air. The other people didn't even fucking notice the damn car!

LSD built the Trabants for that tour. We had guys doing engineering drawings and figuring out how you take a car and make it safe to hang over pop stars' heads and how you transport it around the world. The cars were completely real. We took the engines out and took out all the weight we could, but we added strengthening stuff and hanging bars and safeties inside them and built custom lights that were mounted inside them. That tour was one of the most rewarding tours ever for us because it was such a ground-breaking show, even though it was a hard tour to support: LSD's gear got trashed because of how it was hung on those vertical towers without any weather protection. PopMart was a brilliant concept, and the unique design made it an enormous challenge. The process of putting it together was as much fun as any tour. I took on the ropelight as a personal project and enjoyed working with Richard Hartman figuring out how to do the ropelight in the arch. I was delighted with the way that element turned out. One good thing was the way Bruce Ramus took to his role as lighting director and brought ever so much more to it than anyone else could have. Another thing that I was very proud of on that tour was our crew. LSD had a dozen people on it, some British, some Americans, some Australian, and they were a terrific team.

The Elevation evolution was fascinating to watch. The show's impact really depended on the song selection because the show was built around sequences of emotions and there were things programmed for each song to convey that message. It was fascinating to see the different impact of different set lists. Bruce was really important artistically in Elevation, because Willie had taken over helping the band structure their shows and communicate with their audience. Willie was unable to do the last part of Elevation and Bruce took that part over, and he did a great job, really helping the show get better and better.

LSD has always made a lot of custom stuff for U2 and one of my favourite things ever was the Dustbins on Elevation, another Willie idea that's simple, strong and incredibly evocative. They perfectly supported the emotion on 'Bad'. It was a fun process to build them. I've gotten over a dozen calls since then asking if we can make something just like them for other projects. We can, but we won't. Come up with your own idea and we'll make that for you! On Elevation, Willie and Bruce came to us and said they needed a beacon that would do certain things. At first we were resistant – we wanted to give them something that we already knew how to do. They wouldn't go for that, so we started thinking about it. We explained our ideas and Willie saw one new use and Bruce saw a different new thing they could do, so we built 33 of them for the tour. The way they used them was completely shocking and stunning to me. Everybody that I have ever seen has put a beacon horizontally so that the light spins like a lighthouse. Willie turned the beacons on their side so they swept through a vertical plane and that simple difference was completely mind blowing. When I saw 'Streets' using those things in rehearsal I wanted to cry! It was so beautiful. There were a number of people who said: 'How did they do that effect? That wall of spinning rainlight in "Streets"?' And I'd say: 'Police beacons.' And people go, 'Nah, it couldn't be.' Well, yeah, it could.

By this tour, LSD was now part of a big company, Fourth Phase. One of the benefits of being part of a larger organization is that we can do more things. For this tour Willie wanted to project onto the audience, and we were able to provide the Pigi projectors. Willie turned them on their backs and pointed them straight up and shot them into mirrors so we could quickly change the focus and have the images appear in different places. These projectors can rotate images. There was a sequence of three songs near the end of the show that used these rotations in three different dimensions: 'Bad' had the dustbins rotating horizontally, next 'Streets' had the beacons rotating vertically, then 'Still Haven't Found' with the Pigis creating rotating vortices in the air.

LSD and Fourth Phase have provided lighting for lots of Superbowl half-time shows. I started on Superbowl XXVIII and have been to quite a few since then, but this one was different. The producers usually try to appeal to a broad demographic, to put in a rock group and a boy band and a country star and a rap artist. The willingness of the producers to take a risk on having just one band is what allowed U2's half-time performance to be unique – but it was the power of U2's performance and the emotional resonance of the projection of the World Trade Center's victims' names on that marvellous backdrop that brought it home. Doing half-time entertainment at a Superbowl is a real lesson in humility because you're the least important person in the entire stadium. The guys who do towels for the teams get better access to the venue than you do. You work for weeks to do an eight-minute show whose purpose is to increase the price of the commercials. You feel like a migrant video worker.

The wonderful thing about working with Willie is that he demands that you be really creative. Willie wants to come up with something that nobody's seen before and he wants help doing it effectively. That's a delightful experience for somebody in my position. And the band is great. They want to do the best show in the world – and what could be better than helping them do that? The main reason that I'm so proud and happy to have been even a minor part of all this is that, of all the shows that I attend, U2's have consistently been among the very best at connecting the band to the audience and with the things that make life worth living. The importance of U2's production is not that we built a bigger screen or had more ropelight; it's that we helped people feel better about their situation and their lot in life. Somebody bought a ticket in the hope of seeing a great show, and on the way out the door they say, 'God, that was great. That was so wonderful. I feel good about the world.' And we hope that feeling lasts, and they think, 'Man that was fun. Let's go to another show next week.'

Newbury Park, CA, January 2004

Light and Sound Design's technical contributions have included customised lighting for ZooTV's Trabants and Elevation's 'dustbins'

Bruce Ramus

Lighting director, Zooropa–Present

Above: Bruce Ramus directing the lighting from his desk on the Elevation tour, Madison Square Garden, New York City, June 2001

To make art, to seek spirit, to take the piss massively, what more?

Everybody who is a part of a U2 tour, from the crew to the crowd, knows they're sharing in an incredibly creative energy. It's led by the band, but it's driven by the characters, Willie, Fintan, Pete the Greek, Firmin, Bits, Dallas, Joe O ... great characters, great parties, great football, great vibe. U2's shows always feel like a significant spiritual exchange between the tour and the audience, and in my opinion, that's part of the reason why they have such longevity and appeal. They're willing to risk spirit.

I have a wonderful job, and it has played out with U2 on the Zooropa, PopMart and Elevation tours. On the last two, I directed the lighting show. During the show, I operate the lighting console and call the spots. Calling spots is a challenge which involves trying to get a number of local operators to do my bidding exactly when I want it. It involves talking, almost incessantly, during the show, to spotlight operators, positioned all around the building, who may or may not know the music and may or may not be interested in our show. So I develop a rhythm during the show, it's a cue-calling cadence by which the operators learn to react to my 'go's at just the right moment. I will elongate the 'go' if it's a slow fade that's needed (say, at the end of 'Bad'), or I will bark a short, sharp, 'go' (beginning of 'Sunday') to make the operators react all at once. This can be difficult because everybody reacts slightly differently, and it does come down to a difference of a

quarter of a second between being on the beat, i.e. part of the music, or being late, a distraction. It's a blast though when I get a good bunch of attentive spot ops (on PopMart, there were 26 of them; on Elevation, only 15); it can really feel great.

The console is the computer link between myself and the rest of the lighting system. I operate this as I'm calling spots. This works on an entirely different timing and rhythm and with it I can make slow cross-fades between scenes or rapid changes. My favourite is the 'Streets' 'BANG' cue. After the stage gets plunged into darkness, and the punters' pupils are nice and wide and they're leaning forward to try to catch sight of the band, I get to hit the button that lights the entire place up, and sends the audience reeling backward like they've been struck. You can feel it. That cue, in time with that music, is a powerful moment. Willie told me when I was learning the show on Zooropa back in 1993, 'This is one cue you can never miss.'

So that's the best bit of my job. It takes two hours of each show day. The other 22 is taken up by Bus 3, load-in, football, a little bit of sleep and my least favourite part, tour politics. Tour politics are territorial skirmishes between departments. There are frequent clashes as each member of each department tries to exert some influence on the proceedings or at least define their own job description. I shouldn't say much more about that, though, as it's a tricky game, but I hope I'm learning to choose my battles more wisely.

All in all, it feels like my gig involves creating an environment that aids the band in effectively communicating their music. This happens all day, every day on tour, either with the actual show gear in the arena/stadium on a show day or with the vibe of the people on tour on a day off. It's all part of the road, and I love it.

As Jack Kerouac said: 'Our battered suitcases were piled on the sidewalk again, we had longer ways to go. But no matter, the road is life.'

Vancouver, January 2004

Show Video Production

Pat Morrow

Nocturne Productions Inc., lighting suppliers, Joshua Tree;
video suppliers, ZooTV

Frank Barsalona had a classic approach agenting. A little story of a Palladium gig is a perfect example. It was the old Academy of Music, renamed the Palladium, and Ron Delsener was using it for headliners and small headliners, mid-line acts and acts coming up. Capacity was about 25,000. When you get really big you go to Madison Square Garden. When U2 came on the Boy tour, early on, they had the strength in New York maybe to play at the Garden, almost a full Garden, maybe, if you really pulled out all the stops. Instead, Frank persuaded McGuinness – and Paul wouldn't do anything without Frank's blessing because he knew Frank knew what he was doing – to do the Palladium one night, put it on sale, boom it's clean, second night added by popular demand, boom it's clean. You've got two sold-out nights at the Palladium. So imagine, the next day you go to school and a friend asks, 'Hey, how was the U2 show?' 'Oh, it was great, it was packed, it was heaving.' If you'd gone to Madison Square Garden you'd say, 'Oh, the show was great, but it wasn't sold out.' Right away, in your mind, U2 is not a sell-out act. Frank designed the right gig for the right reasons.

When U2 came, we, with Journey, were playing at the Nassau Coliseum two nights sold out. I was the tour manager and Herbie Herbert was out as the manager. Herbie brought Paul and Frank to the gig and had me show them all the production at the sound check. One of the things that we focused on was making a gorgeous production, but keeping it small. In other words, the stage is fairly modest in actual physical size, which also means that your artists don't shrink into the set; they dominate the set a bit more. And then you added front-row seats at the highest price, increasing your yield. And that's a manager's job, to create opportunity, to maximize the yield. And that's what Herbie and Frank and I taught Iredale and his people. After the Journey gig, we went back to the hotel and McGuinness hung out with us for a couple of hours. He asked about crew and salaries and putting together tours. He was watching me function as a tour manager and recognized that you have to have someone who is a clearing house for information on a tour to make sure decisions are executed properly. The next thing I know I'm striking up a friendship with him and with Iredale. Some months later I called Paul. At first I went to Herbie and said, 'You know these guys are going to be huge. We ought to get involved with them. They've got to be the right act for us to start our little production company. Steve Iredale's got nothing to do for six months, he's a really hard-working guy, a nice guy, let's bring him out, we'll train him and pay him a cash per diem and maybe it'll lead naturally to

ongoing participation in U2's tour production.'

U2 came with this incredibly gifted audio engineer, Joe O'Herlihy, who had spent his early years mixing sound for Rory Gallagher. Joe really, really knew how to get the sound right from Irish pubs up. And so here U2 are, right off the bat, hooking up with us and getting pointers and a push in this direction and that, and maybe putting the training wheels on Iredale a bit, to the extent that U2 really knew what they were doing. U2 took the impetus of what Frank showed them and what we had shown them and took it to hyperspace. War and Joshua Tree really did it. That's where they got on track. From the beginning of the War tour right through all of Joshua Tree you saw production value grow, innovation grow. Willie Williams was nothing if he wasn't always innovative. I think the most important thing that happened was U2 started doing sound with Clair Brothers and the lights with Nocturne. Clair Brothers is a wonderful company. They do by far the best audio work; they do everyone from Madonna to Michael Jackson and back again. With Willie and Joe at the helm, and Steve Iredale organizing the production, Nocturne would do the lighting. After we sold our lighting operation to Light & Sound Design, Nocturne became exclusively a video supplier. This was after Joshua Tree.

Musically and artistically, U2 was making such an enormous impact. In addition to that incredible musical success, their tour production and design were innovative with sound as good or better than the record you've listened to. I could name many acts who, for financial reasons, toured with a fairly standard rig: just the lights in the air, and the music's the focus. You get your money's worth and it's a great ticket. This happens with lots of artists, but with U2 you always got more production. There's a tangible, physical, economic and psychic impact that comes from production values that can't be supplied in any other way. You see it in the theatre, in political rallies, on television. Production values are simply about immense attention to detail and a thoroughly articulated and realized artistic vision that has broad appeal. That's how I define it.

The real climax for Nocturne was ZooTV. You can't say enough about what Willie's vision has been over and over. His work is sublime and very much its own thing. Wonderful artistic mind, and a brilliant guy. For Zoo, Willie called me from Dublin and said, 'They're talking about doing video.' The sale of the lighting operation was happening with LSD, and we were moving into video. At the time we were doing tours for Lynyrd Skynyrd and David Bowie and the Police and the Purple Rain tour for Prince. We're busy establishing ourselves as by far the market leader and most innovative company for large-screen video reinforcement; Barco screens. If you saw them against the screens that are used today you would just laugh. Soon we'll be using

Bono in front of the massive ZooTV video wall, Feyenoord Stadium, Rotterdam, Holland, May 1993

liquid flat screens that are absolutely perfect in daylight. ZooTV made our bones. It was the best tour, probably the best project, I ever booked and participated in. It was huge for Nocturne and for all the video companies. It really put video on the map in the biggest way because it was the focus of the production. Since then, many acts have done variations on the theme, and you've seen video become more and more important.

One of the reasons why ticket prices are so high is these productions cost a fortune to mount now. U2 did the same thing that Journey did: they influenced other artists and influenced the buying public, the expectations of the ticket buyer. Nowadays you'd better have a really good show for these people. The consumer's an utterly sophisticated being. They're not dumb kids smoking too much pot.

All through my involvement with them, U2 have remained utterly consistent. Real road warriors. There was never any question in my mind that they knew how important it was to keep the production paramount, keep the political message. Paul, Principle, Bono and Larry, all of them, have a lot to be proud of. They haven't allowed themselves to be sucked into that Hollywood syndrome and become cartoons of themselves. It's an Irish trait: you might be drinking Guinness, but you tell the truth. It's pretty straight, it's not bullshit. There is a very low level of bullshit in the Irish character. Paul's been very fortunate to have such key advice and key guidance early on. To his credit, he always had the good sense to listen to good advice. He worshipped Frank, and I think very rarely questioned any guidance or direction from Frank. And Barbara was the steward of all that, the executive officer. They knew, as we did, that these guys were not going to go away. Paul McGuinness's career is a spectacular achievement, and he should be very, very proud. I don't know what the band's interpersonal dynamic is, but points to them for the success, too. Never, ever going off message. You've got to give them credit. And I think it's a lot to do with them as people.

Berkeley, CA, July 2003

PopMart: a polite moment.

Monica Caston
Video director, PopMart; assistant video director, ZooTV

ZooTV went through four incarnations to end up as the Outdoor Broadcast, as they called it. It was a big vision. Huge. There wasn't a manual or a book to tell us how to do this. It hadn't been done before. So a lot of technical stuff was worked out in Lakeland, Florida. It was very difficult during the month of rehearsals. The biggest challenge for us was to figure out how to make it all work by computer – instantly. There was a lot of research and development on the road. Experiment as you go. Very stressful, really overwhelming and highly emotional, because a lot of people worked 24/7 to make it happen. Part of what I loved about it was that many of my colleagues came from different backgrounds. I think that made the show more visually interesting. I'm very TV oriented, so there's a bit of 'No, you don't do that' sensibility. (TV people are big on convention.) But it's okay to break the rules. That's what U2 wanted to do as well. Things like taking very expensive camera equipment and making the images look like they were produced with home-movie Hi-8 cameras. Back then, it just wasn't done … and we simply had to get over ourselves.

The band was very hands on through all of it. They wanted to look at everything, and had a lot of specific ideas. Occasionally one of those ideas would come from a mistake. Or what we thought was a mistake. For example, the band was on stage rehearsing and we had a video playing of flames for one song. All of the sudden the video wall lost synch, which is what controls the image on the wall. It started rolling and turned different colours. Edge turned around and said, 'That's it! That's what we want! We don't want the flames; we want that.' Then we had to figure out how to do it on purpose, because you can't simply pull synch on the walls every night! (Unless you wanted to kill the engineer.) So we pulled synch, recorded a bit of it, built a loop, put it on a laser disc, and then played it back during the show. We found a way to push the envelope – dependably – without the nightly risk that it all was going to go horribly wrong

So how do you top ZooTV? You develop and design PopMart. To begin with, more than 70 LED panels made up the PopMart screen, which was 150 feet wide and 70 feet high. Before it was finished, Willie Williams and I sat in a sheep pasture in Belgium, probably about a week before we loaded into Las Vegas for rehearsals, and saw four panels up and running that we played footage on. That's all we ever saw before we got to Vegas. Willie said, 'Best-case scenario, this is really gonna knock your socks off; worst case scenario, it's gonna be a huge lighting source.' There isn't anyone who wouldn't have been overwhelmed by the enormity of that screen, and of the show itself. But U2 had a lot riding on uncharted waters. And, of course, there are very few artists who could actually pull off performing in front of a canvas like that and still hold the audience. But no one knew for sure. We had to figure out the speed of the data going from one side of the screen to the other. How long does it take to go from here to there, to send electronic information through? Then it had to be built. It was very long hours, and a huge leap of faith for the band to spend that much money to make such a big statement.

ZooTV, PopMart and U2 gave all of us the freedom to try stuff. The fear was there, but it got easier because the band were so gracious and so open to trying anything. It was a fantastic opportunity for me, and for everybody else, because we were handed this giant box of cutting-edge tools for the show and told to create, to make it up, have fun! What an amazing playground! And part of what made it fun was that it was such an incredibly collaborative process, in which a lot of people had information, ideas and input. It was always changing, always different.

In that way, PopMart was as much revolutionary as it was evolutionary. We spent a lot of time in pre-production, but then all of a sudden the tour was due to start. It took some time for the band to get comfortable with the staging and screen, for the crew to get comfortable with the technology. But once we did, the engineers rewrote software, made it faster and better. We stretched as we got more confident, as we wondered, 'Okay, how can we make it different, what can we do?' Then we'd do it. I love the fact that friends who came to see PopMart early in the tour came to see it six or eight months later, and were blown away by how much it had changed. And not just visually; the performance by the band had changed too. The set list changed. That made PopMart all the more unusual and exciting.

With six cameras, three screens and a canvas the size of a football field, it scared the hell out of me how dependent we were on computers and technology. The band challenged us to do our best every night, and together we made PopMart a landmark in tour production. Audiences simply went crazy for it. But I also realized something else – that at the end of the day, it's still about those four guys and the music. And what we did to enhance that experience for the band, and for the fans, was icing on the cake. Still, every time I do a new show, ZooTV and PopMart are the standard. It's where I set my creative bar. And I'd do it all again in a heartbeat!
Los Angeles, February 2003

Carol Dodds
Video director, ZooTV

After studying acting and directing primarily in improvisational theatre, I designed lighting for concert tours and took my earnings to play at the Experimental Television Center in New York. It was really video art. Then the Bruce Springsteen tour asked me to direct the live video. Once I found I could make a living at that, I shifted to combining it all.

Prior to working with U2 on Zoo, I had worked with David Bowie on the Sound and Vision tour, which is where Willie and I found we enjoyed working together. I was on Paula Abdul's tour using the first touring video-wall. Willie and I would chat on the phone about possibilities and dreams. Then U2 asked me to come work with them on Zoo to help make happen what we had envisioned. In order to work with U2, I had to leave the Paula

Abdul tour early, which they reluctantly but graciously allowed me do.

U2 is a unique working experience because they are one of the few bands that will pay for ground-breaking technology to push the performance into previously unexplored areas. They are also interested in integrating visual art. At the time, it was the most adventurous use of video to date and I totally embraced the openness to artistic vision they supported. At the same time, the band was very cost conscious, so it involved finding that balance.

I managed all the video, from the playback already in progress to creating additional pieces. I organized the playback content, mapped multiple feed routes, synchronized live and recorded material to the live music, and chose the nightly satellite feeds. I also acquired the additional broadcast feeds for use in the show, directed the live manned cameras, remotely controlled cameras and various point-of-view cameras, recording day of show for use that night. All this in addition to overseeing the video crew and managing the entire lot as far as what goes where and exactly when and making that happen. We also had outside broadcasts, which I produced and/or co-ordinated. And the band was in a constant state of creativity that needed attention to keep everything revised and updated. As video was such a large part of the tour, I was asked to do a good deal of press too.

We all wanted to put together a living video entity. This was the most difficult endeavour. I had been working in the art world with organic video and wanted to transform that into the touring monster. The band was totally in concert with this idea. It was a constant tussle with the technical mechanics of the form and broadcast tradition. The organic quality of the entity ended up being the people working on the project rather than the hardware. It twisted a few heads. Ultimately, we all had to get into a ZooTV frame of mind because, more than anything, it was the whole video crew – Richard Davis, Dave Neugebauer, Michael Pentz, Bob Loney, Monica Caston, Bruce Ramos, Mike Tribble, Jay Strasser, J.D. Williams, Dave Lemmink and Lisa Loney – more than any one person, that made the monster work. This was a bear tamed only by the hard work of all concerned. Some wrestled a bit more than others but everyone worked overtime, all the time. We were making things up as we went along and coming up with new ideas every day that our crew would figure out a way to make happen on tour at each show. We had daily live satellite feeds, which was unheard of at that time. We recorded the audience as they came in and used them in the show. The rules of the game changed each day and we had fun with playing each night.

Having come from the world of lighting design myself, using the video as a lighting source has always been in my video palette. Willie was open to this as well as the band. He and I worked together on the overall visual. It was a wild swirl of living dreams and desires, decisions and surprises, deliberate successes and wonderful failures. Most challenging was the constant change – juggling the desires with needs. On the one hand we were capturing the performance of U2, and on the other

*Above: Video as lighting tool on ZooTV
Bottom: Jake Kennedy, Carol Dodds and David Stalbaumer discuss video matters on the ZooTV tour*

releasing the same energy to be the political or petulant, posturing or passionate animal it was. It was slaying the Hydra every day and having it rise like a phoenix again at the next show. Overall, it was a great group to work with. Although we had hundreds of people on tour, there was a familial quality to the overall production. We were taking the newest equipment available and making it roadworthy at an accelerated pace to do things that had no real relation to any accepted norm. Between legs on the tour, we made new content to keep it up to date and to keep turning the band's ideas into realities, sometimes reflecting the differences between US, European and UK audiences.

I have had an amazing number of people tell me stories about the effect Zoo had on video use. Ultimately I think Zoo and U2 have had a substantial effect on video and the future of the video industry. I'm glad I didn't realize that at the time. It would have been overwhelming.

USA, December 2003

Frederic Opsomer

System Technologies, video screen suppliers, Zooropa, PopMart

When we came into contact with U2 for the first time they were planning the Zooropa tour and System Technologies was just a small design and mechanical engineering department in a Belgian rental company. We developed a new video-wall system that matched U2's requirements for the tour: a back-projection cube that was fully closed, thus eliminating much of the influence of ambient light. Over 200 of these cubes were installed in a single day at the Zooropa venues, fully adjusted and show-ready. Just hours after the show, the screens would be back in the trucks travelling to the next destination. The total surface area of the video screen was around 100 square metres, divided over three screens.

In the summer 1996 U2 was planning PopMart. This time the set was even more ambitious. The video element of the set design was a 706-square-metre video screen serving as a back-drop for the stage and we were asked to design and manufacture it. In those days, the biggest transportable video screen was 80 square metres in size and considered by many to be unworkable: it took over one day to build with gigantic cranes. The PopMart screen had to be lightweight, transportable, bright and able to be rigged and de-rigged within hours at every venue. Transportation had to be easy: the whole screen should fit into three artics.

I knew that the only way out was LED, which would offer high light output combined with low weight and low power consumption. Full-colour LED video screens had not yet been invented, but someone had heard that having a blue LED would make this possible. I had to find someone who could produce the type of electronics that the mechanical design required. I went to Japan, the United States, Taiwan, Korea, Hong Kong, Germany, Italy, everywhere, trying to find a manufacturer with enough know-how

and guts to embark on this adventure, but the results were disappointing. Then Paul Amenta from MultiVision in New York told me about a company called Saco in Montreal. Saco had little experience with video screens but their president Fred Jalbout was keen to accept the challenge. The fact that he had never been anywhere near a concert stage was probably an advantage for him to make this assessment! Just a couple of weeks later a first presentation was made to the band and management, and System Technologies and Saco were given approval to design and manufacture the screen. In Belgium we worked frantically on the design. Vertical aluminium tubes holding the pixels, mounted on folding panels, were to comply with the requirements: lightweight, reduced wind load, fast rigging and de-rigging, low volume in transport. In Montreal, Saco's engineers designed the electronics, PCB strips with the pixels mounted on them, which would fit into the aluminium tubes. The driver electronics for each panel would be located in the folding panel. Saco also had to develop a completely new processor to drive the screen.

Before the start of the PopMart screen project, System Technologies had been a small family company; now we had several engineers, CAD designers and 30 temporary employees to cope with the production deadlines. The crew worked night and day, weekends and holidays. At Saco tremendous efforts were also made to get the electronics finished on time and the processing system operational. Finally, in April, the screen was shipped to LA for rehearsals. Many technical problems occurred but, considering that we had used a 706-square-metre untested prototype of a completely innovative product concept, it is simply amazing that in the end everything worked out. From the first minute of the first show everyone there knew that the world of video screens and rock'n'roll touring would never be the same again. The PopMart screen toured the world for over one year, receiving an enthusiastic reception wherever it went. LED now ruled. The U2 screen served as a reference standard and showcase for LED technology. What Formula 1 is to the motor industry, U2 has been, and hopefully will continue to be, to the video-screen industry.

Belgium, November 2003

Top: Setting up PopMart's video panels. Bottom: Sign outside backstage video world on Elevation tour. Right: Close up of the LED clusters in the PopMart video wall

Show Video Content

Catherine Owens

Visual collaborator, ZooTV; curator of screen imagery, PopMart, Elevation

My working relationship with U2 started when the band rehearsed for the Joshua Tree in Dane's Moat. I wasn't long out of art college at the time and the band asked me to paint a series of political wall hangings for their rehearsal room as inspiration while they wrote and worked on their album. I met Willie Williams when I was living in New York. We were introduced by Marian Smyth, the band's wardrobe person at the time, backstage at Madison Square Garden at a Joshua Tree show. I think I was introduced as some sort of creative relation of the band, and it wasn't long before we were dreaming up projects between us.

The underlying idea behind the ZooTV tour was to reinvent the concept of TV in a three-dimensional space and take it round the world, tying together ideas that related to U2's music, their videos and their live performance with a conceptual version of entertainment. 'A multi-layered audio-visual roller-coaster ride' would be an apt description. At the time Willie was looking for an artist to customise a set of Trabants that he was going to reconfigure to use as a source for lighting as part of the set. The Trabant idea originated with Anton Corbijn. He had used them in Berlin while shooting a video. My favourite one is the text car, which now hangs in the Rock and Roll Hall of Fame. The idea for this was simply to ask tour personnel for a bit of text off their daily 'to do' list and reprint it on the car. The result was a lovely ramble of dialogue. There was also the girly car, with long red hair and a naked body, which was my self-portrait, a fish car, a charm bracelet car, a David Wojnarowicz 'Smell The Flowers While You Can' car, a Keith Haring yellow baby car, a star car, a mirrorball car, a personal ad car, and the list goes on. At the same time, the band were sourcing imagery for their screens. I recommended some of the video-makers I knew or knew about in New York and suggested the band talk to Mark Pellington. The connection was made and Mark was just fantastic. His segments for ZooTV really became the signature look for the tour. The style that Mark brought to the ZooTV tour is still being recreated in other shows I see. There was also a group of performance artists from Providence, Rhode Island, called E.B.N., Emergency Broadcast Network, whose work I liked, and they made a series of pieces for us, the most successful being our opening video segment for the whole tour. As the audience watched and waited for the band to come on stage, the screens would crackle and hiss into life like and old television screen tuning in for a picture. Out of this haze of 'shash' came George Bush Senior sitting at his desk in the Oval Office. E.B.N. had edited his speech to make it look like he was repeating the lines from the Queen song 'We Will Rock You', music and all.

I think one of our most lovely achievements while working on ZooTV was the relationship we developed with David Wojnarovicz. David was a well-respected downtown artist in New York. An artist's artist. His work was controversial as it dealt mostly with issues relating to being a gay man who was dying of Aids. So David's work was pushing some important boundaries in building an awareness of the illness. The band already owned some of David's work, and Bono wanted to use his images in the show and on the CD cover of 'One'. David was very ill at the time, but agreed to work with the band in any way he could if it was going to raise the Aids awareness level. He allowed the band to reproduce the image of three buffalo falling over the side of a cliff.

The collaborative success of ZooTV allowed the band to think and dream even bigger on PopMart. The PopMart tour was a little like a Mars exploration, and there is much debate on just how successful it was on various levels, both within the organization and from the outside. It was a mind-boggling production, and perhaps before its time, given the technological advances the tour achieved in terms of scale, show build, LED screen development, and so on. PopMart was a pure collaboration between the band, music, video, art, fashion, performance, celebrity, product, madness and extremes. When I look at some of the video images from that show I am still amazed not only that they pulled off such an event, but that they were able to pack it up, move it to the next location, and start all over again a day or two later.

Where ZooTV had been a conceptual reinvention of television, PopMart was to be an exploration of all things surface; it would examine ideas relating to personality as product, advertising the self, the cult of celebrity, scale, colour, performance, style and technology. I suggested that we move from pure video and focus instead on animation. The band had talked about the possibility of using some of Roy Lichtenstein's imagery from the 1960s so we made contact with Roy. He gave us permission to animate his famous 'Takka Takka' fighter pilot painting for the song 'Bullet the Blue Sky'. I found the perfect animator in London to make the piece, a very talented man called Run Wrake whose work was already influenced by Roy's use of line and colour. The results were beyond what we were hoping for, and Run went on to make the equally successful closing piece for the show, a series of Keith Haring's images animated for the song 'One'. This way of working, of matching animators with images, songs and segments, was in general how I would programme the content. We had a great group of animators on this tour, including Vegetable Vision from London, who also made the visuals for the Chemical Brothers, another UK group called Straw Donkey, and Jennifer Steinkamp, an artist from LA. She was our digital guru. She made these great abstract emotional colour experiences, almost trance-like journeys. In some ways her work was an anchor for the other work to be built

around. John Maybury, who was already well known in the video world for his portrait of Sinead O'Connor in Prince's song 'Nothing Compares to U', gave us a set of completely mental, wonderful pieces of video for our show, the wildest one being footage of the performance artist and nightclub legend Leigh Bowery, not a small man, belly-dancing while wearing not much more then a tinsel wig. As soon as we saw this piece we knew it would look fantastic huge. It was almost like a 'product gone wrong' version of the belly dancer from the ZooTV tour.

At the time, Willie liked to call our band meetings the Dog and Pony shows. The meetings were always a bit crazy as we were more often than not sandwiched between a production meeting and a PR meeting or a wardrobe meeting – and usually while the band was having lunch or a hair cut!

In retrospect, it is easy to see the clear line of communication U2 have had between their world and the art world, even as far back as the late 1970s. At the time when my brother Kieran was managing the Virgin Prunes, he was also working at the Douglas Hyde Gallery in Trinity College, Dublin. The Virgin Prunes played a gig in the gallery, sort of performance art meets punk, meets fashion event. It was an important moment for all of us as it high-lighted the possibilities for multi-media interactions between the music world, then performance world and the art world. In many ways this extended group relationship set an early precedent for how U2 would shape themselves and their shows in the future, often working closely with people over long periods of time who could grow together. There was something in the idea that experi-mental music and performance could and should be art, and that art could and should be experimental music if it needs to be. This way of thinking seemed to leave all doors open. In many was this is very much the way U2 still works today, and that collaborative energy is what drives most of us to continue working with them.
New York, July 2003

Bono observing a run-through of Zoo visuals at Hersheypark Stadium, USA, August 1992

Kevin Godley
Film director, contributor, ZooTV

I was a U2 fan. There wasn't anybody else making that kind of sound at the time – making that kind of 'soul' music. They meant what they said and said it with lots of repeat echo. The album and movie of *Rattle and Hum* got critically panned at the time for being too American. I didn't get it. I loved it. I share their enthusiasm for Americana. Then they disappeared to 'dream it all up again', as Bono put it.

When the time came I did what I always do: I listened with my eyes. I immersed myself in what they were about. They were doing all sorts of interesting tests and meeting up with all sorts of inter-esting people, experimenting with visual stuff in preparation for what would eventually become the ZooTV tour. So their mindset was in a completely different place from the U2 I knew. This was a postmodern band that was digesting everything to do with media and spitting it out in a U2 way and I found that fascinating.

If the things I did for them initially had any influence at all, it was maybe because I was familiar with the media montage thing before. When we shot 'Two Tribes' for Frankie Goes to Hollywood we played around with visual cut-ups, deconstruction and slowing things down, colours getting fragmented, that sort of thing … That whole distortion thing was already part of my vocabulary.

Working with U2 was quite different to working with any other outfit. Normally you don't really get to talk to the artist that often. You get a brief from the record company or video commissioner saying the kind of thing they're after: 'Please come up with an idea by such and such a date.' But U2 are in control of everything. So my wife, Sue, and I got an invitation to visit Dublin and have a chat.

Sue and I sort of work together. We're each other's support system. Over the years we've both become close to everyone in the band, which is lovely. It's like a family thing. The band love meetings. It felt like the band, the management, office staff, the road crew, everyone that works for them, including their cousins, aunts, uncles, mothers, fathers, were all there chipping in. Probably not exactly, but that's how one remembers every meeting with U2!

Later on I directed 'ZooTV: The Outside Broadcast', for Channel 4, based around the US leg of the tour which rehearsed in Hershey, Pennsylvania. U2 wanted to put together a live TV show, but they wanted it to be different. I just felt at one with what they were trying to achieve. I wanted to do a show that took ele-ments of TV that didn't belong in a live rock show. I wanted to throw it around, put it in a blender: everything about television, everything about music, hit the switch and spew something radi-cal and unique out the other end. So I wrote a 15-page diatribe on how I saw ZooTV working. And I got a nice thing back from Malcolm Gerrie and Principle saying, 'At last we have someone who understands what we want to do.' I thought we were just going over there to see rehearsals so I could get to grips with cam-era positions and track lists. But it didn't actually turn out like that, because the whole show was such a massive undertaking. Picture this: Gavin Friday and I sat at the mixing desk with clipboards while the band rehearsed, video played on 20 or so big screens, everyone going through the motions. We'd meet them after rehearsal and talk. We were their audience. What did we think? 'What order should the songs be in? What do you think should happen here? Willie, what do you think? Kevin what do you think? Gav?' Suddenly I was no longer just the director. I was part and parcel of the creation of the damn thing. It was deep-end stuff again. Bottom line is U2 find people they're comfortable working with and challenge them, time after time.

If anyone was going to do it right, they were. It was tricky, though, because it was such a huge undertaking. There were some things that didn't work and some things that worked extremely well, better than your wildest dreams. The whole tour from beginning to end was in a constant state of flux. I think my favourite contribution to the show was the notion that perhaps U2 could perform 'Satellite of Love' with Lou Reed, and everyone thought, 'Cool. We've got a TV station here. Lou can be in New York while we're in Baltimore!' But it didn't work like that. Once the idea was on the table, Maurice Linnane, 'on-board' travelling stage screen director, made a nicely fucked-up film of Lou singing the second half of the song that was played into the overall presentation of 'Satellite of Love'. So, in effect, it looked like Lou Reed was singing, as it was said on the show, 'from the moon'. It was magical. Zoo was the biggest paint box in the world, and all the relevant technicians and artists and God knows who else were there to make it happen. It sounds self-indulgent now, but it wasn't. It was deftly experimental and incredibly exciting.

They broke the mould after ZooTV. It's difficult to categorize. It had documentary, drama, advertising, mock advertising. It was, as advertised, a TV station on the road. There was Zooropa and PopMart later, but they were smartened-up versions of the original. For my money, the original was so hard-core and dangerous. Perfectly imperfect. They were the live show Zeitgeist.

Every night on the tour, even while we were filming, Gavin and I would sit there with our notebooks. I'm sure people wondered who the fuck we were: a couple of inspectors with clipboards making notes which we would then discuss with the band. The show was mutating all the time; people would submit ideas for the screens and on they would go. We'd watch them that very evening. We'd comment on them after the show, and they were in or they were out. It was like a jukebox. Someone would say, 'Well, what if we did this instead? What if we parade six giraffes down the street and shoot them in slow motion in black and white?' 'Okay.' So off poor old Ned O'Hanlon would go and find six giraffes, or whatever, and Maurice or myself or Mark Neale would write some dialogue for them. I remember some pretty hairy edit sessions; 24 hours non-stop; Maurice editing in one room, me in another. There was a lot of cross-fertilization going on. Wonderful madness.

While all this went on, the band were concerned, quite rightly, with their performance. They knew they had a bunch of people around them, an incredibly creative support mechanism, if you like. Between me, Maurice, Mark Neale and Willie Williams, and God knows who else that joined the circus along the road, they knew that there wasn't a great deal that could actually go wrong.

If something didn't work one night, they'd sling it and try something else because the talent was there to create it. They would dip in every now and again and get involved, see how you were getting on and check up and see what's looking good and what's looking bad, and then duck out again.

Zooropa was a completely different tour, and I'd kind of bowed out by then. Then I did the video for 'Numb'. That was an interesting one. True to form, I got 'the call': 'Come out to Berlin, have a listen, what do you think?' Come up with some thoughts. Send the ideas back, have a chat with the band. 'Okay, none of these are quite right, but come out to Berlin anyway,' which is where they were. It was the night before the proposed shoot, and we were having dinner with everybody and we started to work out what we were actually gonna shoot. 'Okay, well, we'll do it as a locked-off camera, as if the camera was a TV set and Edge is looking at the TV set and what should we do?' 'Well, I don't know, but maybe a couple of feet come in from the side …' 'Oh yeah, I like that … and what if Morleigh [the dancer] pops up in front …' It was a funny video too. It was a pretty brave move because it was Edge, not Bono, singing and the look was very different for them.

All the guys in the band are different. They're all equally involved, but they come at it from four different angles. Larry is droll and dour. Typically, his comment on the whole ZooTV experience was: 'Fucking hell, all these people pay good money to see U2 and all they get is to watch television.' Here's Sue's take on them: there are five members of the band. There's Adam, Larry, Bono and The Edge, but there's also U2, and U2 is a separate entity. Each member of the band may have an opinion but there is an umbrella opinion that's more important. More dominant. U2 collectively sense, however they may feel individually about something, if an idea works for U2. They know instinctively what makes the bigger clock tick. You can nuance something the wrong way and a fundamentally good idea ceases to work for them. Or you can push it a little the other way and it's perfect for U2. It takes U2, the band, to know the answer to that question. I think she's right.
London, November 2003

A ZooTV landscape in rehearsals at Hersheypark Stadium, USA, August 1992

'Smell the roses while you can': David Wojnarowicz's buffalo image used on screen during the song 'One' on ZooTV

Mark Pellington
Film director, contributor, ZooTV

My work at MTV involved developing the style and emotion of their identity. I made a spot in 1986 which just said: 'Words. These are words. Blind people can't see them, deaf people can't hear them, foreigners don't understand them. But you can. These are words that can be saying: "people like to use these words in commercials to communicate a message." There are words that could be saying something funny, interesting, or cool. But they're not. They're just sitting here – just like you.' Just very small, tiny words on a black screen. It was basically an attack on the passivity of the audience. I just made it, and it went from idea to air in 36 hours. This was before marketing meetings, before ad sales, before the age of 'Well, let's test it.' This was like a lab.

It was so free, and for somebody who wasn't trained as an artist or a film-maker, it gave me, in the first four years of my career, confidence to trust my instincts about the way I see the world, in the way that I put material together. I would take a theme and make a collage and say, 'I can take any source material and marry it to a theme and put it through this hyperactive, dense, collage blender and use lyrics, anything I want.'

At the time, Jon Klein was working at MTV Europe as the news director. MTV married my ideas for a thematic collage show with Jon's idea of a global show and 'Buzz TV' was created in 1988. It was truly ahead of its time. MTV said, 'This would be a great show to help brand us globally.' This was before the Berlin Wall came down, before TV was seeping into everywhere. It was really a smart move on MTV's part. It was co-produced by Channel 4 in England and MTV US. We got into all sorts of problems because it was cut so fast that they would be like, 'We found a subliminal frame of a swastika next to Queen Elizabeth!' The stuff was going fast. We couldn't even examine it frame by frame. It was just intense acid television wallpaper. Very subversive. 'Buzz TV' ran for a year, 13 episodes, got a lot of press, but it was just too weird for people and too expensive for MTV. They started worrying about ratings and I said, 'Guys, this is an art piece.' I'd say the 'Buzz' buzz probably lasted for me until about 1996. It had an impact until then, which was considerable.

I returned to NYC … Adam Clayton had seen a $10,000 video I had made for the band Disposable Heroes of Hip-hoprisy. I made a seven-and-a-half-minute, railing anti-television diatribe, 'Television Drug of a Nation', for them. Adam saw it and said, 'Wow.' It was very much in the school of Buzz. I then got a call from Bono and talked to Willie Williams. They were upfront and said they were big fans of 'Buzz', were influenced by 'Buzz, and wanted to make a multiple TV screen huge assaultive 'Buzz' in an arena. Mark Neale and I had already produced a five-screen multi-media projection piece with a Spanish performance group, La Fura Del Baus, which means Rat from the Sewer. William Gibson was involved and Brian Eno. It was like the culmination of media bombardment and was called the 'Memory Palace'. I'm almost certain it was in the beginning of 1991.

'Buzz' influenced ZooTV. ZooTV precipitated the Internet explosion, the media multi-channel universe explosion, the proliferation

One of the many thought-provoking messages used in ZooTV's multimedia show

of imitation, of speed, stuff that 'Buzz' was only hinting at within the MTV culture. ZooTV precipitated mass culture, entertainment magazine culture, tabloid television culture, media feeding on it, regurgitating-itself culture, just beginning to bloom and explode both in America and globally. There was a whole other discussion about collage and cut-up theory, and using other people's material to make your own: images from people's videos, and text, and re-contextualizing them in ways to make statements that were ultimately corporate statements, but came across as hip, subversive, anti-authoritarian, rebellion. Those were the watchwords.

In the 'Buzz' pilot, we included a piece on Jenny Holzer, the influential American text artist. Bono, I think, was into Jenny Holzer, so the first video by Jon Klein they did for 'The Fly' was a Holzer-inspired piece where text messages and the lyrics from 'The Fly' came across as aphorisms at Piccadilly Circus, or on different signs. Then they came to me. In a cool way, they were hiring me to give me their juice. They're smart. They're going to artists to say, 'Do your thing, go to town, we'll pay you some money and it's gonna be seen by a lot of people. I had created fast single-word text pieces where it was confusing: they wanted this feeling of not knowing. 'Oh wait – did it say,"Bomb Japan now"? ' It said, 'You are the bomb Japan is this', but people – because this stuff was flying by so fast and then the assault of seeing it on big screens – thought they saw 'Bomb Japan now'.

That was just overwhelming. I'll never forget, and all I did was sit in a little room with the guy. I remember the first time we played it loud and Bono and The Edge came in; it went really fast and then for the choruses it would slow down to just one word, and very haunting or even sad or simple messages. U2 also got turned on by Disposable Heroes, who they had open the tour for them. They were into 'Buzz', into 'Television Drug of a Nation', so they went for the guys who made those things.

I did 'The Fly' and 'Zoo Station'. I went to Dublin for a week and spent all my time in the edit room – didn't get to see any of Dublin. We started talking about ideas, and with 'The Fly' it was like: 'We want to have a barrage of words.' So I started doing tests with loops of words, working with the Windmill Lane editing people. Maurice Linnane was involved, and Ned O'Hanlon, part of U2's creative team. I wrote a bunch of stuff. Bono wrote a bunch of stuff. All I had was a rehearsal track of the song to make the piece with. Ten days after we finished those two songs, I was in NYC and they asked me to go back to do another piece for 'One'. All they said was, 'We're gonna fax you this painting.' It was an image that the late artist David Wojnarowicz made of these buffaloes falling over a cliff with the phrase: 'Smell the roses while you can.' Got on the phone with Bono, and he goes on eloquently and beautifully – and you get it. When Bono has a vision of something he doesn't tell you exactly what to do, he just tells you the inspiration, and he was very happy with what I had done up to then. The tour hadn't started yet. They were still putting all the pieces together and deciding on the rhythm of the show: 'Okay, after a fast piece we want something mellow,' or 'We need something meditative, plaintive.' So I got hold of some old footage of buffalo, and images of flowers. I had this idea of draining colours from flowers and having it come back and forth and the word 'One' in simple type in many different languages. Since I knew we were using more than one screen, I had to provide them with several elements. The 'One' piece they loved. So that was like: 'Here's an image, make a piece.' And it was very much trust your instincts.

When I first saw a show using all the screens, I hadn't had a hint of how cool and insane it would be. I'd seen sketches, but the spectacle and power when the first screen lit up just hit you. 'Zoo Station' came up and that was cool, but, I tell you, with 'Everything You Know Is Wrong', with the first assault of colour (it was all colourful words and outlines on the white background), I got a shiver down my spine and a rush, having created it. Overwhelming.

When you make a movie and you see fiction in your mind brought to life, it's pretty powerful. You see the magic of cinema. This was the magic of spectacle. You see that assault on 40 big screens and the way that Willie had designed it, choreographed it to the music, was brilliant. It was incredible. And I heard that the 'The Fly' knocked people's socks off. Then there was all this hoopla about 'Bomb Japan Now' and people saying there were messages in it. Nobody ever came to me, though. U2 had to bear all that. The visceral response to the music and the imagery was pretty overwhelming. Whether it was beautiful and so sad with 'One', or totally aggressive with 'The Fly', it was the best of both worlds. It was your kick in the face, and the stroke, the touch on your heart, in equal measure. The Zeitgeist of what U2 did with ZooTV at the time, considering where media was, I think was just spot-on. U2 were right at that cusp, pulled artists in and opened up the floodgates.

I will always feel proud of what I did, proud of being involved and having a small impact on their thing. They always were respectful and always acknowledged that they were inspired by things. It was a nice nod to our little show, 'Buzz', that was kind of forgotten.

Los Angeles, February 2003

Mark Neale
Film director, contributor, ZooTV

I have a very minor walk-on part in this whole thing. In 1991 Brian Eno happened to see work I did for a show called 'Memory Palace' for the World Expo in Spain. At about that time I also co-directed a series called 'Buzz' for Channel 4 and MTV USA with Mark Pellington and Jon Klein produced by Malcolm Gerrie and Initial TV in London. The day after I had seen the ZooTV show in Barcelona, I got a call from Malcolm who told me they wanted a writer for the show. I thought, 'Well, this is perfect.' I was a genuine fan of the band and I loved the show. And there was the Mark Pellington connection, and conceptually what they were doing was familiar to me.

It was Edge in particular who decided that they needed a writer. At that stage I didn't really understand what the writer would do. I met Paul McGuinness and I had to go to Dublin to meet Ned and Maurice who just checked me out – we watched videos together. The first thing I wrote was something called: 'Bono to Say, the

Creed of Everything', something that he would recite at the end of/in the middle of the song 'Desire' on all the Outside Broadcast gigs. It began, 'I believe in the sky above me and the silver boots at my feet. I believe in poetry, electricity and cheap cosmetics …' and it goes on like this, a mad rant about believing in random things. Bono read it and said, 'I like your poem.' At the first gig he did it. He tried to memorize it, very gamely, and did well. And Willie was great because as soon as Bono launched into it, Willie ran it on all the LED displays that used to run the stockmarket prices all round the stage. Bono drifted far from the written words as he went along but that was okay. I felt like I was being paid to come up with really ridiculous ideas. Some of them got to happen. I would write 20 pages of ideas and present them to the band, to Kevin Godley, to whoever wanted to look at them. We would try things and sometimes they would work. I came up with the idea for Rex Fox, the ZooTV newsreader who spoke in cut-up gibberish.

My lasting contribution was the video confessional, a customized Portaloo. For a while, the band had wanted to find a way to involve the audience. So one day I suggested having a video confessional. I thought it would be good to have a way for the audience to interact with the show. Bono immediately agreed. By the end of that day we had the camera and I was crudely spray-painting the Portaloo. I got a camera with a wide-angle lens on it and we cut the hole in the outside and spray-painted it with colour bars, like TV colour bars. It got decorated better over time, by Catherine Owens. This thing was set up on the floor of the stadium near the stage but in a public area and anyone could go in. You had 30 seconds to say your piece, to make your video confession. During the first part of the show we would cut together the best bits and then in the interval we would run the best minute or three minutes on the screens and through the PA. It had to be shut down on the first day because somebody actually did use it as a loo. It took off from there. It was in every gig from the beginning of the Outside Broadcast tour to the end of Zooropa. It went all around the world. Willie said, 'That was the one thing in every show that would bring the truck drivers out up front.' They would never watch the show but they would always come and see what the video confessions said. I was always looking for things that would become part of the show rather than just add-ons.

As a show, Zoo simply kept getting stronger. It was such an open concept, which people might not necessarily understand in any coherent way, but everybody understood that they were basically going there to freebase media. The performance was always the thing. That always blew me away, how the band was still the hub, the heart and the soul of the thing. There was quite a lot of debate within the inner circle about whether the show was too glossy or too big. I think it was just something that challenged them in a fundamentally coherent way. U2's heart and soul against the media machine. That's powerful. The more confident they got at playing with the machine, the better it got.

It was so exciting to be given the opportunity to make that stuff. For all the agony that you go through, you have a lot of fun doing it. Nobody else has done what they've done. I haven't been involved with the other shows but that one was perfect for its time, and I was very lucky to be involved in it.

Los Angeles, February 2003

The video confessional booth – an integral part of the show in which fans came clean every night. Zooropa, Rotterdam, Holland, 1993

Show Filming

Top: Bono with Malcolm Gerrie, whose TV show The Tube and 'U2 Live at Red Rocks' *concert documentary helped to define U2's early 'eighties image.*
Bottom: U2 on the Tube TV show

Malcolm Gerrie
Film producer, Under a Blood Red Sky, U2 Live at Red Rocks

In the late 1970s I presented the local kids' Saturday morning show for nearly two years at Tyne Tees, which was part of the ITV regional companies. I became something of a TV presenter as well as a researcher, and we did a lot of music. At this time the whole punk thing was going on: The Clash, The Jam, The Police. I was obsessed with how boring and dull and homogeneous music on TV was then. It was either the worst end of pop or it just ignored punk altogether, as if punk never happened. They were still playing The Eagles, Jackson Browne, middle American rock, when The Clash were massive. They ignored almost completely what was going on here in the UK, which was a music revolution, out of which came U2.

In 1979 Andrea Wonfor, my mentor at Tyne Tees, said, 'I think it's about time you produced your own show', and I said to her, 'Why don't we do a programme which features new bands?' My idea was to make the studio into a live gig: 'They've got to perform live, no lip-synching, have a live audience. We'll have a bar where people can get pissed and the band can drink, and the band can play as many numbers as they want. It's unscripted, and if they want to collaborate with anybody they can.' It was called 'All Right Now' and it caused absolute eruptions. Some of the old boys refused to work on the show. The word got around. Tyne Tees was completely independent, struggling to get programmes on the network and Andrea put her neck on the block, to say, 'New producer, Malcolm Gerrie, never produced anything, radical left-field music show, which is obviously not going to be networked.' Andy Allen, who was the managing director, said, 'Malcolm, you'd better make a good show, get some big names on it and we might get it on the late night network.' This was where the big four TV companies took regional programmes late night as a bit of a sop to the little pimply companies up in the northeast, like us. So I said, 'Don't worry, I'll get you the big names, Andy.' So, we did a pilot, and on the pilot I booked two bands. I was in the edit suite the next day, putting the programme together, when I got a phone call to go to Andy Allen's office immediately. Andy said, 'Malcolm, how the fuck do you expect me to get this programme on the network if you're going to book these no-account, fucking no-hoper, mean fuck-all-shit-useless bands? What the fuck are you doing with my money and my studio and my airtime?' And the two bands were The Police and Dire Straits in one studio, together, never been done before. I said: 'Andy, I'm sorry. If you want someone to book Elton John and Cliff Richard, then I'm not the man for the job. Then it's not the show I want to make, and I don't think it's right. And it's boring, and I think you're wrong.' And he said, 'You do, do you?' It just mushroomed, and the bands we had on were remarkable. The Clash only ever did

two television shows in their whole career. When they came up everybody said, 'Oh, God, they'll be taking heroin and they'll smash the place up.' I remember driving past Tyne Tees and they were sat on the stairs at nine in the morning waiting to go in, eating bacon sandwiches. They were as good as gold, and they just did the most blistering set, which has become a historic piece of TV.

In 1981 it was announced that the government was launching a new terrestrial channel: Channel 4. Until then, there were only three networks – no Channel 5, no MTV, no cable. Monopolistic. So Andy Allen said, 'Right. Here's your chance guys. None of this spiky-haired punky stuff. Here's our chance to get the show on Channel 4. Jeremy Isaacs – who's going to run it, wants programmes from the regions, a "Ready, Steady, Go" for the 1980s. The weekend begins here. They want 20 one-hour and forty-five-minute programmes. Totally live, all from Newcastle, starting on Bonfire Night, the week the Channel goes on air, to run for half the year. So sit down and come up with something.' So we gave him this idea of a show called 'Jamming'; we did a pretend running order and one of the bands in the pretend running order was a little-known band from Ireland called U2. 'Get on a plane, Jeremy Isaacs wants to meet you for lunch in Charlotte Street tomorrow.' So I don't sleep, fly into London, Charlotte Street, sit in this bloody Italian restaurant. In comes Jeremy in a huge puff and bluster. 'My commissioning editor's seen this show you've been doing called "Now It's All Right" or whatever it is. Loves it. Gotta be much bigger and much braver. More mad names, extreme and let's get into trouble with this. I'm gonna say two words to you: make it live and give it balls!' He just slurped the glass of red wine down and went. That commission was the biggest thing. Tyne Tees had never done anything like that, ever. We didn't have enough cameras! I mean, where do you begin? We launched on 5 November 1982 – 'The Tube' in all its glory with Jools Holland and Paula Yates. And the house band became U2.

There was just the most enormous buzz about them. They were on Island Records, who we had a fantastic relationship with because most of the Island acts were perfect for 'The Tube'. Island was the coolest label: the best label, the hardest label, the savviest label, the sexiest label. You needed to have those palm trees in your record collection whether you were in the northeast of England or in Kingston. So there was a bit of a parallel going on. Like minds. I read so much about Chris Blackwell and I thought, 'God, what this man has done for music.'

In early 1983 I got a call out of the blue from Paul to say, 'Malcolm, I've got this idea. I want your advice on it.' He said the band were playing this remarkable venue where Indian tribes used to meet, and no rock band really had ever performed there before on this scale. They wanted to know whether or not I thought it was possible to shoot a special video there. At the time, I thought he was talking about a four-minute song, a promo. He asked me to think about putting it on as a little bit of a 'Tube' special, so I said, 'It sounds amazing.' Then the penny dropped that what he was talking about was a whole hour-long special. I said, 'Well, I've got to sell this to Channel 4, Paul, because 'The Tube' isn't a one-band show.' U2 weren't mega then. They hadn't cracked America and I didn't know if the channel would agree to it. Paul said, 'Even if they don't, we'd like to tape it. And we're going to pay for it and were going to own it.' I said, 'With respect, Paul, what if it doesn't work out?' And he said, 'Well, Malcolm, that's why I brought you. It's got to work out; otherwise we are no more, because all the money we've got is going into this.' So I was like: 'Oh my God.' He said, 'What I'd like to do is give you the rights to show it and we'll talk about some kind of deal for the transmission of it, and we'll give it to Channel 4 for free. So whatever money you get from Channel 4, you take the money from Channel 4 to help make the show.' So we did this classic Paul deal, a brilliant deal in which everybody has an upside.

Initially it was a 15-minute programme within a normal show, and then, because it became such a historic piece of music television, we showed it as a whole thing. It was historic because of what happened on the night. The weather was so bad, the heavens just opened. Electricity was arcing from one speaker column to another. If that had hit they would have been dead. Barry Fey, the promoter, took one look at it and said, 'It's off. Forget it. I'm sending the crowd away.' And so the band were fucked, basically, because they had all their money in it. I had no TV show so I was fucked. We all were. It was a disaster. Paul was on the phone sorting out another venue, and he asked me if we could keep all the crew. We had a helicopter with an ex-Vietnam pilot who was mad as a hatter, who was flying – with our cameraman on board – through the flames. It was like: never mind the weather. So what happened was the atmosphere of it: because the mist descended, and we managed to keep half the crowd, the light … something really weird happened with the light and the fire, you know, and the whole thing just absolutely had an ethereal, magical quality to it, which you couldn't get by any special effects or filters.

There was a real debate, because Paul wanted to put it out on video. Back in 1985, MTV was just starting to come over to Europe. But in America it was big; very, very big. It was breaking acts left, right and centre. Their sister company was called Showtime, which was very grown up – Barbra Streisand, Billy Joel, you know. And I managed to persuade them to show *U2 at Red Rocks*. It was a joint deal between MTV and Showtime, because MTV showed it and then Showtime showed it. It was extraordinary that they took *U2 at Red Rocks* – and it just opened the door for the band. Steve Hewitt, who was running Showtime at the time, was a U2 fan. I showed him some of the rushes and he loved what he saw and was prepared to take a punt. And the band didn't want any money for it; they just wanted to get the exposure. See, Paul was brilliant. So it was just the most fantastic experience. *Billboard* and *Variety* gave it rave reviews. It was one of those happy career moments where it's a really good thing for everybody involved. It was great for Channel 4, it was great for 'The Tube', it was great for the band, and it was great for music on television. That really made me proud.

McGuinness was very clever because he sent his Irish road crew to learn the American ropes in San Francisco. He was watching what was going on in America, and that's another reason why I think maybe it was easier for U2: they learned their ropes on the road. They learned how to play the game that way and then bring it back. It seems to me they were the only band who actually did it that way. What they realized really quickly was that America was actually 50 countries – different radio stations, different promoters, different press – and they made friends in every damn state. That goodwill and that hard work paid huge dividends later on. At the end of the day they just won everybody's trust and got people to do things for them over and above what they might normally do. And that's very clever.

There are two remarkable things about U2. Number one, they were probably the most intelligent, articulate and driven of any band I've ever met. Number two, they had one of the most intelligent and sussed managers of any band I'd ever met, and by this time I'd met quite a few. There's absolutely not one jot of difference between them then and now. Paul runs that band in a completely business-like, professional way, but with a soft touch. It breaks every rule in the book because while it is run like a very well-oiled machine, at the heart of the machine is a heart. I've stayed at Bono's house, I've been pissed with them on airplanes and all sorts of clubs, and still when he meets me at a gig he runs over to me and hugs me and twirls me around like a long-lost son. I know he does that with loads of people. It's loyalty with a capital 'L' and the result of that is they get people to do anything. I will do anything for U2 because, apart from a professional level, I think of them as friends. They're fantastic people and their music is just brilliant.

The number of times they've reinvented themselves! My job is about putting music and pictures together, and nobody since Pink Floyd has done what they've done in terms of stagecraft. There is nobody to touch them. Nobody comes anywhere near to their stage shows in terms of ambition, risk, danger and being ahead of their time. Television is all about stories: soaps, dramas, news stories, heartbreaks, tragedies, love stories, and U2 encapsulate all of that because their music and their beliefs and the way they present them are fantastic stories. So, selfishly, from a TV producer's point of view, this is manna from heaven because you are always, always, always – 10 times out of 10 – going to get a fantastic soundbite out of Bono. You'll get an extremely lucid and intelligent and often controversial point of view from McGuinness. You'll get a heartfelt insight from Edge. You'll get a down-to-earth, gritty, shoot-from-the-hip statement from Adam and Larry. But there's always a story. The problem with U2 is actually getting them to talk about when they're releasing their record and when they're going to tour, because they want to talk about everything else. They're the antithesis of your day-to-day pop band, in that it appears as if the product is bottom of the agenda.

If you could write a TV producer's model band which would tick all the boxes for controversy, politics, fantastic music, spectacle, worldwide domination, you would come up with U2. There are certain individuals who get very near it, but you've got to think hard about who they are. As a band, I think, they're unique in that respect.
London, July 2003

Red Rocks 'fired U2 like a rocket in the sky'

Gavin Taylor

Film director, Under A Blood Red Sky, U2 Live at Red Rocks

I was the studio director of 'The Tube'. Paul McGuinness had told Malcolm Gerrie that he had this ambition for the band: there was a brilliant venue in America called Red Rocks just outside Denver in Colorado, a natural amphitheatre in the Rocky Mountains, and he wanted to film a show there. Red Rocks was just basically a concrete base, some rocks around it and tiered seating. The altitude was very, very high. If you went to the back of the auditorium, you'd have to literally gasp for breath – there was so little oxygen and the air was so thin. We took a skeleton crew: my PA and my two chosen cameramen from Tyne Tees that worked on 'The Tube', and that was it. I'd never been to America before, and apart from Gateshead this was the first sort of major outdoor rock concert that I had done. We had devised a particular style of shooting things in the UK on 'The Tube' and I think that our style had something to do with the reason why Paul McGuinness chose us to do it. It was a new mode of bravery, breaking all the rules, when the cameramen operated cameras hand-held. Hand-held cameras were quite in their infancy in those days. They were tube cameras, and if you pointed a tube camera at a light it used to burn on the tube. It was caught, and if you moved it there would be this great trail where the lights had burned on the tube and then would slowly disappear. We had a number of American cameramen; I think we had about seven cameras altogether, which was a lot in those days. We also had a camera flying in a helicopter that did some aerial shots of Denver, but because of the appalling weather he only managed to do one or two passes over the venue. Those bonfires were burning and it looked just absolutely stunning, the big flames on the sides of the stage.

If I played any part in it, it was the fact that I wanted a stage to be built. I wanted the band to be elevated from just playing on one sort of concrete level, so I insisted that we should build a stage about a metre high. Because of Bono's personality and charisma, I wanted to break down the gap between him and the audience, because he's very much a person's person, a part of the audience. So we built this walkway into the audience so they could be around the walkway. I knew that it would work with U2.

The mist was down and there was a fine drizzle and it was cold. But when Bono was singing he was boiling hot, so there was steam rising from his body, and his breath was clouds of steam. It was the combination of the band, the location and the weather conditions, which were absolutely appalling, but which in a way made that concert. The helicopter shots, the drizzle, the mist and the flames. The reviews afterwards said, 'Is this a rock concert or is this a religious gathering?' *Live at Red Rocks* really kick-started their career, particularly in America. It fired them like a rocket in the sky.

London, February 2004

Ned O'Hanlon

Film producer, virtually all live performances since 1992; Dreamchaser Productions, 1991–2003

My first connection to U2 was through my wife, Anne-Louise. I'd seen them a couple of times in the Dandelion Market when they were playing there in the early stages – I just sort of wandered in off the street. I didn't think a whole lot of them then, thought they made a lot of bad noise. It really wasn't until Anne-Louise started to work with them in 1983, which was the year before we were married, that I met U2 personally. They were very solemn young men. As musicians they were desperately committed to being as good as they could be and very serious about what they were doing. They were definitely not messing around. The first time I really saw one of their shows was in Earl's Court in London on the Unforgettable Fire tour. I was mesmerized by the energy and charisma that came off the stage. The music was fantastic; really, really powerful. There was nothing on the stage. That was in the days when there was just the four of them: no gadgets, no tricks, just three chords and the truth. That's what they built their campaigns on.

I was working in Windmill Lane as a producer, and the work that the company was doing was mostly music-oriented simply by virtue of the fact that there were music studios there. I started working with U2 just at the end of *Rattle and Hum*. We shot a video and then worked on the Irish segment of that film. It progressed from there. The first thing I did with them as a producer was a video for one of the songs off *Rattle and Hum* called 'All I Want Is You', which we shot on a beach outside Rome.

Out on the road when people are touring with U2, there's a joke that represents what the 'U2 family' is all about. It goes, 'There's no going home until you get it right', and the unsaid part of that is, 'It's impossible to get it right, because it's never right!' All U2's touring people who've grown up with the band have learned their craft working with these guys, and they've all floated with that boat. They have all, in their turn, become the best at what they do, and within the industry they're universally acknowledged as such. There's a parallel that goes with this as well, which is the technological advances in touring. As it became clear that it was possible to fill stadiums with big acts, the technology had to follow to allow that to happen. And these guys embraced it. Bono loves his crowd, and bigger is always better. He's one of the few people who can reach the back row of a 90,000 superstadium. Whatever that ingredient is, he has it in truckloads. I mean, you want to smack him for it sometimes, but he does have it – shovel-loads of the stuff. He always had that charisma.

With *Rattle and Hum* they had the toughest time when they were shooting because they wanted to make this huge movie, but they didn't want to see a camera anywhere. They were saying, 'We are about the live show. This is what we're doing here and we don't want any of that stuff. But we do want a great concert film.' There's an inherent contradiction there. Nowadays filming the DVD on a tour is an integral part of the whole package to do with the live show. It's part of the second crack of the whip, purely from the sales point of view. So they went from the *Rattle and*

Hum days when they were kind of video virgins, to ZooTV where they became terrible sluts. Maurice Linnane likes to say that they went from virgins to being complete tarts. They just couldn't get enough of it.

In September 1991 I had been taken on as an overall pro ducer for all the visuals that were going to be within the show. That was a co-ordinating job because there were a lot of people all over the place: Brian Eno, Mark Pellington, Mark Neil. Eno did a lot of the pieces, some of which were the most enduring. One particular piece, the Starfields, started off on ZooTV for 'Love Is Blindness', was then used in PopMart and re-emerged as projections in the Elevation show. At the time Maurice Linnane and I were doing a documentary for MTV which goes by the catchy title of 'The Videos, the Cameos, and a Whole Lot of Interference from ZooTV'. It was a catch-up basically for MTV viewers, where they'd left off from the Unforgettable Fire through Love Town to the start of ZooTV with what had happened in the meantime. The end of this documentary was meant to be them taking the stage at the first show of the ZooTV tour. So Maurice and I went out to Lakeland, Florida, to shoot the first show and finish off the documentary. We were supposed to come home the following day and ended up coming back two years later. That was the first time I went out on the road. When I got to Florida they gave me a bag tag and I knew I was in trouble. Number 13, I should have known.

Arriving at the production rehearsals my main recollection is feeling pure terror. It was absolute heart in your mouth stuff. It was the heaviest night of my life up until that point. That whole rehearsal hall was very, very fraught. Willie Williams and Brian Eno were very involved in the intellectual/conceptual side of ZooTV. The band was deeply involved in it. There was a lot of serious artistic and intellectual rationalization going on about what the meaning of it all was. It was like an out of control locomotive, but it could never be any other way. Until they'd actually done a couple of the shows they were never going to put limits on it. We did a full dress rehearsal the night before the show and it was just dire. It felt entirely contrived: it was just like flashing lights and nonsense. Tensions and tempers were running very high. A lot of people had been working their tails off to try and pull it together. I learned that subsequently this is what U2 do: they wind everybody up like a coiled spring so that it all works on the day. I don't think it's intentional; that's just the way they are, because they take it all so seriously.

The first night, that show was incredible, and it all just worked! Then the work started. That's what kept us busy, throwing stuff out and making new stuff on the road for the screens. The experience was entirely unique, and a real eye-opener for myself and Maurice because we became a guerrilla TV crew. We'd watch a show, then we'd all have a post-mortem afterwards where we'd decide what needed changing. You had these constant ongoing kind of think-tank things – Gavin Friday was another big collaborator in all of that. Gavin would be like the 'Cool Hoover'. He'd stamp around the place with a notebook and a pen and go, 'That's a bucket of shite.' Not one to stand on ceremony, Gavin. The Video Confessional was part of the show. Essentially it was

a Portaloo. This was an idea that came up the day before the outdoor leg of the tour in Giants Stadium. I was in charge of finding a photo booth in 24 hours and kitting it out to be able to film people the following day at rehearsals at Giants Stadium. I hadn't managed to get a photo booth. All I got was a Portaloo and a camera and a light and had it installed in one of the concourses. This was deemed not to be good enough and I got into terrible trouble.

ZooTV was very, very heavily staged, but in a way they were being spontaneous as well. From a design and a technological point of view, we were doing things that the technology said you couldn't do. We were doing mad stuff. A lot of the material we made was TV stuff around the show for television. That's where ZooTV became an actual ethos, a vibe. The whole point of it originally was to use a television channel that didn't broadcast. And the tour became a magnet. There was a large, ever-changing team of people who became involved as it moved around, who just came along and said, 'I have this' or 'I can do that' or 'Have you thought about this?' And then we'd be launched off to do some other mad stuff and stick it in the show. It was very much a travelling circus, and certainly for myself and Maurice it was such a learning curve. That was the first time I'd produced a show of that scale for TV and one that went live pretty much everywhere. We had a virtually limitless budget. There was never a question of 'How much will it cost to do this?' It was 'Just do it!' *ZooTV Live from Sydney* was a huge, huge, gargantuan production. The whole show is in NTSC – we were shooting in a PAL country, so we had to ship everything in to shoot. A lot of money, a lot of pressure and a lot of satellite problems.

The PopMart show was a much easier one to shoot because we were more kind of standing back absorbing what was going on; as opposed to ZooTV, which was more integrated, because we were trying to shoot that show in a ZooTV manner while still making it coherent for the punter watching it at home. There were more layers to it. On the Elevation tour they completely reinvented themselves again. They've got the temerity and the cheek to do that. They've got two audiences: one who's just discovered them – kids in my son's class are big fans – and the guys who've been hanging around for a long time, people my age. I suppose the typical audience is probably somewhere in their 30s to 40s and pretty much a white audience.

I suppose the band have a certain sort of ethos. They've never been a kind of big classic rock act – it's not sex, drugs, rock and roll, girls backstage and all that sort of stuff. They're very low-key. They like to party, but it's perfectly innocent. I guess that comes from self-confidence as well: you don't need to live that life in order to be serious about what you're doing, and they've always been serious. They've changed in their presentation, but the message is the same. They're serious about being ironic. They're serious about taking the piss out of themselves and everything around them. They take their music and their business seriously, and it's to their credit that they've never let any of that slip. They're on top of it, they're interested, they're engaged, they're involved and nothing really happens regarding them as a brand, an entity, a unit and as a band that they're not fully conver-

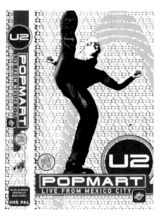

Top: 'Achtung Baby: the videos, the cameos, and a whole lot of interference from ZooTV' produced by Ned O'Hanlon, directed by Maurice Linnane. Centre: 'ZooTV Live from Sydney' 1994, produced by Ned O'Hanlon and Rocky Oldham, directed by David Mallet. Bottom, 'PopMart Live from Mexico City' 1998, produced by Ned O'Hanlon, Directed by David Mallet

sant with and happy about. So, is that rock and roll? Probably not. It's more like big business. U2 set very high standards for themselves and for everybody around them and they've always been completely focused on the music. At all times it is the band, and the band is made up of four separate, distinct, individual, and entirely different human beings. It's a classic case of where the whole is greater than the sum of its parts. Their strength is as a unit, and they've never ever gone away from that. They are, without question, unique in the world of rock and roll.

Dublin, January 2004

Maurice Linnane

Video director, Dreamchaser Productions, 1991–2003

In the late 1980s I was an editor at Windmill Lane, working with Ned O'Hanlon. U2 were one of the clients at the facility. Principle Management also had their offices in Windmill Lane, so everyone kind of knew everyone else. In 1991 Ned and I started our own company and we were called in to do publicity for the *Achtung Baby* album. Then MTV wanted to do a documentary of the tour when that happened, and we were asked to do that. I pulled together all this stuff from the year dot and put together a soundtrack in a kind of a greatest-hitsy kind of a way. It was beguilingly called the 'History Mix' and opened the MTV documentary, which was initially supposed to be aired just before the ZooTV tour hit Europe on the indoor leg in May 1992. That was the plan anyway. But as we would soon learn you could never really depend on the plan. Ned and I went out to Lakeland, Florida, purely to finish the MTV documentary, because the documentary we had pitched was to finish with the band walking away from us onto the stage as everything faded to black. We were supposed to be out

'We were credited as being the guerrilla TV crew, we were there to put out forest fires and act as kind of a SWAT team!'

there for four days to finish shooting and then go home to Ireland to edit it and have it ready in four weeks. We arrived and McGuinness asked us to stay on for another couple of weeks, which we did. Then he laughingly asked us to stay on for another couple of weeks and laughingly we agreed, and the long and short of it is that we stayed the whole tour. We went down for two weeks, stayed for two years.

Within that period, the show changed hugely. My role in particular changed. That first indoor leg in America was just a mad dash – it was 40 shows in 40 nights. We were credited as being the guerrilla TV crew: we were there to put out forest fires and act as kind of a SWAT team. If stuff needed to be done we were the ones who were called on to do it. Ned and me, Gerry MacArthur, the world's greatest cameraman, Richard Kendrick, who was then Gerry's soundman, and, initially at least, Barry Devlin, who'd seen it all and done it all several times before and without whom I wouldn't have made it past the first week. For chunks of time I was more of a satellite to the tour: I'd shoot things, run away and edit them, run back and show them, run away and change them. Come back, be told it was wrong – 'Everything We Knew Was Wrong' – be told it was a new thing, go and shoot that thing and start the cycle again. I ended the tour credited as the artistic director of Zooropa. It was quite a journey.

It was a great time. We got to grow and stretch and see the world, though occasionally at a price. It was a pretty uncompromising, unforgiving place at times. Nobody applauded mere effort. Things had to be right and the definition of what was right could be changed while you were out of the room. But I wouldn't swap it. At that stage I'd been working for six years in the business. Dublin is a great place to do this kind of work because there's great work that gets done here. But you're in Dublin – not the biggest place in the world – and you want to see if you could cut it elsewhere. That was the whole thing for me. And Ireland at the end of the 1980s wasn't the kind of prosperous Celtic Tiger-driven place it is now. Back then people were leaving and not coming back, in their thousands. So we went off as part of ZooTV and found out that we could stand up to be counted. Heady days. They came along and they just pushed the bar up really, really high. So high that the only ones who have ever come close to clearing it since have been themselves. You've got to applaud that.

Dublin, February 2004

Wardrobe

Fintan Fitzgerald

Wardrobe assistant, Joshua Tree; stylist, head of wardrobe Love Town, ZooTV; wardrobe co-ordinator, PopMart, Elevation

I started with U2 in 1986, when they were making *Joshua Tree*. The woman entrusted with their styling, costume and wardrobe at that time, Marian Smyth, got me in to do a few jobs for her. Catherine Owens had recommended me. U2 were recording the album up in Danes Moat in Dublin. It was great to be around the band and get a feel for the process, hear a bit of the music. At that stage I was still very peripheral.

The first gig I ever did with them was Self Aid, a project in Ireland for unemployed people. It raised money and awareness. I had worked with some small Dublin bands, but I had never done anything like that before. I had just never been in an atmosphere like that. I remember Bono asking me, early on, if I knew much about the band. Well, years before, I used to live in Amsterdam and heard about this band out of Dublin, and I brought a bunch of friends to see them at a small venue called the Milkyway. It must have been in 1981 or 1982. And so I told Bono this: at the time I thought they were really rubbish and we left halfway through the gig! He smiled and said, 'Well, you know, that's good. You'll do for us because you're critical, you have an opinion and a point of view.' From then on I became more and more part of the family. A few months before the Joshua Tree tour Marian stopped work to have a baby and the band asked if Judy Williams and I would fill in and do wardrobe while they looked for someone else. That's how touring started for me.

U2 have a very organic approach to their work. There's a process. A lot happens in between where it starts and where it finishes. To be even on the periphery of that as a stylist, you get good sense of what direction they're heading in. Then you can service the look of the show or the tour a lot better, in the long term, rather than if you suddenly turn up at the end of that process and are simply told what has gone on before. You get a better understanding. Costume and wardrobe are very personal. As well as being about the show, it is very much about people feeling comfortable with what they wear onstage. So you need to be fairly close.

It's not like fashion styling. You can't just say, 'Put this on, you're gonna look great.' There's a lot of dialogue involved about what feels good, helps give people confidence for their performance. If you have to walk out on stage in front of 10,000 or 20,000 people and you're going to be the focus of attention, you really need to have confidence that you're looking your best. And you need to have confidence in the person who is advising you or helping you with those clothes. So trust is important, as well as a good and honest eye.

There's a lot of preparation. You don't just go out the week before the tour and find what you're looking for. Sometimes you have to have things made, which are very seldom 100 per cent right the first time. That's time-consuming. There are fittings, choosing fabrics, getting the colour palette right to work with the staging and lighting, the visuals. And, for a tour, you're also trying to supply enough clothes for perhaps a whole year. You need sets of clothes. It's also a constantly changing, growing project. U2 continually try to change and improve everything throughout the tour.

Working on Joshua Tree was a baptism of fire for me. It was a time of great excitement and chaos, because everyone was on new territory. There was a lot of fan frenzy. They made the cover of *Time* magazine. Everyone wanted a piece of the band. It was quite scary, but exciting – a sharp learning curve for everybody to have to deal with.

On the tour there was an incredible amount of press interest, so there were photo shoots all the time, as well as all the wardrobe preparation for the gigs themselves. We shot two or three videos during the tour. And then there was a decision to make the film, *Rattle and Hum,* which added more work. It was an intense two years. But the only real pressures I've ever been aware of, working with U2, have come from the band members themselves and their need to get the best possible work done. It's never been anything to do with the demands of, say, a record company, or a film studio, or the 'suits'. It's never about the money or the profit, always about the quality of the work. Those guys, they're workaholics. They don't ever stop, and they're constantly trying to push their own boundaries. They really want to do the work. That's their life and that's what excites them. That ethos, as long as I've been around them, has always been the same. It certainly hasn't dimmed. If anything, it gets more intense. But I think they're better these days at giving themselves a little space, some time out.

At the end of 1990 I got a phone call. The band was working in Berlin, with Brian Eno and Danny Lanois, recording the new album. I went there for maybe three months to see what's going on, the process. There were some photo shoots. Anton Corbijn came in to document the U2 Berlin period. They were rediscovering themselves and wanting to do something new. And out of it

MacPhisto's boots, Zooropa tour, Rotterdam, Holland, May 1993

came *Achtung Baby*, which was very European and quite modern, taking into account certain things that were going on in music at the time. The music was more urban, more industrial than anything they had done before. One of my main ideas for the tour wardrobe was that we should go with one designer to create a much stronger feel from the clothes to tie in with the new sound.

I went off and I started researching and narrowing down who would be the best designer for the job. It had to be urban, modern, European, totally different than anything that had gone before. There was this sense of the onslaught of media and advertising, so many visuals in people's lives. How were we going to portray that and how would the band look within that, how would it mix visually? Finding one or two key pieces is always the great clue. Then everything else builds around it. I had found these big fly bug glasses from the early 1970s in an old junk shop in Soho. I brought them to Bono and he started wearing them all the time, even in the studio, and he started developing this persona with them. Out of that grew the Fly character. It seemed to work in with the whole emerging Zoo concept. Next, I found this old naugahyde second-hand jacket. We used it for the first video, which was 'The Fly'. It went with the glasses and this persona. So we had this Fly character and that was the start. I think everything came from that, costume-wise. That jacket actually self-destructed. During the making of the video it started to fall apart. By the end shot the thing had ripped apart. It was like a metamorphosis or something.

The Fly was a great character, so I went looking for designers who would be able to develop this. We narrowed it down to Joe Casley Hayford. I thought it was a very good marriage. We started with the Fly, obviously, buzz black fly. All black leather. That stayed throughout the tour. We made a red leather version, which we never really used much. You usually try and have one definitive look and then maybe two or three variations. You try to narrow it down in the first weeks of the tour and then you start adding to that. And as the shell changed, or the structure of it, so you add or subtract different looks. Like MacPhisto. Before MacPhisto we had Mirrorball Man on the US leg of the tour, a mirrorball cowboy, a flashy preacher man, the TV evangelist who blinds people with flash and steals their souls. It was a play on those ideas. During the show, for 'Desire', lots of Zoo money came out into the audience, and Bono took on this preacher-man persona. I suppose it was a comment on TV evangelists in America. Around that time there were a couple of big scandals involving hypocritical TV evangelists, modern-age medicine men hoodwinking people out of their hard-earned cash. Joe Casley Hayford made the suit. I researched and found the fabric, which was from a group called Space Time Fabrics, who made great three-dimensional fabrics here in London. I put the fabric people and the designer together and, with the ideas from Bono about the Mirrorball Man, we came up with this and it really worked well. But we dropped it for Europe, and he became MacPhisto. Bono thought he needed a character point in the show, and the character was MacPhisto, the Devil, a very theatrical character. It was the first time he had done a character like that. And then we came up with a gold suit and red lamé, a ruffled shirt, the make-

up and the Devil horns. Bono really took on the persona and got into character. Personally, I think if he wasn't the great musician he is, he probably would have made a great actor. I think the character himself came from Bono and Gavin Friday. Somewhere along the line they conceived this character, and then Bono asked for a costume for it. There was a big debate about the horns for a long time, whether it was too theatrical, or just too comic. We played around with loads of ideas.

Other outfits in Zoo included a character Bono wore for 'Bullet the Blue Sky', a military/SWAT team guy. In a U2 show, you can't have too many big costume changes. This was probably the first tour they had any costume changes in fact. They were necessary for the different moods and different elements of the show. It was a concept show. But it's not a costume drama. It's not Diana Ross and it's not Beyoncé! It's a rock and roll show. The only time, later in the tour, that we changed everything was for *Zooropa* the album. For the song 'Lemon' the band came out in four more or less identical royal blue costumes and, again, it was about *Zooropa* and it was about Europe and the unification of Europe, and, I suppose, the potential dangers of a united Europe. What does it mean? It could go one way or the other, you know. It's so not like U2, but it worked for that one song. It worked well in the video and it worked well in the set. I think it was the only time that they all wore the same thing.

Sometimes you need to make bigger statements on stage visually than you would off stage, simply because everything's further away, or on a screen. You need to make it a bit more theatrical. But it's a fine line: if you make it too theatrical, it can look silly. If you had followed U2 up to that point you might have thought: 'What the fuck is going on?' But I think they gained a lot of new fans who had not been interested in U2 before. I think it was a brave, dangerous step, but on balance it worked. It was thought-provoking and it was challenging.

I think Zoo rewrote the rules for live performance. I still go to shows today and see things that we did in 1992 that hadn't been done before. For example the ramp into the middle of the audience; so many bands use that now. There were so many ideas in that show, and the great thing about it was that it changed almost weekly. And when it went outdoors I think it really worked on that level as well. You could see the excitement on people's faces in the audience. It was a total visual and aural experience. On the Zoo tour the wardrobe team was myself, Helen Campbell and Nasim Khalifa. Everybody had to muck in. Generally one person would travel with the crew on the buses and would load in the wardrobe cases and everything, organize the dressing rooms, set up everything during the day for the gig. The other two would travel with the band. It depended on what was going on. If we had a photo shoot or something like that, then obviously it made more sense for Nasim to be with us, because there would be basic make-up to be done. The person at the gig would set up everything, get the wardrobe room ready, do the ironing, put out clothes for that night, which would be the four stage outfits, plus some alternatives and back-ups for any emergencies. The dry-cleaning would have to be sent out, the washing done, repairs and alterations. We usually travel with washing machines and dryers. A million and one little tasks have to be done before every gig.

Principle Management give us a schedule of upcoming events, shows, interviews and so on, and we have to prepare what the band are going to wear. Normally the band come off stage and, if they're not staying in town that night, they go straight to the airport and change clothes on the way or when they get there. A lot of it is just routine servicing of the clothes, making sure everything's put out ready to wear: the jewellery, the glasses, etc. And, before a show, setting up what we call the quick-change room, which is beside the stage. It has its own ambience. Everything's in there: drinks for the band, towels, mirrors. All the water is room temperature because cold water is bad news for singers. This room is separated from the stage, wherever it's convenient for them to come off. It's very busy in there when the band come off stage. There is not much time. You've got two or three minutes and you've got to get people out of one set of clothes and into another. If they stood still! And during the show you watch all the time because you never know when somebody's trousers are going to split! It's happened on several occasions. Clothes go through a lot of wear and tear during a performance. This is something that we emphasize to designers. These clothes go through intense heat and sweat and stretching and pulling. Bono in particular gives a very physical performance. He climbs things, jumps around, often gets into the front rows and people start pulling and ripping the shirt off his back. Things give, so you have to make sure everything's super double stitched and that you have back-up outfits standing by. There was one show on ZooTV where Bono's leather trousers just ripped from the crotch all down the leg, mid-song. He kept on performing as he had to and we just had to wrap his leg up with gaffer tape, black gaffer tape on black trousers, while he was still singing. All the crew are watching out for the band during a show. We are all in radio contact with each other. It can be pretty full-on, but after a while it almost gets to be routine; that's the dangerous time, when you think everything is going along swimmingly. This is of course the very time something will happen and it's of course the one thing you haven't prepared for.

The break between Joshua Tree and ZooTV seemed longer than the break between ZooTV and PopMart. I think PopMart took ZooTV to its logical conclusion. I thought PopMart was amazing, but to be honest I thought the sheer size of the show constantly threatened to consume the band. It was such a huge stage, it was so overwhelming, and I think it must have been difficult for them to stand in front of such a huge screen in the middle of all that stuff. It was hard to pick out the band in the landscape. But that's them, you know. They'll just try the most difficult thing and go at it until they make it work. And I think they did make it work.

Sharon Blankson became the stylist/head of wardrobe from this point on. I really only came in for the tours and worked on the day-to-day running of the wardrobe department. One of my jobs on PopMart involved being in the lemon. It was one of my more unusual jobs in life: riding in a lemon with four rock stars! It was very funny. There was an entrance at the back, so the band went in, I went in, the hatch was closed. I was in radio contact with the people controlling the lemon from the outside, the lemon driver, etc. We would talk to each other as if we were on an Apollo mission. And I did have a big red button to press in case of an emergency. After the band exited the lemon, I had a 20-minute rest, spinning around with 50,000 people outside, and then the lemon would go back and I could get out again. So it was great fun as long as everything worked!

There was one incident where the lemon got stuck; it didn't open all the way. It was inevitable that it would happen at some stage and it was amazing that it happened only once throughout the whole tour. But it was a *Spinal Tap* moment. The machinery broke and the lemon only opened about a foot and a half. I've been told it looked quite funny from outside because all you could see were the band's legs. Inside it was pandemonium! Edge was trying to look out of the base, and the others were saying, 'Don't do that Edge!' And they were shouting, 'Hit the red button, which I was, but nothing was happening. Eventually it had to be opened manually and the band had to exit out the back down a ladder. They climbed down, went round and carried on with the show. It happened in Oslo. I've been in many funny situations with U2, but that has to be one of the most surreal: spending a year in a giant lemon three or four times a week, being spun around in the middle of thousands of people all over the world. I often thought about bringing a book and sandwiches but never got round to it.

London, July 2003

The U2 boutique, circa 1993 (top) and 2001 (bottom)

Fintan Fitzgerald and Sharon Blankson, backstage, PopMart

Sharon Blankson

Head of wardrobe, PopMart, Elevation

Fintan and I both use the expression 'baptism of fire' about our respective first shows because ZooTV and PopMart were productions of such an overwhelming size and scale that making the clothes hold their own and stand up to the staging was a challenge in itself, never mind projecting out. We really had to work not just hard, but very smart. The clothes not only had to embrace the mood of the elaborate staging set, but add to it and work with it.

Styling a band for stage work is a completely different thing to fashion styling. In styling a band you have to think about how people actually wear things themselves. The clothes have to work. They have to be able to move. The clothes have to project on stage to an audience of 70,000 people and you never really know what is going to work until they're performing and you see the whole picture. It's beauty, form, function. There is no formal approach to styling a U2 show. On the surface the band have quite a loose approach, though underneath that, it's actually very focused. With *Pop*, the band took me into the studio as they were working on the album and let me listen to it. It was very experimental with a lot of dance influences – Howie, Nelly, Flood; it was completely different to anything they'd done before. I met the set designers, saw the vision for the staging, and realized that we have four people, but we have a production 200 times the size of them. How are we going to make this work so that they don't get lost in the production? How does it work that they will actually not be lost within the monumental aspect of it?

The tour was scheduled to start in the summer. I started my research with the Paris fashion shows. I was looking for something that would complement that, support it but also stand up to it, and take it on. I went to every single show in Paris that year and visited a lot of designers in the UK, including Maharishi, who was just starting out and worked out of his girlfriend's attic. I took videotapes of all the shows home with me where I watched them on my own, and with Bono.

As we narrowed it down with the band, a Belgian designer, Walter Van Bierendonck, stood out. His show that year and the clothes in that collection had the kind of cartoony cyberpunk effect that fitted with PopMart and with what I think the band were feeling at the time. Outside of his day-to-day design talent Walter could actually get the bigger scale. He had what it took to produce the stage costumes with the grandeur needed to compete with the size and scale of PopMart. I had realized by this point in time that one designer, one vision, was the best way forward, particularly in light of the tight time frame.

We flew Walter to Dublin for a production meeting with the band and the stage designers Willie Williams and Mark Fisher. From there we worked instinctively, taking on board everyone's personality. Bono is a very physical performer – he needs to be able to move freely. Edge has always been a cowboy. Adam was the glamour-puss. From a practical point of view for drumming, Larry has to have things that actually fit him quite well, but are

not going to interfere or be restrictive. No sleeves. He has to be able to move. Bono has an instinct for things. He will say something that's in his mind, it may be a tiny thing, and I will take it from there. At the time he said he loved the idea of Action Man, so I started doing research into Action Man dolls. I discussed this with Walter and he came up with the designs for the Muscle Man T-shirt. He developed the design for Action Man, but the idea really did sprout from Bono.

As soon as we had developed one Action Man character, we realized we wanted four. So Bono was Bono Man, Adam was Pop Tart, Edge – Mr The Edge to You, and Larry was Hit Man. We collaborated with Walter as we went and this is a good example of how a show's look and feel evolve. It's listening to the music, someone hitting on an idea, the idea developing, briefing and re-briefing, one new design triggering an idea for another. Bono came forward with the idea of Lop-Sided Man. He had this idea that he could start the show in a suit, which he could peel off to reveal the Muscle Man T-shirt.

In keeping with the show, we were using very modern fabrics, man-made, hi-tech, which looked amazing but often proved impractical. I remember at one point being faced with what I can only refer to as the Incredible Shrinking Suit. It was for Lop-Sided Man, and the fabric shrunk as soon as it got hot, which meant it only lasted one performance and had to keep being re-made. It kept disappearing before our eyes. The problem only became apparent with the first few performances, though. There's no way you can predict that kind of thing in advance. So we had to resolve it as we went, and that's a good example of how a tour evolves. What you start with may grow, or may have to be completely reinvented fabric-wise if you are to retain it within the show.

Outside the four main characters we developed other elements to the show. We decided Bono would make his entrance as a boxer does, walking through the arena with a hooded boxer's robe on. We bought the boxer's robes from official suppliers and customized them.

During production rehearsals, it became evident that we required something more casual for the second half and the hoodie was developed. Again this was something that wasn't planned; it just became clear as we were rehearsing. Walter wanted something really special for the encore and came up with Discman – a futuristic *Mission: Impossible* meets James Bond cartoon character. Like Lop-Sided Man, this costume would test us all, particularly Fintan and Karen. Covered in oversized sequins made up from large plastic discs, each piece was carefully hand sewn on to the suit to great effect. We hadn't allowed for the physicality of Bono's performance however, and as he moved and jumped and stretched, sections of the jacket would just pop off. After each show, we would have to scour the stage for the missing sequins, which would have to be sewed back on. Every time.

The PopMart tour schedule was on as grand a scale as the show itself. In the space of a year and a half we toured North and South America, Europe, Australia and Japan. The team on PopMart was Karen Nicholson, who was my assistant, and

Fintan Fitzgerald and Helen Dean on grooming. Karen and Fintan were responsible for all pre-show set-up and post-show get-out so their tasks included making sure the clothes got into the venue on time, the dressing rooms were ready and that the clothes were packed away and tagged after each show. They maintained the clothes across the tour – doing repairs, washing, pressing, dry-cleaning and organizing replacements wherever necessary.

Elevation couldn't have been more different than Popmart. If Popmart broadcast from cyberspace beaming out in a Technicolor blaze of cartoon glory, Elevation walked the streets, blending easily, moving freely. I wanted the clothes to be in context with the music, to speak the same language. As with *Pop*, the band brought me into studio and allowed me to listen to the music. I decided I wanted to maintain their personalities from the street to the stage and back again. I didn't want one overall designer look. I liked the idea that they could walk straight off stage into a bar and blend in; that they were clothes the audience could relate to.

At the same time, however, the show clothes had to be aspirational. They had to project, but I realized this could be achieved through clever and subtle use of materials, design and customization. I wanted to create a wardrobe of ordinary every-day clothes that you could see everywhere but buy nowhere. Unlike Popmart, I had more time, and because I wanted an individual look for each band member, I decided to use a series of designers rather than just one.

I started with Bono. Off stage Bono is most comfortable in a leather jacket and trousers so how did we take that and bring it to a higher level? A year before Elevation I met Todd Lynn, a final-year St Martin's student, whose work with leather clothing was extremely impressive. He contacted me just as I was beginning my research for Elevation. I looked at his work and loved it. I brought him to Dublin to meet the band and we took it from there.

The leather jackets were a key point to the Elevation tour. They're iconic. Think Elvis, James Dean, Marlon Brando. Todd and I decided to pull on this, and then researched Amercian uniforms for style, structure and general references. A lot of the imagery on the sleeves and the back of the jacket would come from our research on the American Civil War. We wanted the jacket to say everything while saying nothing. The stripes on the sleeves, the red star on the front – these symbols represented different things to different people. Privately for us the Black Panther represented Malcolm X, the White Dove Martin Luther King – both united on one jacket as they were on one issue, their two very different approaches, however, being symbolized in the Black Panther and the White Dove. But it was all about subtlety of messaging. We didn't need to spell it out for the audience. Put the jacket against the heart-shaped stage, the simple street-style of the other band members, the light show that reflected mes-sages of love, war and peace, and it all just worked. It gelled into the music, the audience and back again.

We decided the black leather jacket in the first half would change to blue leather in the second half – again, soft, subtle changes. I have no idea how many jackets we made in the end –

a lot because of what they had to stand up to on stage. Fine leather gets trashed with the actual physical performance and the amount of perspiration. But they all had unique things. We did a special version for the band's performance at the Superbowl with elbow patches that were shaped like American footballs laced up as the football would be. If you were to look at the jacket, it embodied American football and it ended up on the cover of *Time* magazine. Lining a version of the jacket with stars and stripes fell together in America before 9/11, though it would become hugely symbolic. We had decided we needed something to make that jacket kind of work inside out.

I looked at Edge and thought, 'What works for him? Jeans and a T-shirt.' That's what he wears and like the leather jacket they're iconic. So I thought: 'How can I make the jeans work on stage?' How can I make them have an element of Edge that says something about him, that works in the context of an arena, but has his stamp?' I needed to add a little glamour. I came up with the idea of flames going up the leg and spoke to a friend of mine, Jay Maskeray, who had patented skin jewellery. We customized Edge's jeans with Swarkovski crystals travelling up the legs in flames, which worked extremely well on stage. Karen Nicholson and I then created a series of T-shirts, scouring vintage shops, customizing what we bought and then designing our own separately.

Adam has his own very unique sense of style so we just pushed that out a bit further. I wanted an eclectic mix. We had Todd's designs, we had our T-shirt creations, there was a good selection of vintage and we'd customized a lot for Edge, so for Adam I brought in high-end designers like Gucci, Yves St Laurent and Dolce & Gabanna but mixed them with some general streetwear so they still felt accessible: the end result was exactly what I wanted: the four individual personalities coming through. A strong stage presence delivered tangibly, the clothes in context with the music.

When we arrive at a venue we begin preparing the band to go on stage. We have a set time period for that. Then, at a certain point it's a quieter period, and from that time until the show, there's very little access to the room. There would just be the band and the three wardrobe people, and maybe management. I try to make it as calm as possible because they have to get focused. They still get nervous. The fact that they still get anx-ious about getting out there and performing is a good sign. It means they still love it. They still want it. It's the thing of try, try harder.

We have a kind of a general routine. I would give a 20-minute warning. Bono would do a vocal warm-up, there's a final five-minute warning, then showtime. I think the key factor about the band is that music comes first and foremost. They have hand-picked a strong team around them and will listen to their views. They are respectful of the people around them. They have a huge amount of grace. For rock and roll, that's unique.
London, June 2003

Todd Lynn's leather jackets for Bono on Elevation

Band Crew

Stephen Rainford
Guitar technician, The Edge, 1983–1986

Early in 1983 U2 came to Liverpool for their production rehearsals for the European leg of the War tour. Joe O'Herlihy and I had worked with Rory Gallagher in the past so when I heard they needed a guitar tech I went over to the Royal Court Theatre and said, 'I'm your man!' And they said, 'Okay!'

They were really a three-piece band, and a three piece when it's tight sounds wonderful. The gear was very simple at the time: a piano, probably five or six guitars, and a Yamaha synthesizer. But things grew pretty rapidly. The War tour was the transition. They were figuring out how to do larger venues on the fly because the demand was there. Everybody who got involved felt like there was something special there. It wasn't easy to understand, but you felt like it was going places and you were going along, too.

One of my favourite shows was at Red Rocks in Colorado. We had different challenges: just the load-in was difficult enough because it was a steep hill up a windy road; they had little flatbed trucks to ferry stuff up from the parking area. But once we were in it looked like a really beautiful spot, and we were enjoying being there. Then the weather conditions changed and the clouds dropped. It wasn't hot and humid, it was misty and cold. During the show we had helicopters flying in low cloud with cameras and spotlights on them – you know, it was like, 'How dangerous do you want this to be? You'd like to light a bonfire on the top of the hill now? Okay!' It was very tense. That was a very small group – maybe eight or ten of us on the crew. It wasn't exactly safe: what with everything being so wet, the stage netting was literally electrically live that night. That night was a magic, magic night. Everybody knowing there's a lot on the line, and going for it. In those days I was on stage with them. Right there.

At the larger venues, guitar-world was off to stage right and was usually two or three feet lower than the main stage. I was very in tune with the performance on stage. It was easy to read their live performance from the side of that stage, and to be connected to what they were doing. I had to keep my head on a swivel and my ears on their mixes too. Their on-stage monitoring requirements changed quite a bit over time and I ended up providing a monitor mix of Edge's equipment and a vocal and guitar mix to Larry, independently of the rest of his drum monitoring, which was provided by the normal stage monitoring system. Larry listens to the guitar because the timing is so integral to the music, rather than the bass, which could be a bit loose sometimes. So, they needed what they needed and the equipment became more sophisticated. I was heads-up all the time.

I was tuning guitars and triggering things every few minutes. Maybe it seemed to them that I was the brain. I don't know.

On the Unforgettable Fire tour I continued to look after Edge-world. I learned new technologies as I was given new challenges and helped to bring them into the computer age for both studio and live performance. It was an interesting challenge for me. It was the beginning of what's now called MIDI (Musical Instrument Digital Interface) control for instruments. *Unforgettable Fire* had been recorded with a lot more electronic synthesis and we needed a system that could record and reproduce electronic music to make the live performance both flexible and richer sonically. MIDI and sampling are still a big part of their live shows. Brian Eno was quite a big influence from the synthesizer point of view also. He liked the Yamaha DX7. We used quite a lot of Yamaha equipment, mainly because it was technologically advanced and available. Eno used to say: 'Embrace this, make it your own.' He liked things that were broken too. I've seen him push a keyboard over and say, 'Oh, just leave it for a few days.' Just lying on the floor going, 'Wooo', making some oddball noise. If there was something about it that he liked he would record a piece of it and maybe use it as a soundscape later. He was an interesting influence and one of the most interesting people you could meet and talk to. It didn't matter what the subject was, he had some great points of view about everything you were involved in. Edge likes simplicity most of all, I think. It's about the path of least resistance to the musical outlet. He always says he feels like he has the best gigs when he doesn't remember doing it, when it's automatic, when it flows. I think that the technology helped make it possible to increase the flow, help guarantee the flow.

There was a lot of anxiety about the MIDI technology at first. We went out on the Unforgettable Fire tour and we had a complete double set of keyboard equipment set up and ready to roll at every venue, just in case there was a failure because we didn't know if it was going to blow up or if it would just stop working. Adopting new technology has never been a barrier for the band. The question is, 'How's this going to work out live?' Edge always had a way to stop or start the MIDI sequence track that was playing. We'd have a discussion about how to control a new bit of equipment during a show. And then live I would do whatever it took to bring it in on time. I was the quality control guy for the keyboard gear. In August 1984 we went to Australia to tour the *Unforgettable Fire* record. In fact, we went there and did essentially the same War show we had toured the year before. We only did two songs from *The Unforgettable Fire* record because, while they had just recorded it in the studio, we didn't have a practical way to do it live yet. The technology wasn't ready. Australia had never seen U2, so the band felt they would be just as strong doing the War show. We visited New Zealand on that tour too. That's where we were all amazed by Gregg Carroll. He jumped at the opportunity to come on the rest of the tour with us. He was such a dynamo of energy and a positive force. He became Bono's stage minder. He would track Bono everywhere he went, which Steve Iredale had done previously. We miss Gregg.

On the *Joshua Tree* record I worked on all of the demo recording, up to the band going to Windmill Lane. I worked there 24 hours a day sometimes. You could have Bono there till 1.30 in the morning, jamming on something, and then he'd appear again at 8.30 in the morning and want to play blues for a couple of hours before the band showed up. Bono blew me away a couple of times coming in early. He didn't do it every day, but a few days a week he'd come in early and I'd facilitate whatever he wanted to do. He came in one day and started playing classical piano. I said, 'My God – where'd you get that from?' He said somebody had showed him a few things, and he was literally just making it up, but he was making it up in a genre that somebody had just given him an insight into. He was doing the same with the blues at the time. I think the whole B.B. King relationship grew out of his perspective on blues music and American culture.

The venues we played had changed rapidly: from theatres to arenas to venues like Giants Stadium. I think my favourite was somewhere in the middle. Edge said to me a few years ago that he much prefers to play in larger places. It's probably the all-encompassing sound he can create with such a huge sound system. Maybe it's just the enormous spectacle of it. They must feed off that a lot. If you looked only at the tours, you might think those were their main periods of work. But really they work all the time, with very few weeks off. Maybe a month off in between a tour and beginning something else.

What's different about The Edge as a guitar player? Well, he never tried to mimic other guitar players' sounds. I think it's about his sense of rhythm; he's a great rhythm player, of course. He embraces innovation and it makes him completely unique as a guitarist. He's a great singer too.
Gloucester, MA, May 2003

Dallas Schoo
Guitar technician, The Edge, 1987–Present

Top: On-stage sound disscussion with (left to right) Dallas Schoo, Dave Skaff and Niall Slevin. Bottom: Dallas Schoo talking guitars with The Edge, PopMart 1997

Edge expects me to look after his guitar department with as much responsibility as if he himself was operating it. No more, no less. Edge wants consistency, but he also wants you to know the U2 library of songs well enough, so that when they call upon a song not on the set list during the show, you would be able to know what guitar in what tuning and what guitar sound are needed. It is an understood reliance and it's been developed over the many years of us working around one another. Of course I've learned after so many shows when he needs help on stage, whether it be for a guitar need or for a monitor-mixing need. Sometimes I'm incorrect, but not that often any more.

He'll never say everything is right, everything is good. My point is, if it's good, you'll never hear from him. If it's not good then he wants some help. Edge just uses so many guitar sounds and has so many bits, which is fantastic and he sounds fantastic, yet all this comes at a price. The potential for electronic failures or a 'melt down' is incredible and that we don't have many is unbelievable. My job is very intense and U2 can be very intense.

He's The Edge and he has his own ways and I've got my own ways. You know, I'm an athlete and I spend my days chasing swimming pools in every country in the world trying to stay in shape and battle these late rock 'n' roll hours. That's what I do. As far as Edge, he pretty much will chat with you when he's ready. Not a lot of jabbering and idle conversation. My take on it is something like: the man has two and a half hours each night performing and two hours plus added on with U2 sound checking, getting his head around a new venue sound and attempting to dial it all in. He's the lead guitarist; to me, he's the musical director of this band. He doesn't have a lot of time for a lot of 'Everything's going great' or maybe 'My hat doesn't fit that well tonight on stage.' But Edge is my friend and my boss.

U2 Joshua Tree tour. When I think of those days and that long tour, I think of physically holding on to the underneath of the stage during 'Streets'. You literally had to hold on. The people were pushing up against the stage so hard in that song that every night it just began shaking and swaying back and forth. I just knew then and there, that this was the greatest band I could ever have been asked to work with. I'll never forget it. It was the most powerful thing I've ever been a part of. To this day during U2 shows 'Streets' still evokes a tremendous arena response. I remember U2 wearing the long black coats and I remember that day in downtown San Francisco when they showed up and just blew everybody away! It was the first time I'd really been a part of 'Yeah, you think we only play arenas? Watch this!' Bill Graham put together this great event in his home town, one afternoon and did not announce it. On a flatbed truck stage, no less. That was for *Rattle and Hum*. Watching the crowd slowly gathering, just like The Beatles on the roof thing – everybody slowly hearing this music from somewhere and leaving their offices and houses and coming out to try to figure out just where this tremendous music that was filtering through the street

Left (Left to right): Daniel Lanois, Rab McAllister, Sam O'Sullivan, Stuart Morgan warming up at Elevation production rehearsals

was coming from! It was simply brilliant. That's the way it happened that day. As they kept playing, you could see from the stage behind the band the crowd growing to thousands. We were all very, very young, and I just was so proud to be with them.

The PopMart tour to me was a tour of huge production experimentation. It was just too in your face, too massive. I felt almost like the music was secondary. I remember having trouble on the guitar exchanges over Edge's tall cowboy hat, his guitar strap catching on it. The agreement between Edge and I on these quick guitar exchanges was that he would take the hat off and hold it while I put the guitar over him. That tour took me to a different U2 understanding; I had to learn that they were being tongue in cheek. And the lemon! I really never knew when Edge would exit out of that huge lemon during the show if his guitar was going to be on or not! The wireless guitar transmission was a variable that became a constant challenge. On a tour of great complexity, you get employed and paid to be able to remedy a technical problem quickly. To be able to get plan 'B' going quickly. How fast can you move when he's in trouble, when his plan 'A' is off the air? There was one time during a PopMart show, out at the middle of the stadium small stage during the song 'Desire', where Edge's guitar went completely off. The only way to help him and not let the song suffer was for me to get another guitar working on the main stage, strum the predominant guitar chord and run it out to him and exchange it for the non-working one. It never happened again but I thought on that one occasion I was going to freeze up. Edge of course was the coolest candidate. He just kind of kept walking towards me with this confidence, I guess, that I would get him back on the air. Great guy to have in your corner when a stage crisis surfaces.

Dublin, April 2003

Gibsons, Fenders and Rickenbackers loom large in The Edge's guitar arsenal. Top: PopMart, Kansas City, May 1997.
Bottom: Dallas tuning The Edge's guitars, understage Elevation, Las Vegas, November 2001

Recording

Chris Blackwell
Founder, Island Records

The first time I saw U2 perform there were about ten people in the audience – and I think most of the ten people worked for them or worked with Island Records. But they played as if they were playing to a full house. Although I didn't immediately respond to their music, I really responded to them as people, to their passion, belief in and commitment to what they were doing. I just really believed in them. It's one of those things where you feel, well, 'I believe in these guys. I believe they're really smart, I believe they're really basically quality people and genuinely committed to what they're doing. And if this is what they want to do, I'm sure it's going to be very successful. I might not hear it right now, but I'm sure it's going to be successful.' They also had a very good manager, which was a key side to it. Paul McGuinness was very good. Signing an act is a little like a venture capitalist investing in a business. You want to know who's the management, what is the product, all that kind of thing. So I instructed the company basically to follow their direction because I really believed in them. And that's pretty much how we have always operated with U2. We didn't really do that much for them, except give them support and the freedom to pursue their vision.

Whenever you start with a band you feel something can be big, but you never know what global impact a band might have. It's impossible for anybody to see ahead like that. There are so many obstacles, so many things that can happen. Bands can break up, things can not work as you planned. You can never have any idea where it might lead. U2 have made their own course. They're not like anybody else I know. I first saw them in 1980. Here we are 23 years later, and anybody who works with them will tell you that they're the most honourable, extraordinary people. All of them. Normally with bands the more you get into it, the more rotten the core is in many cases. This guy's wife hates that guy, and the other guy's wife, etc. They're at each other's throats and everything collapses. With U2, they're just solid. Bono's the most visible, but all of them are incredible. The one who's the least visible, as you probably know, is the leader of the band, Larry. They've never lost their heads through all this. Always kept their feet on the ground. Never lost their roots. Just regular people. Believe me, it's more than unusual. U2 are definitely the only band who have ever lasted that long in the same unit. The Stones have, of course, been around for ages, but they've had personnel changes.

Frank Barsalona was a key individual in the beginning for U2. Frank was 'The Man' of rock and roll agenting. He represented everybody, and he had an incredible network of promoters working with him. To have him in your corner was a great stamp of approval. I had a strong relationship with him because I'd worked with him

with other bands and artists. In fact, I helped him finance his business when he started. U2 were a live band. They loved to play live. That was at their core. And Frank is all about live bands. His policy and whole concept was to work with the same promoters in different parts of the country. To work with those same promoters and let them stay with the bands, becoming bigger themselves as the bands got bigger. It was a great way to work. He believed in the long-term relationship. So U2 and Frank was a match made in heaven.

Steve Lillywhite was at that first show I saw. He had already connected with U2 in some way. At the end of the show he came over to me and he said, 'I would have thought this would be a band you'd produce.' Because at that time I was still producing. But I couldn't have brought anything to the table. It wasn't something that I felt I could help guide. For me, over the years, there are some things I've produced and some things that I don't produce. And the things that I've produced are more things that I have a feel for, where I know how I can help get it from A to B. I love what U2 do, but I couldn't perform that function for them. Steve himself has a good sense of how to get the most out of a song. He was very important to U2 in those early years and pretty much all the way through, if not for a whole record.

When the band suggested working with Brian Eno as a producer, at first I was very against it. I love Brian Eno and the records that he made for Island. He was with us first with Roxy Music, and then as a solo artist, and we released some great, great records with him. So it wasn't that I didn't think he was good; it's just I'd never associated him and his work with a rock band who were looking to sell a million records. Brian was always a much more esoteric producer. Brilliant records, but much more esoteric. So I flew over to Dublin to meet with the band and Paul McGuinness to discuss this, because they really wanted Brian and I was against it. And they persuaded me. Their reasoning was that they wanted Brian's intelligence in the mix, his intellectual approach. They didn't want to make just a straightforward rock record. I was persuaded and thought it was very smart to think that way. Of course, Brian did bring to the mix exactly what they wanted him to, an intangible essence, which has kept them moving and kept them doing interesting things.

Personally, I think the key is to make a record that makes you want to go and see the band. Many records are brilliant, but often you know that the record is much better than the band would be live. You want to be left with the impression that you just have to see them because they're going to be fantastic. I think U2 have had that in pretty much all of their records. They have been able to do something which is very difficult: to keep their early fans, who are now in their 40s, and also to appeal to those people's children. Normally that's very difficult, because the essence of

Chris Blackwell and Bono

rock and roll is that it's music that your parents hate!

Originally I wanted Jimmy Iovine to produce the record that U2 wanted Brian Eno to produce. Jimmy ended up producing the live records for Red Rocks and *Rattle and Hum*. Now he runs a record company. In my opinion, he's really probably the best record guy of this generation, of this era. He knows the studio, he knows how to make a record, he knows the root of everything. He knows artists, he likes artists and he knows how to deal with artists. But he also has a tremendous promotional and marketing sense, and sense of event. He's put together a great record company and he's found incredible talent.

I was on tour for some of *Rattle and Hum,* which I thought was great. I would see three or four shows on every tour. I saw the Joshua Tree more often. I love to see U2 live. They're fantastic. That's the root of everything. It's the way I view the record business. My style of record business is that it's an investment in the artist and the long-term career of the artist. The records are merely milestones in the artist's career. The records aren't the be-all and end-all. So you have people who've lasted a long time, like The Stones: they have some good records, they have some bad records. The Stones keep rolling on. For U2, it's the same kind of thing, except that *Pop* is the only record that they didn't get exactly right. And we at Island had no real model existing to help them, because we always just supported their vision. So there was no model in place to say, 'Hold on, this doesn't sound right,' or 'This doesn't seem right.' There was also a rush to get everything out in time for the tour. I think it was the irony of the thing – which is what Pop was all about. It didn't really translate; certainly people in America didn't get it. Announcing the tour at K-mart, for example. All I'd read was 'What are they doing? They've sold out, the band has just sold out.' So that was the only thing they'd done which didn't work. But they bounced right back from it.

In the old days people would tour all the time. Count Basie toured all the time. Artists would make records now and again, and those records would bring some attention. In those days they never made much money on selling records, but the records enhanced reputations, allowing artists to charge an extra thousand-odd dollars a night for their live appearances. Nevertheless, a record is still something that gives a focus for press and for everything else. Touring is not really undertaken to promote the record; the record is there to promote the tour. And of course they promote each other.

Rock stars and bands have a lot of followers when they tour. When they play to 20,000 people, they have a captive audience of 20,000 people. U2 feel it's an opportunity to get a message across now and again. And they don't do it by preaching, they do it by entertaining, words here and there. They don't bang you over the head or bore you to death with their messages. I think they feel they're in a position where they can reach a lot of people, and they should and do use that position well. I've seen others join some cause just because it'll be a good career move. There's nothing wrong with that, but it's a lot less genuine. U2 have been active in this way right from the beginning of their career. And they've never sought publicity for any private charitable work they've done. Bono and his wife worked in relief camps in Ethiopia, for example. They are totally genuine people.

New York, November 2003

Jimmy Iovine

Chairman, Interscope Geffen A&M, a division of Universal Music; record producer, Under a Blood Red Sky *and* Rattle and Hum

I'm attracted to the overall heat and intensity of everything U2 do. I don't think there's ever been anybody who's accomplished what they've accomplished, as far as retaining the quality of their music, and the commitment these guys in U2 have to each other is remarkable. The lyrics and music are extraordinary, how rock it is, how intense it is, yet how punk it is. They've managed to build a career over 20 years that is unparalleled.

I'm very proud of the two live albums which I produced for U2. They are powerful pieces. I didn't actually go to the Red Rocks concert. I went to Ireland, and we worked on these tapes of the show which resulted in the album *Under a Blood Red Sky.* This came out months after the movie of the Red Rocks concert did. With *Rattle and Hum* we recorded quite a few shows. I would go to the show – stay in the audience and feel the power of it – then do what we could in recording and mixing it to make it feel like that: to get the essence of what they were doing. I think we accomplished that on both albums. It was a combination of trying to get the up-close sound that sounds so great when you're on stage. But you have to hear the hall as well. It is hard to do. We had more control over *Rattle and Hum* because we had more time, and we actually did the recording ourselves. We combined live stuff with studio stuff, so it was both a live record and a studio record, which I was really jazzed about doing because a record hadn't been really done like that before. We had to make the studio pieces and the live parts make sense together, so we used a lot of the technique of recording live in the studio. We had monitors in the studio, for example, rather than headphones. And we set up a very live situation in most of the studios we went to. We travelled around a lot. We did some overdubs and stuff like that, but we tried to make it feel like they rolled off the stage and into the studio. I think one of the best live recordings on that record is 'Pride'. That and 'Helter Skelter'. I think they're two fabulous live recordings.

With *Rattle and Hum*, U2 were paying tribute to the culture of American music. We followed them around. We got to work in Elvis's studio, we did something with B.B. King, it was great. We went to Harlem, we did a few things with a gospel choir. It was a very exciting project, but it was long and tiring and, of course, there was a movie attached to it as well. It took a lot of detailed work to create different effects for all the different projects. The live album and the movie sound different, as they should, because you have to do things differently on a CD, when you don't have the luxury of looking at the film. You're using different senses: sight and sound rather than just sound. So the DVD actually sounds different than the live album, but it's supposed to.

I started Interscope after that. That was it. They're on Interscope now and I'm really proud to have them. I love those guys, man. They're tougher than me, they're stronger than me. They're an unstoppable force, the four of them. It's incredible. Any band that starts out now, U2 is the blueprint. It just is. Period. Everything that you think growing up that rock 'n' roll should be, and could be, is how these guys have done it. They've written their own rules. Drive, dedication and consistency. Yet Bono lives in the face of danger all the time. He is a superior human being. You have to understand that. There's no one I've ever met like him. No one. And he automatically drives you. And he changes you. After you've experienced him, if you don't change, you're numb. And so what I learned from *Rattle and Hum* is that I really didn't want to make any more records myself. That was the last album that I lived.

ZooTV was one of the most ground-breaking things that ever happened to live music. It was every bit as effective as Pink Floyd's The Wall, every bit as effective as any of the early Sly Stone shows. It was a turning point in technology and in concerts. And that was all based on their commitment to their audience. That's all it was based on. So whether you see them in a small place or a really big place, if you can focus you get a very similar thing from them. A different kind of energy, but a similar impact.

I can't say enough about these guys. They've truly inspired me, on a personal level and on a professional level. They know what emotion sounds like. That's the trick to any kind of greatness: you've got to know what it sounds like. It can't be blurred by money or houses or new girlfriends or anything. U2 manage to keep all of that out of the mix. The more people express what they feel through music, rather than thinking what they should write, just writing it naturally, the more success they will have. No matter what happens with MTV or the video channels or anything like that, there's still a personal emotion when you go to your first concert. It's as close as you're gonna get to the first time you had sex, if it's the right concert, and I think that as long as we have ears and eyes we're gonna be going to concerts. *Los Angeles, January 2004*

Brian Eno

Musician; record producer, The Unforgettable Fire, The Joshua Tree, Achtung Baby, Zooropa *and* All That You Can't Leave Behind; *video staging concept,* ZooTV

During your work in the studio with U2, do any points come up about how the music will be performed in a live context?
Occasionally in the studio there's a realization that a certain aspect of something would make a good live moment, but it's not much thought about. The only general context that's set, which is an ongoing argument that we're always having, is that we need some fast songs, we need some powerful songs, because they work well live. Whereas the soft, more reflective songs don't communicate well to large audiences. This is the theory – though I disagree with this myself.
So in general you're presented with a palette of songs, and you help them to decide which songs go on to an album, bearing in mind that live performance aspect?
Yes. Well, it would certainly add plus points to big, loud songs, do you see what I mean? They would be given an extra 'credit' for their live potential.
What was your involvement in the creation of ZooTV?
For ZooTV, I was trying to come up with an idea where you could essentially improvise with the visuals. You still have complex and rich and interesting visuals, but done in such a way that you could improvise with them to follow the band rather than the band having to follow the visuals. I suggested working on video, on laser discs. The material we made was transferred to four laser discs, so there would be four players active at all times. Whoever was controlling the video could cross-fade between them so they're not stuck to the length of a programme. For instance, if one song looks like it wants to be longer, it's getting longer and longer and you're running out of video, you simply cross-fade to the same video material on one of the other discs.
Was ZooTV the first time that this had been done?
I think so, yes. I also made a lot of the images that we used. I was very concerned to try to make something that was lo-tech and handmade, rather than the clever stuff that comes out of computers. So I did some very simple things. On the tour there was one piece where this lady's head rocks back and forth. She's on several screens at once and each head is rocking like a pendulum. I made that image simply by cutting a picture out of a magazine and filming it on a potter's wheel with a rostrum camera. I just moved the wheel back and forth. It was simple to make and I could immediately see the results. So I was trying to make the video in the same way as I would try to make music: always being able to keep my hands on things and respond immediately, rather than getting trapped in some big technological honeycomb that I couldn't extract myself from.
It must have been a unique experience, artistically as well as musically, working with U2 in that period.
Yes, well, the visual side I did quite separately. I worked alone on that in London. I made a whole lot of stuff and sent it to

Left: Brian Eno made these 'rocking pendulum' images for ZooTV screens by cutting an image out of a magazine and filming it on a potter's wheel with a rostrum camera

them. I also had this other idea, which became a theme of that tour, and that was not to have one point of focus. We had lots and lots of things to look at. I thought it would be really exciting if it was very confusing, if you didn't really know where to look, and if there was just too much going on all the time. That was the feeling I wanted, rather than this single-focus thing that you so often get.

How did the star field projections come about?

That again was done very simply. It was just a zoom on a rostrum camera with a big star map I bought in London at a map shop, again on a potter's wheel. So I'm slowly turning the star map as the camera slowly zooms in, which gives such a beautiful feeling of motion, I think. It must have been the cheapest piece of video ever made for a major rock tour! It cost me about £12 to make it. The potter's wheel turned out to be a very useful tool.

U2's studio crews have mentioned how Bono and Edge are always aware of how a song will 'look', whereas you are focusing on the actual production of the album. Do the ideas bounce back and forth between you?

When I'm working on a record I'm not thinking of tours. I don't think of tours, I don't like them. I'm not good at them and U2 are! So certainly their consciousness of what it's going to be like, how it's going to translate on stage, is entirely different from mine, and I completely defer to their sense of that. On ZooTV it was a rather different situation in that they asked me to get involved in the visual side. I took that on as a separate project: okay, these are the songs you're going to do; okay, let's see what we can do with them. There's one song called 'Light My Way' that used this deaf and dumb lady, Rachel Bastikar. That's my favourite song. I had seen her on BBC Television translating some programmes into sign language, and so I wanted her to sign the whole song. I thought she gave such a new feeling to that song. I thought it was very strong. It made the song something different from what it had been. It wasn't just a nice little add-on, it expanded the song somehow.

When you're in the studio with U2, how do you work with co-producer Daniel Lanois, and what do you bring individually to the creative process?

Dan's extremely good at working with musicians, as he is a very good musician himself. He understands what aspects of a situation you need to focus on to get a good performance from people. He has a real talent for that. He pays a lot of attention to details. Our roles overlap a lot, but if you had to characterize them simply, I'd say I tend to look at the thing as a whole, to look at where it stands in time. And, like Dan, I contribute quite a lot as a musician too. I play a lot on their records. That's a hard question to answer, we've been doing it for such a long time.

London, January 2003

Brian Eno's 'Starfields' design contribution to Elevation, originally conceived for ZooTV

Daniel Lanois

Musician; record producer, The Unforgettable Fire, The Joshua Tree, Achtung Baby *and* All That You Can't Leave Behind.

I was working in Canada with Brian Eno before U2 recorded *Unforgettable Fire.* Brian was working on ambient records, so all our time was devoted to experimenting in the studio and creating these sort of sonic textures. It was a wild new frontier for us. We were fascinated with manipulating sound – taking existing, quite pure sounds and rather than doing overdubs, we would modify those sounds and enhance them and build on them with different octaves and different echo settings to the point where you've built up this amazing sonic identity. It's almost like a way of turning an Andy Warhol sketch in to a multi-layered image. It's largely Brian's driving force that created this. Brian came into my world. I was highly skilled and ready to sink my teeth into something. What I admired most about his approach was his dedication to what he loves. It was not about catering to the marketplace. In those four years we made six records. One track, called 'Deep Blue Day', turns up in the *Trainspotting* soundtrack. If you listen you'll see how the experiments of that time made their way into *Unforgettable Fire.*

Those were years not only of experimentation, but also of intense concentration. During that time I decided never again to dedicate any of my time to something I didn't believe in 100 per cent. So when the time came to do U2, the U2 boys not only employed a couple of pretty smart cats, but a philosophy and a dedication to experiment. They wanted intelligence around them. And rightly so, because if you're trying to reinvent yourself soni-cally you want to make sure that you're doing something that's gonna last. Brian is a pretty smart cat. They were oblivious to my existence; I only turned up via Brian's invitation. The ploy was that Brian would introduce me and he would walk away and I would be producer of U2, but Bono, of course, talked Brian into doing it and we became a co-production team. At the time, U2 had already established themselves as an Irish rock band. Smart people with something to say, with a hard-hitting sound. They had not really broken as big as they would in the next few years, but they were already poised to do well. Brian and I were meant to bring in a new way of looking at things.

Coincidentally, I had become somewhat disillusioned with the recording studio as a place to record bands. So I had also been experimenting with recording in different kinds of locations in Canada. I was over the dead, padded sound of the 1970s. To my ears, bands always sounded best anywhere other than the studio. Only in the studio would you ever hear problems. It'd be 'Oh the bass pedal's squeaking, the drum's ringing, the guitar's buzzing.' All these problems only ever appeared in the studio, and I thought to myself, 'I want out of this problem box.' One of the things that came up in our initial meetings with U2 was that they also wanted to record somewhere other than a studio. Someplace where they felt inspired. That's what Slane Castle was about.

I could tell they were dreamers – as I am – optimists who just want to know what's on the other side of the hill. So very open to experimentation, sonic discoveries. They were fascinat-ed with some of the great rock and roll records of the early 1970s, you know, Iggy Pop, the Berlin years. They were interest-ed in making their own discoveries so that this *Unforgettable Fire* record could be regarded as some kind of ground-breaking sonic record – not to repeat what other people had done, to find a thing that they wanted in their work. And I think we did – I think we made the unique atmospheric U2 record.

When we're finishing a record obviously the subject of touring comes up and certainly I've put in my two-cents' worth. We'd talk mostly about the tracks that have a sonic identity on the record that would be hard to replicate live. For example, some things we work on in the studio for days, complex background details – as on 'With or Without You'. The only way you can then bring them into live performance is if you mix them off the record and bring a gridwork for U2 to operate against. So it's like a fixed tempo: Larry gets 154 in his cans [headphones], and the band then has access to all kinds of computer sounds that Eno might have come up with. I've not been heavily involved in that, but that's how it works.

Brian has a knack for having the band look at their songs in a different light. In the case of 'Beautiful Day', it was pretty much a rock chord sequence and rhythm that The Edge came up with. It's as rock and roll as it gets. Brian and I always come into the studio early, a few hours before the band. One day he came up with a more German way of looking at this rock and roll: quite stiff, kind of metallic, with a little piano. Then I played this harmony guitar over the top, and we laid that down. The band came in and were excited – 'Hey this is our song, but we have a chance to play it in a different fashion now.'

'With or Without You' would be another example. The begin-ning was a technological one. At every stage of working with U2 we've done our best to bring in sonic technological discoveries. So on 'With or Without You' the infinite sustained guitar sound, that high, beautiful, almost stratospheric sound, it's great. It's ethereal. That was made with a guitar called the Infinite Sustain invented by Michael Brook, my Canadian compadre. He's worked with Brian and me in the past. That tool had never been used on a record before. It allowed The Edge to redefine the guitar on

The combination of Daniel Lanois' roots and Brian Eno's ambient styles inspired the recording of The Unforgettable Fire *at Slane Castle in 1984*

Work in progress at Hanover Quay Studios, Dublin, 2003

Joshua Tree. What had been the more textural guitar on *The Unforgettable Fire* – which was largely putting The Edge through the atmospheres that Brian Eno and I had created in Hamilton, Canada – now became this beautiful sound that they had been unaware of before.

Edge discovers sounds himself too. It doesn't matter who brings them into the studio, as long as we're making an effort. During *Achtung Baby* time, Brian brought in the Whammy pedal. Sometimes the cheapest little box will bring about a great result. And then I brought The Edge my little secret weapon: my little distortion wah-wah pedal used at the beginning riff of 'Elevation'. Sometimes a cheap trick used in a novel way will allow you to have a completely new sound. Then we'll discard those tricks so that we don't repeat ourselves.

The difference between Brian and me in the U2 studio is that I have the patience for trench work. I will go through ten vocal tracks and find that golden moment that's hidden away on the one that nobody's paying attention to. I'll make sure that the gem is brought to the forefront. I will make sure that it is per-fectly balanced and re-equalized even though it was done in a different room, different mike. I will make sure that it sounds like the same moment with the preceding line. I have the patience and the know-how and still the interest to look after those kinds of details. Brian, on the other had, he's over that. He wants it but he would prefer that I do it. Brian, while I'm doing that kind of work, will be looking ahead and have a vision about how another track might sound. So he's much more interested in drumming up another way of looking at things regarding the next song. So I'm still happy to do some of the trench work, because I'm anticipating that Brian will bring in a very innovative way to look at the next track.

We have two work areas when we record an album: one is the band room and the other is the control room circle. The control room circle is a great innovative place because it means that people aren't holding their usual positions. So we've got couches and chairs and different kinds of tools around. That's where the acoustic guitars are. Maybe Larry will play just tambourine, or maybe there'll be an electronic kit. He doesn't want to play an electronic kit in U2, but sometimes it's convenient just to have something different at hand that creates a sort of living room circle. And that is usually the area where interesting overdubs are created, the quieter way of looking at things; maybe that's where the lyrics are fine-tuned. It's kind of like the thinker's circle. Very, very important to U2 records. A lot of the brainstorming has happened in that circle. Then you have the band room. That's where the conducting happens. That's where the band turns up and it's more like a stage setting. That's where you never know what's gonna happen. The band room is where the drums are. The band room is more raucous and tends to provide what we love about U2 in that sense of: okay, you've started up the engines and you're off! You're out to sea and now here comes a wave. Move over here and you don't know what's gonna happen and something may start coming into focus, something you hadn't anticipated. That's where Bono will usually say, 'Hold that, keep building it, keep building it,' and then when it reaches a sort of fever pitch it might inspire him to sing a certain kind of phrase or melody. And those are very, very important compositional moments to U2. And in my opinion, in regards to *The Unforgettable Fire, The Joshua Tree* and *Achtung Baby,* that area, the band arena, has been responsible for a lot of the compositional bends in the record.

A couple of years after we had finished *Achtung Baby* I had a chance to hear it unexpectedly and it really struck me how innovative that record really is. I'm very proud of that record. It was very hard work and expectations were high, as usual, in the U2 camp, and I think we really did it. It's ground breaking. It's fantastically out of control. It's wild, you don't know where it's coming from, it's bizarre and it's rock and roll. I love it.

I'm usually in the band room with them, egging them on. Playing percussion, guitar, whatever it takes. Singing. It doesn't matter. Just giving a sense to the band that somebody's there looking after them. I won't leave the room until they've got something and they feel it, so that they don't want to leave the room either and then it snowballs.

That process didn't exist so much on *All That You Can't Leave Behind,* because the band room means screaming for hours on end from Bono, singing in the upper end of his range. It's very demanding on any voice. On this last record he had burned out that part of himself a little bit and didn't want to be conducting and screaming all the time. He wanted the blueprint of the thing already to be designed before he got there. In my opinion, it made for a very different record. I miss the band room's ecstasy. It's passionate, it's real and it's unexpected. You don't know what's coming round the bend.

Live performance isn't necessarily like that, though I think it used to be more that way than it is now. In Miami for the Elevation rehearsals, for example, they brought me in just for my advice regarding the sound, any kind of arrangement suggestions I might make. I told them that I felt that they would do very well to operate off the gridwork more than they were, because when you're operating on the gridwork you can't be spontaneous about arrangements. Intro is 8 bars, not 12, because if you do 12 you're gonna be out of synch when the next section of the song comes up. You get the benefit of reliability with your songs, but you undermine spontaneity and any chance of a sort of rock and roll excursion.

So, for my taste, I prefer more renegade versions. I would be willing to do away with some of the familiar sonics of the record in anticipation of a more rock and roll rendition relative to how they were on that night. To be honest with you, I miss that part of U2. I remember hearing them on the Joshua Tree tour and being very moved. It was emotional for me to hear music that we put so much time into brought to the stage and for it to work. To this day U2 manages to strike that nerve in me. It's just a combination of it all. Even if I had not been involved in the U2 records I think they would still reach me in that same way, but it's lovely to have been there at the birth and see the kids out there doing well.

Touring itself sometimes bleeds into the next record. Sometimes the band gets new ideas on tour from sound check recordings brought to the table for the next record, perhaps as possible beginnings of songs. Sound checks are a low-pressure setting – you're really meant to be just getting sounds and if an idea pops up during sound check it's sort of regarded as a bit of moonlighting, so you don't have the pressure of the studio. You have all the freedom to try out some new ideas. Over the years many things have been brought in from sound check recordings. On *All That You Can't Leave Behind* there was an amazing warren that I'm not sure even made it to the finish. And The Edge is always knocking them out at home. He's the archivist of the band.

The scrutiny of songs and the brainstorming, especially at the beginning of a tour, are really about how can we make the tour better. They're looking for broad opinions and I've often given them mine. It's the same with the after-show huddling and brainstorming. Still, I think the sound check recordings can be major contributors to the next batch of composition. You're out on the road, you're gonna hit on something – not just during sound check, maybe in the hotel room. Wherever new ideas happen to come up, they're important.

I've pretty much seen everybody in the band grow up – or maybe grow sideways! I don't know if anybody ever grows up. I've seen them through various chapters of their lives and it's great. I saw them go through some of the things that I had gone through. But you know, you don't say anything about it, it's like 'All right brother, whatever.'

I believe the respect that exists between the U2 folks and myself is largely philosophical as much as it is, you know, 'Aren't we good in the studio.' Like there's just something, some chemistry or some sense that there's a greater power at work here and we're servants to the operation. I'm a spiritual person and they know that. We have a different kind of belief system, but nonetheless I believe they sensed that there's something. I had the capacity to raise the spirit, as they do, in my own way, and they like that I bring that to their table. The Edge once said, 'It might be uncomfortable to have a searching soul, but it keeps the good work coming in.' You know it's not easy to be constantly questioning and wanting to be innovative and wondering what the hell it's all about and wanting some kind of a moral fibre at the bedrock of what you're doing. You're just not knocking out rock and roll records in the name of pollution, you know. You try to put something out there that some listener will draw something from and it will enhance their imagination, if not their life. You want substance at the bottom of it and I think they sense that, if nothing else, there is at least dedication to care and attention to detail and wanting to do good work and just kind of old school values. I believe they sense them in me. It's not just 'Where's the hook?' and 'What's the beat?' and 'Wowie zowie we're in the charts!' There are plenty of people who can do that. I think that's probably the foundation of our relationship beyond technical skill.

Over the years, U2 have stuck to their thing. The feeling you get from their music is largely due to who they are and what their sentiments, their lyrical sentiments, are meant to be.

Some music rises and falls more quickly. That's not to say that it's not great, but if the sentiment of a track is 'Let's get up and dance and have a great night and it's only rock and roll and we like it that way', that's fine. You can never criticize that, but it's a spontaneous combustion. It's like, the next morning the party hat gets put away and you get on with your life. So the more spiritual driving force a piece has, the longer term the content. It doesn't go out of fashion.

You take every little chapter of evolution and put it in your pocket. You're thankful and you move on. I'm sure that the U2 boys have got a little Daniel Lanois in their pockets and I've got a little piece of them in mine.
Los Angeles, February 2003

Top: (left to right): Joe O'Herlihy, Jo Ravitch and Daniel Lanois, Elevation tour production rehearsals, Miami Arena, USA, March 2001. Bottom: The Edge and Bono performing with Daniel Lanois on Elevation tour at Madison Square Garden, NYC, 2001

Flood

Recording engineer, The Joshua Tree *and* Achtung Baby; *record producer,* Zooropa *and* Pop

Flood during recording of 'Zooropa' May 1993, The Factory, Dublin

I got this phone call at work. Somebody said, 'Bono's on the phone …' and I thought, 'Yeah. Somebody's on a wind-up.' Finally he phoned up and got through to the control room. He wanted me to come out and do an audio interview. I was 26 years old and it was the single most career-changing experience I've had. Up until that point I'd been a studio engineer; I'd done a few things with a few people. That's it.

I was working in Trident Studios most of the time. I'd worked on one of the early Virgin Prunes albums. Bono asked Gavin Friday about different engineers for *The Joshua Tree*, and he suggested me. Dan Lanois had done most of *The Unforgettable Fire* but wanted to move more into production with Eno. So Bono put the word out, Gavin suggested me and said have a listen to what I'd done with Nick Cave. Bono heard it, asked me over and I went for two weeks. They were camped out at Danes Moat. I had never seen anything like this before because I was used to standard studio practice, one instrument at a time, etc. They were writing it as they went along. It was like, 'Well, this is an environment we feel creative in.' So my job was just to enhance that. We ran two studios. Brian would go to one, say, with Bono to do singing, and Danny would be in the other one maybe working with Edge on guitars, or percussion or whatever. To be quite honest, with hindsight, I think I was out of my depth for most of the record. I was just hanging on by the skin of my teeth. It was such a mindblowing experience. And you either went with it, or you went back to wherever you were. At the end of it, because the album had overrun so much, I couldn't mix it because I was going off to produce Erasure. And that was the hardest decision I think I've ever had to make. Do I stay and mix *Joshua Tree* or do I go off and produce Erasure's second album? I'm glad I did what I did, but it was difficult.

Later on, I was over at the Giants Stadium to see Depeche Mode play. I was sitting in the press box, very drunk, having a whale of a time. I wasn't working, there are 70,000 people all going absolutely bananas. I'd just finished working with the Jesus and the Mary Chain. So all the bands on the bill I'd just finished working with. I was lording it for a night. Then Anton Corbijn came into the press box and said, 'Oh, I've got a couple of friends to come and see you.' And there were two dodgy blokes with hoods on. They took the hoods off and it's Bono and Adam. I was very, very drunk at the time. We just started talking and then they said that they really wanted to try doing something different, to break out of where they were. Bono was fascinated with Berlin, and because I had spent so much time working with Nick Cave, who worked a lot in Berlin, he asked if I would be interested in starting to work with U2 again. I said yes because I'd gone through a very rapid ascent from being an engineer into being a producer and I wanted to sit back and take stock of what producers I respect – Brian and Dan – would do in certain situations. As a producer, you can't learn unless you go back to being an engineer. So this seems like a perfect opportunity for me to go back, to be an engineer, but still take everything on board.

It was very clear with *Achtung Baby* that Bono wanted to break the mould. And when you're in that sort of situation you can't just walk into the studio one day and say, 'I've discovered the wheel. This is it, this is the way we go!' You have to go through the things they don't want, things they do want, and then avenues open up to you. So there's a tremendous period of turmoil. And at that time, they were all under incredible pressure. They had been touring for ever, they were right on the top of the tree, and they wanted to turn the whole thing on its head, to reinvent themselves. And they wanted to do it in Berlin, which was still divided, but on the verge of being reunified. We were out there about three months, on and off, and it was hell. Then it was decided that we'd go back to Ireland. Over the Christmas period they found a house on the coast, right on the sea, in Dalkey. Joe O'Herlihy, a couple of the guys in the crew and I got all the gear set up, got the building rewired so the band could walk in within about two or three days. That's where 80 per cent of the recording for *Achtung Baby* was done.

Danny and I were in the trenches. Eno would fly in, do his magic and then leave. Danny and I would just sit there and look at each other. It was really good because I felt confident enough to try loads of things, from the engineering point of view, that were much more than just, 'Let's record.' And so Danny and I built up a really good rapport. We covered each other's back. And then Brian would come in and he would sense that and take everything to the next stage. It was a really productive team. Nobody had any egos that pushed anything too far, one way or the other.

The studio environment, sonically, is so different from what goes on live that you really just have to use the studio recordings as guidelines. Eventually the live music forms its own self. When we were mixing *Achtung Baby*, Joe O'Herlihy was around all the time. He was there making sure everything was sorted, and acting as a studio tour boss. It was great. He got a true feeling for what was going on. Then he could take it and do it in his own way live, which is vital.

I saw the ZooTV tour two or three times. Everything about it just blew my mind. Really, just 'Wow.' I don't think anybody has surpassed that, including U2 themselves. It captured the right amount of accessibility and humanity. *Zooropa* came about when U2 took a little time off during the middle of the ZooTV tour. It was weird because it started as an EP, and then it grew into an experimental album. It was an embryonic thing. Bono and Edge wanted to do it, so we just kept on going. Then it got to a point where they had to tour. The tour was booked. It was insane. By the end I'd start at, say, 11 a.m. Everything was constantly on the move, so I'd spend about two hours getting things to a point where the band would come in. They'd listen to where we were at. Then maybe they'd go down and see Brian, who might be in a different place on another song. And then they'd go and fly off to wherever they were in Europe, do their gig and fly back. We worked according to their instructions during the day. They'd usually get back anytime between 11 p.m. and 1 a.m. Then they'd come in, have a listen, make more comments. I can remember doing vocals with Bono for 'Lemon' at 4 a.m. Insane, insane hours. It nearly killed all of us. We were constantly in this state of stressed caffeine hallucinations, hiding in the studio. It was ridiculous. Suzanne

Doyle was there to help everybody, but it was insane to do those hours. There was me, Robbie Adams and then the two assistants: William Manion and Rob Kirwan. Rob is one of my closest friends and he said that after that album he hated me. It's quite understandable.

I see my role within U2 as a strange one, because I've come up through the ranks in the organization. And on *Pop* I'd been sort of moved to the top of the pile, but because I had started as the junior there's a hierarchy. There's Brian, then Danny, then it's me. Nobody says anything, and it's not deliberate at all, but it's human nature. So there was a period of time where I think nobody was quite sure what was going to happen with *Pop*; whether it wanted to be another new direction, or whether it wanted to be an extension of what had gone before with ZooTV. This was what was strange: there seemed to be a lot of intellectualism going on, but the spirit wasn't quite 100 per cent there. It was almost as if everybody was in a period of change and reflection at the same time. So there's a bit of, 'Well, why are we here? Can't we have a bit of a break? We've been touring for ever.' I can remember June 1996 sitting next to Bono and saying, 'Look, don't get caught by the fact that you've got this humungous tour booked.' It was very difficult. Nobody completely lost their temper, nobody walked out, there were good days and bad days in the studio, but it was all in an air of democracy when, ultimately, a bit of cuddly fascism was needed.

It wasn't like *Achtung Baby,* where the band nearly split up with all the tension in Berlin. That tension was healthy. It was creative. And I think that was the problem with *Pop*. And the ultimate dictator was the tour. I remember sitting in a meeting with the record company and the management and the band and arguing that we needed more time. And everybody saying, 'Well, we can extend it here, but we can't go any further.' And I just said, 'I don't think it's going to be finished.' It was a really, really weird experience because everybody knew that it wasn't finished. The creative process is a gamble, and you hope that you get the chemistry right. There was frustration, there was disappointment for the process, a sense of failure within myself too, that I hadn't delivered what I could have. And then you go through periods of resentment, anger, depression, blaming everybody else. I think for me it was probably about a year, maybe 18 months, later that I could finally sit down and see my own part in it, and how it was really just a collective. It was a moment in time and it happened. And if it hadn't happened, then they wouldn't have made the next album. You can't be creative and stay at the pinnacle of success all the time. You have to have the lows in order to have the highs. I mean, people forget about *Rattle and Hum* because critically it was a dip. That enabled *Achtung Baby* to be where it was. Totally. *The Unforgettable Fire,* I think, was a bit of a dip compared to what had gone before, and then *The Joshua Tree* comes after that. There is a pattern. I think it's just creativity and life.

Larry is the man of the people. He's the completely flamboyant, individualistic drummer, at least from a drummer's point of view. His style is totally unique. And yet, if he can't hear the song, he's got a problem with it. He can't pick up an acoustic guitar and go, 'La-la-la-la-la, this is how it goes.' So he's completely rooted. He's grounded. Adam is exactly the same, but in a different way. He is the random element in the band, when it comes to the music. Some of the things he comes up with – everybody in the room will look at him and wonder, 'How did you come up with this, Adam?' Time after time. And yet, he's the person who's happiest, sometimes, to take the backseat musically. A lot of people give him stick for playing fairly simple parts, but if Adam wasn't there you'd have three other incredible individual musicians on the loose. You've got to have somebody rooting it down. Normally that would be the drummer, but a lot of the time it's Adam. He's the one who's there with his feet down, but he also does these things and you think: 'Where has that come from?' Edge is the total brains. He's called the scientist. His head is somewhere else entirely. Out of nowhere, he will come up with an amazing guitar part, or vocal part. He's the one with the most extreme contradiction, because he's level-headed, even-tempered and he appears like the ultimate scientist. And yet he can just do the most amazing lyrical, artistic things. He's very much the intellectual when it comes to things like lyrics and the ideas of songs and the technicalities of sonics and things like that. But to be able to articulate the emotion of the music, I think that definitely is through the music rather than verbally. Whereas HMV, as we all call him, is inspiration. Bono's one of the few people who just by pushing himself one stage further can inspire. It's very rare and you can't put your finger on it. Bono has charisma. He'd be the first to say he's not the world's most accomplished musician, but his soul, his emotion, it just comes out, and it touches people.

One of my lasting memories of them was during the PopMart tour. We were in Sarajevo. Bono had put himself under so much pressure because it meant so much to him to bring some release, or relief, to the people of Bosnia and Sarajevo. It was a real personal thing. So the world's biggest tour ever comes to Sarajevo. I was in the outside broadcast truck, and there were armed guards, UN soldiers. Bono came on stage and they start to perform. In about the middle of, I think, the second song, I could hear his voice start to go. Now, because I know his voice so well, I was able to predict this about five songs before it was obvious to most other people. I was able to cover it up, as far as the outside broadcast was concerned. If I had a criticism of the PopMart tour in general, the band seemed to have become impersonal. The thing with the light show, everything else, was bigger than the band. But what happened in Sarajevo was remarkable. Bono lost his voice and you suddenly had 50,000 people, all with huge expectations, watching this guy go through his own personal hell because of the stress, the pressure. He's lost his voice! You saw this enormous, great big thing suddenly disappear, but there was a total connection between Bono and all the people in the audience who could really relate to his predicament, his stress. It was so emotional. It felt like the first time that I'd seen and heard them play in a club. Bono sang so quietly, and the audience was with him. He sang, he grunted, Edge would come up and sing, and the audience was totally with him. That shows the real spirit and integrity of the band and the way that they connect.

London, October 2003

Cheryl Engels

Recording quality control, all U2's records since Rattle and Hum

I was the director of quality control for A&M Records, which was owned by Jerry Moss and Herb Alpert, and had the privilege of meeting and working with many artists, producers and engineers over the 18 years I was there. Herb, being an artist, was intensely concerned with having consumers purchase records that reflected the artist's original intent, records that sounded like the mix the artist had approved. At many labels, that is not how records are made. Labels routinely receive mixes from the artist, then modify the sound of that mix through mastering, without the artist's involvement. Labels seldom check the audio quality at each step of manufacturing, where procedures can alter and degrade the fidelity, frequency response and overall complexion of the audio. Master tapes are routinely sent from America to England, where someone makes 30 copies, then sends those copies to 30 other countries. In those countries each 'master' goes to another studio, where an engineer says, 'Well I think that sounds a little too …' and starts turning all the knobs on his board. Not only have EQ changes been made, but every generation of copies is a bit further away from the original audio.

At A&M, we had a quality control department that liaised with all the creative people involved in making the records, and also with label departments and the manufacturing facilities. We watched over every stage to make certain the artist remained involved in mastering and manufacturing. We checked every product until it sounded like the mix approved by the band at the end of mastering. We were probably more concerned with QC than any other record label at the time.

U2 were not on the A&M label, but they worked for months at the A&M Recording Studios on *Rattle and Hum.* Larry wandered into my office, which was in the studio, and asked about my department. He said he didn't think anyone at U2's label, Island, was doing QC on their records. So he sent me samples of previously released U2 vinyl, cassettes and CDs from around the world, and asked that we test them. We did, and, of course, nothing sounded great; not only was the audio quality poor in many cases, but the records sounded completely different in every country.

U2 were quite shocked. Then they said, 'Well, okay. Now we have to figure out how to change this for ourselves.' So A&M said, 'Well, if you master your records in our mastering studio, we'll loan you Cheryl, and she'll oversee QC for you.' Island was not thrilled to have someone imply they were not manufacturing correctly; Chris Blackwell was very upset and actually went to plants and tried to improve things. However, the problem is you need to have one person who follows a project all the way through. Most labels aren't set up that way; Island wasn't prepared for it, and they didn't have people in the technical area that knew how to enact such a comprehensive quality control programme.

When U2 finished *Rattle and Hum*, we sent the album out to various top mastering engineers, including Arnie Acosta, one of the engineers at A&M Mastering Studios. Then, in a controlled environment, we played all the engineers' cuts against one another for the band to decide which one sounded best. The band liked Arnie's. Even Jimmy Iovine, the producer, agreed that the Arnie's master served the music best. Arnie has been the band's primary mastering engineer since, eventually exiting A&M, now working as an independent engineer based in LA.

One of the great joys of working with this band is that they understand the entire production chain and are completely involved in mastering and editing. With manufacturing, we have developed such a rapport over the years that they now trust me to take over at that point, working directly with the record labels and plants.

For every album, the record label submits a list of every company that is going to make tapes, CDs, DVDs, whatever. I approve each plant's manufacturing process and raw materials. They must agree to adhere to our technical specifications before the country is approved to make the product. I send each plant a first-generation master tape on a format with which they can work. Then they send me pre-production tests for approval, before they start manufacturing. With a CD, for instance, I compare the test to the band's original approved mastered mix, and it must be a satisfactory match. Then I take the CD into a laboratory and inspect all the electrical, physical and optical characteristics that must meet stringent industry guidelines. After approval, the label manufactures the CD, prints the booklets, and ships the packaged CD to the warehouse. They send samples of the finished product and I perform the same QC steps again. If the product fails to pass QC checks, then it all has to be scrapped and manufacturing has to start over. Over the years we have re-mastered some of U2's older recordings and re-supplied improved tapes to many countries. We re-mastered *The Joshua Tree* and *The Unforgettable Fire* for audiophile releases. And we have overseen the re-manufacture of many albums.

Some of the members of U2 and their management are very technical and enjoy learning and hearing about that side. Some are more interested in the artistic, creative side of things. I work with The Edge the most. He is the most brilliant human that lives, in my opinion. He has, for certain, the best ears for hearing detail. What he can hear just amazes me, and he is always right. I've never seen him make a wrong choice about anything to do with engineering. And at the same time, he's enormously creative. With him the brain, the heart and the ears are involved and I think that is what makes him so unique.

After *Rattle and Hum* was mastered, somebody from the band's management called to say they needed me to go to the plants in England and Europe to oversee manufacturing of the album to make sure it came out right. I said, 'No, I can't do that; I have a job!' At that time, we were dealing with vinyl, cassette, CD and videotape, all these different formats. My boss, who had been in the business for ever, knew technical stuff I didn't know about some of these formats. So I said, 'Well, I couldn't do that by myself, anyway,' so they said, 'Take your boss with you.' I said, 'No, I can't do that; I have a job at A&M.' Then Larry called: 'We would appreciate it so much if, as a personal favour to me, you would go and do this.' Who could resist such charm and dedication to releasing a great-sounding album? We were on a plane the next day, and went through Europe inspecting many plants along the way.

Rattle and Hum was a massive project, involving not only a double album of live and studio tracks but a theatrical film version. Thousands of reels of tape and many engineers. Near the end of mixing U2 actually had five studios at A&M working simultaneously, a first for any band who had ever worked in our studios. With so many songs and so many deadlines, the only way to make it all happen was to have multiple engineers: Shelly Yakus, Tom Panunzio, David Tickle, Don Smith, Rob Jacobs, etc. The band was over-dubbing even at the very end of mixing. That is how their process works; there have been records where they were in mastering, meaning the mixing was finished, when they decided to go back into the recording studio. And they did, even so late in the game. That's not how most artists work; many give up at that point. But U2 are so dedicated to getting something deep in their hearts and souls onto tape that they will keep digging until they feel like they've reached it. Always. Let's say they want to edit a finished mix and they're in Dublin or wherever. Arnie and I are in LA, all our delivery dates are past, and we really need to ship out the production parts. At this point the band will still find a way to do the work they feel is critical to the song, even putting people on planes to hand-carry tapes in order not to miss the release date.

One of the things that is so fabulous about working with U2 is that they allow you to become part of the creative process. With Edge, after working with him long distance for many years, we've developed a kind of short-hand in our communications. Arnie and I seem to understand what he wants from the mastering, and we usually end up with something the entire band likes. Given just a very brief outline, they will allow us to go off and create something that ends up as part of their artistic statement. Edge will call, for example, and say, 'I'm sending you a mix of a song for the album for editing and mastering.' I ask him, 'Well, what is your idea? What's your vision?' Often there are details that you cannot finesse at a mixing console. If you're a very good engineer, you know what things you can improve and enhance in mastering and other things you have to get the way you want them during mixing. So what I'm asking Edge is, 'Are there things you know you want me to address?' He'll say something like, 'A particular instrument in this mix sounds like the player has a big grin on his face, so watch that in mastering.' I wonder what he could possibly mean, but when Arnie and I listen to the mix, we can just see that band member with a giant smile from ear to ear, and Edge is right, there is a lot of energy in the instrument that needs to be kept in balance within the mix through equalization. He has called when I'm shopping in the supermarket and said, 'Okay, on such and such a song in the first chorus where the melody goes da-da-da, we want to try changing the melody to da-la-da, okay? Bye.' So I'm standing there in the checkout line, trying to draw out the notes on a musical staff on my shopping list, trying to remember what he sang! I love the challenge, and magically it always seems to work out.

When the band is on tour, singles continue to be released. On most singles, we go through the editing process, as singles will usually be a different edit or version than on the album. The band is working constantly on different assignments when not on the stage. And because they work harder than any band I have ever dealt with, finding a moment to talk to them and play things for them over the telephone becomes infinitely more complex.

There was an instance of an edit that both Edge and Bono needed to hear. There was a show, and as soon as it was over Bono was boarding a plane and Edge was going off to do press. As Bono was walking off the stage they handed him a phone, I played him the edit, then called the dressing room, and, because they weren't going to see each other that night, briefed Edge on Bono's input, then got Edge's thoughts, and that's how we finished the song. People think a rock star's life is all glamour and parties. Not with this band. They work! I think they do attend a party or two, but only after the job is done.

As far as mastering is concerned, U2 understand that Arnie Acosta knows how they hear. There are different ways to approach sound. You can approach it in a sonically accurate way that is as hi-fi as possible, for want of a better description. Well, this band is totally not interested in that. They are interested in whatever is right for the mood of a particular song. During the mastering of *Achtung Baby*, we were in the studio with a recording, and we made it sound open, bright and sparkly, sonically perfect. Bono came into the room and said, 'What have you done to my song? It is supposed to sound like you've been in a basement for three days, and you are just walking up the basement steps out into the sunlight, and like how your head feels at that moment.' You can't just give their music to an engineer who goes off to make it 'perfect'. You have to give it to someone who understands what emotion the band is trying to communicate, and Arnie has developed that level of understanding with their music.

The first time that I saw them play 'Elevation' was at a live show for a TV broadcast. They started playing the song, which I'd heard perhaps a thousand times already at that point. So I was singing and dancing along. Then Edge played a different guitar solo section, not what was on the record, causing me to completely lose my groove. When one is so familiar with an arrangement, with every note burned into memory, the slightest change completely shorts out the brain. I went up to him after the show and said, 'What did you do? You didn't play the song right! You can't do that to me!' He started laughing, I'm certain partly due to my impudence, and partly because the creative process never really ends. When they play a song live, the communication between U2 and the audience can transform a song into something entirely new.

Los Angeles, July 2003

Graphics

Love Town tour programme

Steve Averill
Designer of all U2 record and tour artwork

I first became involved when my brother, who was in the same class as Edge and Adam, said to me, 'There's a couple of guys at school who really want to talk to you about being in a band.' I'd been in punk band, the Radiators (from Space), in Dublin in 1976/7. Adam came over to my house basically just looking for advice: what they should do, where they should go, how they should approach the music and what they should do about it. Adam knew that I had been involved in the advertising industry, which was where I worked at the time. Our conversation then evolved from talking about everything in general terms to more specific things like the name and the direction of the band, the look and feel. The difference between them and other bands I met at that stage was that there was an obvious intelligence about what they wanted to do. There was a belief then that they could do it themselves, but they weren't sure how to go about it. People at that stage who ask for advice either take it blindly and don't think about it, or they ignore it completely. U2 would come back and say, 'We've thought about that one, 'We think this one is good,' This isn't exactly the way we see it,' or whatever. So they would sift through the advice they received and find bits that were most useful to them, where they could progress.

It came to a point, around 1977 or 1978, where they were playing some gigs and Adam said that they needed to change the name of the band. They were playing in a contest down in Limerick and had decided to use the name U2. They won. I remember Adam saying that he liked the idea of a name like XTC – another band at the time – and they went away and thought about it, decided on U2. I knew about the spy plane, the U2, but in broader terms the name was more about the expression 'You, too': be involved. It also has a graphic strength because it's kind of universal and simple to write down. I knew that it would work very well on posters. From that point onwards I got involved in the first photo session, art directing and then designing the sleeves for the first singles they made for Sony in Ireland. 'U23' was the first sleeve that we did. Before that we made a street poster for gigs. That was probably the first piece of actual print that we worked on together. It progressed from there.

The photography for the first album was already done. Hugo McGuinness, a friend of the band, had taken the pictures, so we just picked out a shot from the contact sheets that I thought would work and that was the one that was used, quite clear and quite moving. We shot a lot of the pic-

tures on the back in the studio while they recorded the first album. It was quite a brave decision for a first album because the design doesn't really highlight the band's name and the title isn't there. In a funny way, the next album *October* is much more like a first album because it has the name big and the band's picture on the front. But that first album became almost iconic, associated with that sense of innocence they had as a band. For every album cover we've done together since there's been a large amount of discussion about how things work and what they do, it was a very strong path we were following. You've always got to be able to come up with something they like, that they find exciting, that they find is suitable for the music. You can't become complacent about doing it. You've got to be on your toes; graphically and musically you've got to match what they're doing.

My two passions in life have always been music and graphic design and all I wanted was to combine those two things and carry them through. In the early days, they would record in less time and on a much tighter schedule. You would go down to the studio at an early stage and you would hear some very rough music. It would change quite a lot between the beginning and the end. Likewise, the graphic identity would probably be developed at the same time. By the time they have finished working with Daniel Lanois or Brian Eno or whoever, the whole perspective of the music will have changed dramatically. We'd sit and listen for maybe an hour, half an hour, see what's coming out, see how they feel about the music. And then sometimes we come up with initial ideas without ever hearing the music. Sometimes, a strong identity forms itself before you've actually heard the full sound. Albums like *Achtung Baby* had a certain sonic elegance.

October was obviously the sleeve where there they wanted to bring the band a little more to the fore, so that was shot in and around the docks area of Dublin. And it was fairly straightforward. I think there was a feeling from Bono at that point that he quite liked some of the 1960s album covers, where the titles appear on the front of the album, like Bob Dylan and things like that. So it was more or less one shot at the dock. The inner bag had extra shots of people in and around the area. It wasn't that complicated a sleeve to do. In some ways it may be, to my mind, one of the weaker covers. It was the right cover for that time, but I think the choice of shots could have been stronger. *War* was more complicated, in that they had the title early on and talked a lot about whether we would commission photographs by Don McCullin, the acclaimed war photographer, or someone like him. Finding the right image was the crucial thing. We talked about finding an existing shot that represented the whole idea. But that ties you down to one place, to the Middle East or Belfast or wherever. I had seen a documentary a couple of years earlier about the Nazis rounding up people in the Polish ghetto. One scene stuck in my mind: a young boy standing against a wall with his hands behind his back; he was obviously terrified. That's what I was trying to capture, that sense of fear. Initially we thought, 'What boy shall we use?' And then, because they'd already done a sleeve with Peter and they knew him, he seemed an obvious choice. I suppose if I'd sat down and thought a bit longer I might have said, 'No, don't use the same kid – it's too close to that cover.' But, as it turned out, it was fine. The typography mimicked the black-and-red colour scheme on the covers of *Life* magazine.

We've always used a strong, compact typeface to get U2's image across. That was used on different covers in different ways but it still recycles itself every now and then. The logo design for the more recent albums has become more subtle because the band has become much more well known. We've always tried to keep moving on. On one occasion the art director at Island Records was keen to design a U2 cover and asked if I would mind if he presented some covers to the band. The band insisted that I come down to the presentation, which I felt awkward about. So I went along, looked at what was done, didn't say anything. Paul McGuinness called me out of the room and just turned to me and said, 'How quickly can you come up with an idea?' Suddenly you're trying to think. I knew the *Unforgettable Fire* title came from a Hiroshima exhibition and I understood the significance. In fact, one of the covers that they had presented was of an aerial view, with a target graphic on it, of Hiroshima. But we knew it wasn't really appropriate so I tried to think of places or times when fire has created something that in itself is beautiful and different. So I thought about castles and houses that had burned down, where the remaining structure has a presence in its own style. Fire destroys one thing and creates something else. I got a series of maps and over a three-day period looked at a number of castles with the photographer Anton Corbijn. It very quickly became apparent that a lot of the castles were either now in the middle of villages or they were turned into barnyards or they were just not great for photography. The one on the album cover is a place called Moydrum Castle in County West Meath. It's actually an old house, not a castle.

Unforgettable Fire set a tone for *Joshua Tree,* almost bringing the physical presence of the band into a landscape. I think the working title for *Joshua Tree* was 'The Two Americans'. Bono's concept was that the place where the desert meets civilization is a raw place. So we initially set out to find a ghost town that would express that – and we did. The cover was shot in black and white near Zabriskie Point.

With *Rattle and Hum* I went out to Los Angeles with the band and spent time discussing ideas with U2 and the peo-ple at Paramount Pictures. It became quite obvious to me fairly early on that there was no point in me pretending to do anything because I didn't have the facilities in Los Angeles that I have in Dublin and I was happy enough with that. I knew what the cover was going to be, I'd spent about ten hours in editing suites researching through live show footage to find that image of Bono with the light and Edge. The shot came from 'Bullet the Blue Sky' in the show where Bono had wanted almost a war kind of feeling to the searchlight, and it had a kind of hard, rough sound. That came to a degree from his experiences when down in South America. He more or less knew fairly early on that this was the image he wanted to capture. In the end it was re-shot in a stills studio with Anton Corbijn.

Achtung Baby came next and that was a large change in terms of the band reinventing themselves. The sense of irony and of fun, the sense of playing at being a rock star, came into play at that point. And it was probably one of the most extensively photographed periods for them – Santa Cruz, Berlin, Morocco. We started out trying to find a single image that would project what they wanted to do, and slowly the single image became multiple images in order to reflect this whole change. We decided to do a montage, as many images on the cover as we could fit. There are something like 36 shots in the overall package and that's quite an amazing impression. The grid system was introduced, which was followed through in both *Zooropa* and *Pop*. We carried the same theme through all those images on all of those covers.

Achtung Baby was also a time when Shaughn McGrath got much more involved in the U2 projects for two reasons: I wanted another person to bounce ideas off and I wanted someone with a different perspective too. As the band develops and their music develops, everything graphically is changing too. You want to be able to look to other people to reflect that shift. I'm very lucky in having a strong passion for music. Hardly a day goes by when I'm not in a record shop or looking at covers. In graphic design and typography there are trends, just as there are in anything else. With U2, we didn't want to create covers that looked like they were produced in a particular era, or a particular time. I would like to think that the U2 *War* album could have been released last week, whereas a lot of graphic design for other bands is tied to a particular time. You could say, 'Well, that's a 1970s sleeve' or 'That's a 1980s sleeve.' We wanted to get beyond that so that they would be as strong 10 years, 20 years, 30 years after they were released. *Achtung Baby* was a huge opening up of the whole way we did things. *Zooropa* happened very quickly. The Zooropa tour was under way in Europe and they were coming back to the studio in Dublin as often as they could, almost every second day, to work on recording. We spent quite a lot of evenings in their studio working on ideas while they worked at the music. There was an EP and then an album so the title for the tour was suggested. Initially we went down with ideas that were based around the European stars and flag, but there had been one or two covers already

ZooTV Outside Broadcast programme

PopMart programme

like that. Instead, we made an electronic flag using a computer and overlaid images. We picked images from the back cover and overlaid them with titles and all sorts of things. It was also the first cover that we did on a Mac so we were experimenting ourselves with computer technology. Over the years you build a certain rapport with people. You have an idea of what they're thinking or where they're going.

The next album cover for U2 was *Pop,* which we wanted to design in a way that would reflect Pop artists like Warhol and Lichtenstein in a way that was not a homage but more something they might have done if they had the computer technology that we have. We wanted the tour booklet to expand beyond that. The tour itself was so over the top and that cover became a reflection of exactly what was going on at the time. *The Unforgettable Fire* was the first time that we started getting involved in tour programmes and merchandising. The tour products have always been a reflection of what's happened after the album cover and, generally speaking, the tour programmes are developed as they've gone along. A lot of them have two or three editions. The first edition goes out with the first leg of the tour. Then the second edition is updated with photography from the first leg so the sense of it being a live adventure is carried through at a later point. There's a sort of continuous change and development of ideas. The band often changes things at the last minute, but that's the way they work and that's the way we work with them. It would be quite difficult for an outside design company to come in and do it that way, because we're here, in Dublin, and we know how to react. If we get a phone call to come down in half an hour and do this or that, we go. We work at the tempo that they do. When it really gets down to the wire, you've got to be able to do things quite quickly and make things happen, because we do everything in there: T-shirts, tickets, signage, tour programmes, everything associated with the graphic side of things is done in our studio. A huge amount of work is turned out. Willie Williams consults with us to a degree, but obviously he has his own direction and vision with what he's doing. At some point he'll look at what we're doing and sometimes he attends meetings. Likewise we go and attend meetings that he's having on the stage design, so there's a small amount of crossover, but everyone sticks to their own responsibilities of course. Then we might supply Willie with whatever imagery he feels he could translate into what he's doing. And then when we see a stage show we've got to take some of that stage show and put it into what we're doing. So there's a kind of synergy in the way the whole thing develops.
Dublin, February 2004

Shaughn McGrath
Co-designer with Steve Averill of U2 record and tour artwork since Achtung Baby

Although the tour primarily follows an album and promotes that album, the tour also has a life of its own. It's a musical journey and includes far more than just the current album. It's also a historical journey and all that should be reflected in the graphics.

When we start to work on tour graphics we don't really embed ourselves in the current album or singles or whatever. It might only be a word or a phrase and that's all we'll get, then we start the journey ourselves and see what that'll conjure up. At the core of the U2 world are a lot of visually articulate artists – not least all four members of U2 themselves – all influencing the escapade. It can be fun. Part of their philosophy is don't close any doors until you genuinely feel that everything's been nailed, every aspect has been looked at.

When it comes to the tour we may already be partly down the road. For instance on the Elevation tour we had the concept of the heart, which came initially because the theme was the airport and the airport signage from the album *All That You Can't Leave Behind,* and having little symbols to go with each of the songs on that album. It's very graphic, it's an ideal little device, a little icon just to transfer into anything at all, really. In ZooTV we had particular little iconic images which were used everywhere from signage to T-shirts, backstage passes, screen graphics. There is a symbolism and there is a certain universality that lets them work without words; they cross that place between words and pictures. With PopMart, the word 'POP' is just ideal, that 'O', that centre to fill, is just perfect.

U2 have created their own sense of visual language, their own colours. There is that sense of a surface and something lying underneath – the story, the message. Even if it kind of takes a while to get to it, it's there. And likewise for us, the images that work for us are those that work on both those levels: a symbol that quite happily sits as an image on a T-shirt while behind that graphic is a whole paragraph of meaning.
Dublin, February 2004

Elevation crew tour itinerary

Promoters

Dennis Desmond
Promoter, Ireland

I first met U2 in Cork in '77. I was a weekend promoter, because the market wasn't there. My day job was as a petrochemical engineer. The whole industry began to take off around the same time, and U2 were the most successful band to come out of it because they had the bottle to go the full distance; the belief in themselves. I think very importantly they also had the management structure. They were focused.

There have been so many shows, but one of my favourites was when we did three awesome nights in Dublin just prior to Christmas 1982, at a time when there was a slight dip in the band's fortunes. When *October* was at a constant rather than going up. The band had progressed so much that you were looking at them playing to 1500 people, which was the stand-up show. After this we opted for the show on Phoenix Park race course in August '83. I recall when we announced that and people said: 'Wow, that's a bit ambitious!' and it was. Going from three nights with 1500 people a night to a 15,000-capacity open-air show, which at that time were few and far between. We had this amazing line up that was U2, Simple Minds, Eurythmics, Big Country, Steel Pulse and a band from the North called Perfect Crime. It was a cracking gig and the band was brilliant and that was it.

As a band, there's always been a sense of excitement around them. This comes from the fact that they always deliver an incredibly good live show. In every performance that I've seen them do, what comes across with the band is a passion and the fact that it's just four guys on stage. It's still the four guys. That, to me, is what U2 is about. They are that group in the true sense of the word. It is the four of them taking on the world, and Paul there behind them pushing them up that hill.
Dublin, January 2004

Jim Aiken
Promoter, Northern Ireland

There's always been a very strong indigenous Irish music scene. U2 added a thing to the Irish music scene. The difference between them and other Irish bands is that I think others waited for things to happen and U2 made them happen. U2 saw things and went for it and were rewarded for going for it. They did push the boat out and they realized that you didn't have to leave Ireland to do it. That's one of their strengths: they knew they could conquer the world from Dublin, while others thought that you could only conquer the world from London or New York. In early 1985 I happened to be at a U2 concert at the Cow Palace in San Francisco. I suddenly realized the effect that this band was having on an American audience. I remember particularly when Bono sang 'Bad' it made the hairs stand on my head. He had the youth of America in his hands. I was going to do major concerts with them in Ireland that year and I realized that no matter how much we talked about it, there was only one way to promote this concert: I decided to bring the Irish media out to their Madison Square Gardens gig on 1 April 1985. That was the first time that Irish journalists had ever been taken to a gig by the promoter – being flown out, paid for, and used as a promotion element. Representatives of the Irish media saw U2, saw how America had taken them to their hearts, came home and wrote about it. There was no way by talking that I could have passed on what I had experienced in San Francisco. That was the peak of my relationship with U2 because after that they didn't need much promoting! They were self-driven.
Belfast, January 2004

Bono and audience, Phoenix Park, Dublin, August 1983

Tim Parsons
Promoter, UK

There was one Sunday when I rang home and my girlfriend said, 'I've just been listening to this fantastic record you left lying around,' which was *Boy*. I got home, listened to it, went into the office and started talking to a guy called Ian Wilson. He was their agent, and I booked two or three shows for October of '80 and I had dates for £1000 a night. In terms of the performance it was staggering because Bono was such a pivotal figure. He had this way of having his foot on the monitors that was very authoritative, and a way of climbing all over the speakers which was very precarious. It looked punk-ish, but it really wasn't punk, because the songs were just so strong.

They were obviously going to be a big band, just because they were so authoritative. Paul McGuinness was very attentive, and in the mish-mash of punk where the fifth member was the band's best mate who happened to be the manager, he was a little bit different. So, from an organizational point of view they were a lot more substantial. Ian Flooks was quite a classy agent and Paul McGuinness was quite a classy manager. We all knocked each other's rough edges off, in terms of cuisine and wine and the type of hotels we'd recommend to one another. Whatever squares were on me were all rounded off quite nicely by the education I got in life from the Ians and the Pauls! With Live Aid, what McGuinness actually ended up doing was ensuring that U2 got a slot in the UK which was the first slot in America when America came on live. So U2 were the first band seen on Live Aid, in America. That's the type of thing that Paul did that now, 15 years later, probably isn't necessarily appreciated as being what I would consider to be one of the pivotal moments of their career.

They were a very iconic band, and I think that iconic bands are successful in the States. You'd always get a great photograph of Bono holding the white flag over the audience. He used to do that as part of the show, and I think it was only when people started fighting over the flag that they thought it was really stupid and ditched it. And they were always working hard on the intimacy of their shows. Indoors I don't think anybody ever got close to U2. For a promoter the thing that was great about a band like U2 was that they were very challenging for us. We had to interface with the venues to try and create an environment that the band would work in. They were demanding of us and of venues to get the environment which they felt that a) their audience wanted and b) they'd perform best in. For instance, they preferred a standing audience rather than a seated audience and this made us go to the Wembleys and the NECs of this world about not having seats on the floor. U2 started the trend which then ended up benefiting other bands down the line. U2 wanted us to create an environment that was more beneficial to them. They're quite famous for the gathering of the clan, everybody and the kitchen sink. I couldn't get there quick enough, because the lunches and dinners were fabulous. And they also had the most fantastic crews, and you'd always see their sound engineer, or their production manager, or their stage manager on other tours. To my mind, it was a very happy crew.

I never stopped promoting them. But with PopMart there were all sorts of syndicates bidding for the tour which ultimately ended up going with TNA. I think it went for about $107 million in the end, or something stupid, for 100 shows. We were still the promoter working with TNA, but we were getting paid a fee rather than taking any fiscal risk. And then the Elevation tour was owned by Clear Channel because they owned TNA.

I think the Internet's had a far more profound influence on music than MTV. From our point of view of selling tickets, when we started selling tickets on the Internet I used to love it, because we were making money when I was asleep. All of a sudden we could promote in a different way. It had a fundamental impact on the way we promoted. Immediately the Worldwide Web is this dichotomy of a one-to-one relationship with your customer, and a worldwide basis of communication. Fantastic. So MTV: no thank you. Internet: absolutely. I'll take that every time.
London, October 2003

Herman Schueremans
Promoter, Belgium

We were a small independent promoter that did bands that nobody else wanted to do, and we toured them extensively in Belgium and Frankfurt. We have a festival called DNW Rock Werchter. U2 played that in 1982. That's where the band discovered they had the power to appeal and to play in front of a big audience. They were number three on out of seven bands. Bono climbed in the PA wings and the whole audience at that time – 70,000 people – went wild, it was magic. They played the festival again in 1983, and when U2 came back a third time in 1985 they headlined the festival. The festival is always a party, it was always the highlight of the year. More recently I remember them arriving with their plane in Brussels and we were waiting to pick them up in the limo at the private airport. We were able to walk on the tarmac and Bono said, 'Herman, come up here,' so I went up into the plane and he said, 'Look, this is where we are living now!' U2 is about the ultimate power of positivism and believing in what you do and persuading the rest of the world.
Belgium, December 2003

Don Law
Promoter, USA

Anybody who was in the business in the late sixties rode a tsunami change in popular culture.

Bar owners had a stage in the corner and police departments and municipalities were openly hostile to kids. It was a semi-riot environment because it was usually a square-off between the police and the kids, and within about 15 or 20 minutes the concert was over. We really had a tough time breaking through with music, because it was kids with long hair and construction workers and the police thought these guys were obviously nothing other then dope fiends, crazed kids who they wanted to shut down. One of the things that turned out to be hugely important for us was that we convinced the owner of a couple of failing FM radio stations that he should convert them over to album-orientated rock. WBCN, which is one of the cornerstone radio stations in America, was one of them. In 1977 I opened up a club called the Paradise Theater which was a 600-seat sit-down club, and that was probably our main showcase for new talent and still remains our showcase in Boston now, 26 years later. That's where U2 played in 1981.

We always sold U2 out instantaneously. This is an Irish city and U2 made a point of making sure that they were here on St Patrick's Day. With ZooTV they had the walkway that went out into the audience and it was a love-fest on both sides. Bono could have done anything, the audience was with him every second.

U2 did change the face of the music business by their art, by their lyrical ability, by their genius. I don't think that it would be the same music community without U2 and I think everybody understands the intelligence that goes into their music. They're an extraordinary talent.
Boston, November 2003

Gregg Perloff

Promoter, California

The night I talked to Bono for the first time – when they opened for J.Geils at the San Francisco Civic in spring '81 – he said to me, 'I have the vision, I have the energy, I have the commitment. We're going be the biggest band in the world.' I was like, 'Oh, my God.' I mean, this guy's an opening act in an 8000-seater. And instead of taking it as being boastful, I was looking at him and I was going, 'I'm not doubting him.' I mean, this was just some opening act. If anyone else had said it you'd just go, 'Get the fuck out of here.' Nobody ever sounded like U2. I don't know a band where anyone ever said, 'Well, they're kind of like U2.' Think about that.

I remember a date I did with them at the Cow Palace that brought me to tears. They had a kid join them on 'Knockin' on Heaven's Door' by Bob Dylan. Here was a 20-year-old whose life was about to change. He got up on stage and Bono talked about the possibilities of dreaming. That if you believe in yourself and you believe that you can do things in this world, things can change. He was very eloquent. So they bring this young man on stage, and Edge teaches him the three-chord progression, fairly simple. He's so nervous that in the first eight bars he can hardly play, then he starts getting it. Here he is on stage, in front of 15,000 people, with U2, and Bono stops singing and then Edge slowly steps back and stops playing, so you've got the bass and drums and just him, playing now. And for not very long, maybe four or eight bars, they just showed an entire audience what happens if you're willing to try something. It was one of the most remarkable experiences I've ever had in 30 years in this business. I can tell you that if it affected me so deeply, think about what it did for that guy and that audience. Now, if you have the power to do that … How many bands can do something like that and pull it off? How many bands can entertain, teach and stand for positive things in this world all at the same time?

There was the famous free show we did at noon at Vallencourt Plaza which was filmed for *Rattle and Hum.* It's a space that holds around 15,000 people in downtown San Francisco, right on the waterfront. U2 were huge, and we got the city of San Francisco to agree within 48 hours because we had to keep it quiet. At 11.45 Bill Graham said, 'We can't announce this earlier or it'll be insanity.' I mean, people literally ran out of their offices. So we're doing this show and at some point Bono asked for a can of spray paint. Whatever. Then he goes and sprays this sacred statue. Well, to say the shit hit the fan is an understatement. They wanted to ban U2 from San Francisco. So, luckily, the artist whose sculpture it was thought it was really cool and he came public and said, 'This is art. This is great.' So the next night, at the Oakland Stadium, Bono lets the artist spray paint their scrim for Joshua Tree show.

The first show I did after Bill died was the ZooTV stadium show, and there was a second ramp. Paul and I decided for some reason to walk out into that area just to feel what was going on with the crowd. And at some point Bono happens to be walking back. Now you've got to understand, there are 55,000

people that he's entertaining, and he's walking back and he sees us. I don't know how he saw us. We didn't see that he had seen us. He leans over, and he says in my ear, 'Bill would be very proud of what you've done right now.' And I'm thinking: 'How can he do this? How can the guy, in the middle of being so focused, in front of 55,000 people, see somebody? How could he have the wherewithal to do it?' I mean, how long is the break while you're singing? Three seconds? To lean over, say this to me, continue the song, and walk back to the main stage. Now you tell me anybody who can do something like that?

I don't talk about this band the way I talk about most bands. Nobody ever sounded like U2. By 1993 here was a band that wasn't happy just to rest on the quality of the songs, but wanted to connect with their audience in a different way and wanted also to give them a show. Give them an experience.

San Francisco, November 2003

Bono (top) spray-painting the Armand Vaillancourt sculpture at the free outdoor concert in Justin Herman Plaza, San Francisco, USA, 11th November 1987. Bottom: Bono performing in front of backdrop at same concert

Arthur Fogel

President of touring, CCE Music Group; promoter, Canada

Michael Cohl was the founder and chief executive of CPI. In 1989, our company promoted The Rolling Stones 'Steel Wheels' tour world-wide, and that really was the platform from which we launched ourselves into the world. At that time no one had really created a model to roll out globally. A big Stones tour was a dramatic start and it was also somewhat scary because it came down to: succeed and open up an entire new world or fail and there wasn't a lot of margin for air! It was a very brave move and opened up an incredible business opportunity that lives vibrantly to this day.

Bob Sillerman at SFX, later acquired by Clear Channel, had the vision to consolidate the local promoting industry. He went out into the world and acquired numerous local promoting operations in the United States, state-by-state or city-by-city. The strategy was to create a worldwide local promoter platform through consolidation. Because we were a global touring company, when SFX bought us we acquired worldwide rights for artists to tour and to put those artists through the local promote channel.

The key to success really in these global partnerships with artists is creating as efficient and cost-effective an operation as possible, because ultimately that is what turns out to be an enjoyable experience for everybody as well. I'm not quite sure how to describe PopMart, other than it was a sort of different feel than I had known of U2. The approach was very different, it was very irreverent, it was Pop art, it had a very different sort of feel. It was as if they had been coming at something from the right for most of their career, but were now looking at coming at it from the left.

We had a relationship with Paul and U2, which dated back to the early eighties from being their promoters in Canada, and we joined forces in 1997 to promote U2 worldwide in their PopMart tour. I would have to say, when I look back before Elevation and PopMart, and certainly through U2's touring history, that I think what you have to admire about artists such as U2 is that they're always looking to challenge themselves. Elevation was a different tour to PopMart, PopMart was a different tour to ZooTV, but ultimately it was a band creating a show and expressing themselves in a different way and that is ultimately what artistry is about.

Miami, January 2004

Top: U2 stop the traffic (again!) outside Madison Square Garden, Elevation tour, NYC, June 2001. Bottom: Inside, fans await the Elevation show

Michael Cohl

Promoter, Canada

We worked with Barbara Skydel (you only got the blessing of talking to Frank Barsalona occasionally!) U2 were successful from the beginning. They came, they played, they conquered. They made the step up brilliantly, to the point where it was probably better to see them in an arena with 19,000 people doing Joshua Tree and Rattle and Hum. For me, with their energy and exuberance, it was better seeing them in the arena than it was in the club or the theatre. ZooTV was mind blowing. That's the only way I can describe it. That night I went over to Paul McGuinness and I said, 'I really should be your promoter everywhere, like I deal with The Stones and Pink Floyd. I will do it in such a way that a local promoter can't. You put all the apples in one barrel, and what you become is a better marketing tool, and a more efficient production. It's just a better model.' The timing was right for U2 to change after ZooTV.

I loved PopMart. The last night of the tour was actually one of the highlights of my promoting career. Arthur Fogel and I got the 'You know, you guys were right. It works. It was slow for us to get into it. We hadn't realized exactly what it was.' We said, 'Maybe we didn't put the carpet down for you to see the roadmap as well as we could have.' By midway through the tour it was getting better and better, and by the end they looked at it and went, 'It really will work right. It will be great. Next time, we will listen more and it'll be fantastic.'

Toronto, February 2004

Media

Bill Flanagan
*Senior vice-president, MTV Networks International; author of
U2 at the End of the World*

As record companies encounter new problems with free downloads on the Internet and the crashing sales of CDs, touring has again become the centre of the music business. Earlier in the 20th century records were something that you made just to promote your live shows or whatever other career you had – movies, television. It was the baby brother. In the 1960s that all changed and record sales began to explode. Now, in the 21st century, as record companies contract at an extraordinary rate, the energy and certainly the cash flow has gone back into the touring business. And you see this reflected in a lot of ways. Everybody who was ever out on tour is out again now. You can go and see The Who, Paul McCartney, Simon and Garfunkel, The Rolling Stones. You name it. They're out there.

And while the price of CDs plummets, the sky seems to be the limit for the price of concert tickets: $100 is not considered to be particularly extraordinary. So that's where the money is, where the business is. And that's where people can have a unique experience. Tremendous amounts of music come at you for free through the television, radio and the Internet, but going out to see someone play in concert is still considered to be a great night out and good value for money.

In the time that U2 have been on the road they have ridden this shift. And U2 have demonstrated that it is possible for a band to compete on the biggest level – stadium shows, extraordinary spectacle – while maintaining a direct, personal, almost confessional relationship with the audience. A lot of people doubted that was possible. There's always been a puritan streak within rock and roll, that certain things are sell-outs, phoney. Of course, certain things are. But at its best, it can be about the counter-culture coming together, progressive, political ideas, sexual and racial liberation. Big ideas have been attached to rock and roll, and this puritan streak tends to distrust giant inflatable pigs and laser shows. At its worst, that puritanism becomes elitist and that is contrary to the very nature of rock and roll. That elitism says, 'If a lot of people like this, I'm doing something wrong. If the jocks and the frat boys like it, then I must be selling out despite my best intentions.' I think that's self-destructive, but it's always been there. It slid into rock with the old lefties and the folkies who trailed in after Dylan. It erupted with punk rock, with The Clash and groups like that. It erupted with grunge and Kurt Cobain, that notion that if a lot of people like you, you are probably doing something wrong. And if you entertain on a vast scale, if it gets much bigger than a theatre, you're definitely doing something wrong.

It would be hard for anyone to deny that U2 managed to do things that were really big, that were really good, and that retained the core of what their connection was with their audience in the first place. That this is about something bigger than both of us. I remember that Springsteen once said that when he first saw U2 play in a club he knew they would play arenas because the sound was so big. Not just the songs, not just Bono's gestures, which were very big, but the sound made a club sound like it was an arena. The way that Edge's guitar bounced off everything. Springsteen thought that a group with a sound this grand would eventually find a room big enough to make sense. There's a lot of truth in that. By the time of the War tour, with the white flag and the marching and Bono scurrying up the scaffolding, it was clear that U2 was a big group, like The Who, regardless of the room. I saw that show in college gyms and in small theatres, and it was a big show. It almost didn't matter what the room was. It was like going to a Led Zeppelin show. It was huge. And yet, they made everyone feel part of it. So in that sense U2 justified broadness and bigness for a generation that might have been dubious about it otherwise.

It's possible to do a small show in a really big place, and a big show in a small place. You can see Radiohead play outdoors, for example, at some giant festival or over here as they did at the Statue of Liberty, and it's still fairly contained. The music and the way that they carry themselves still suggest an inward-looking performance, and the whole audience leans forward to see what Radiohead are seeing. I think one of the things that made U2 so powerful is that they were never elitist about it. Bono said, probably more than once, that he felt of the bands that came up during punk and new wave, U2 were about seventh in line, and accepted that. Suddenly everyone ahead of them – The Sex Pistols, The Clash, The Police, Talking Heads – all disappeared and U2 were left alone at the front of the line to gather all the energy those groups had built up. Kind of what Madonna did with disco.

One thing that U2 were not precious about that has been the death of so many bands – from The Clash to Nirvana to Lauryn Hill – is that U2 wanted to talk to everyone who would listen. That's the motivation of rock and roll. Elvis Presley and The Beatles and The Who and James Brown and Aretha Franklin all wanted to talk to anyone who would listen to what they had to say. It was about reaching everybody. It was about appealing to the nerds and to the football players as well as to the people who wore all the right clothes. U2 didn't have that Hamlet complex that at key moments caused people from Sinead O'Connor to Eddie Vedder to doubt the worth of what they were doing. Or to look into the audience and say, 'I don't like that person.' And that's one of the reasons that U2 have been so successful for so long.

What U2 have contributed to the music video is like what they have contributed to arena rock: showing that a band with integrity and a band with real art can do these things and not be defined by them. There are very few people who became famous through music video who didn't turn into The Monkees within five years. It's unfortunate because a lot of people, had they come along at a different time and been exposed in a different way, probably would have had longer careers and been taken more seriously. Instead they become nostalgia. There are few people who were part of that first MTV generation who have any kind of career now. U2 are an exception, along with Madonna and Tom Petty, very different artists. Madonna is much more defined by the video. Although Petty had big, big, videos, the video was kind of incidental for him. He was already established when the video hit and just grabbed it sooner than others did. U2 made their first appearance to most Americans through music videos, yet I don't think that anyone thinks of U2 as a video band.

Like most of the rock bands who have had long, successful careers, U2 built their audience one city at a time through their live shows. They came back to America and worked and worked and worked and worked and worked. They toured here so many times between 1980 and 1984. People in Boston thought they were a local band! I think they always saw touring as an essential part of the job, which is another thing that distinguishes them from a lot of people who came along during the 1980s. Other bands figured, 'The video is doing the job, the record's doing the job, the photo shoot's doing the job, therefore I don't have to play to 300 people in Boise on a Tuesday night.' Whereas U2 said, 'Three hundred people in Boise, let's go!'

You have to remember that the record company doesn't control the touring. The band and their management and their agents decide what they're going to do. It's useful, of course, for tours and records to hit at the same time; the tour sells records, and the publicity and attention around the record helps promote the tour. U2 toured so much in the first five years or so, whether they had a record or not.

The thing that's never changed in U2 is the heart of what they do, which is the communication between the band and their audience. No matter how you dress it up, and no matter the size of the venue, that's constant. That's what people come back for and that has never gone away. At times U2 have made themselves and the audience jump through a few more hoops in order to get that, and they've had to adapt it to make sense in a 50,000-seat stadium, but I think that we wouldn't be talking about them if that hadn't stayed constant the whole way through. There's never been a point where they've just gone through the motions.

The PopMart tour, which has gone down as a moment when U2 stumbled, is interesting. This is all pretty well known, but I'll say it anyway. They booked the tour before they had the album done. When the album wasn't done to their satisfaction they cancelled the rehearsal dates and the prep dates in order to get the album done. They still didn't feel they had the album done, but they just reached the point where the tour was about to begin, so they had to put it out. They've said they'll never put themselves in that position again. As a result, the album, which had a lot of really good songs on it, was probably not finished exactly right. But it went out, and it went out with these enormous expectations coming off the most important records they'd ever made, and it didn't do as well as they'd hoped it would.

You could also make the case that U2 had missed a step in terms of how promotion in the US had changed. You were no longer going get four or five singles off an album. The first single had to be the biggest, best song. There was no build. Radio had become more constricted. Television had become more important in promoting music. When *Achtung Baby* was rolled out just a few years earlier, anything U2 did was played automatically because it was U2. People forget that although *Rattle and Hum* may not have been their artistic high point, it was a commercial gigantic point. So when *Achtung Baby* came out, anything U2 did was going to get played. Therefore, U2 could put out 'The Fly' and blow everybody's minds, and then move into 'Mysterious Ways' and have a big video, and then save 'One', which was the clear, across-the-board smash, to be the fourth single and really hit a peak. It was all paced out. It was still an assumption that you had a year, a year and a half, when you'd have people's attention. By the time *Pop* came, the US had changed dramatically. It was now the era of, say, Hanson, the Spice Girls. It was the height of Sarah McLachlan, Lilith and Jewel, and even Hootie and the Blowfish, a whole different kind of music. The media world then had a very short attention span. You got one shot with your first single: 'If the first single doesn't go we don't want to hear anything else from you.' But U2 sort of came out the way that they did on *Achtung Baby*. First was 'Discotheque' and the crazy video where they were dressed up as the Village People. The response was 'This ain't a hit, forget it.' And they lost a lot of their opening right there. They launched the tour at a K-mart, as an ironic joke about commercialism, but people didn't understand it. People didn't bother to try and understand it. I remember Sheryl Crow, who's very smart and alert, saying to me, 'Gee, those guys have so much integrity, I just can't believe that they have K-mart sponsoring their tour.' This was a total misunderstanding of what was going on, but shows how even a perceptive musician could misunderstand it. This tour is called PopMart, it's launched at K-mart, it's like, 'Gee, I thought they had more class than that.' Most people wouldn't read the press release. You would get a quick shot on MTV news of U2 launching their tour at K-mart and people generally weren't paying much attention. And U2 didn't realize the degree to which they would have to reach out and grab people by the throat to make it clear.

Having said all that, U2 ended up sacrificing what would have been the rehearsal time to finish the record. I went out to see them in Las Vegas when they were supposed to be in tour rehearsals. It was just a few days before the first show, but the whole band hadn't even arrived yet. They hadn't played the whole set. They had just barely finished the album. It was pretty insane. And I suppose they felt they'd just pick up where they left off with Zoo. In addition to that, the real problem was that the whole country's media was converging on Las Vegas for the launch of the U2 tour. It had become a media event. Everyone was flying in for it. It wasn't like they were opening out of town where no one would see it and get the kinks out. And they were gonna do a live television special from the first night of the tour. It was on ABC, and just days before they were still figuring out what the show should be.

Another problem was that the tour, as I remember, hit LA almost immediately, hit New York very early, and then continued on for a year. So the impression in America was 'This tour is a drag.' The record wasn't happening, radio wasn't really interested by the time they came with the songs that might have been hit singles. I saw that show a few months later in Spain and it was magnificent. I saw it towards the end of the whole tour, in Rio, and it was incredible. They'd worked out the kinks. So the notion that the PopMart tour was kind of the fall of U2 isn't really true. But in the US it was perceived as a misstep.

At a certain point in your career, inevitably, everyone hits a bad point. Even people like John Lennon and Paul Simon at a certain point said, 'I'll take five years off. We'll ride out this punk craze. 'I don't know that they planned it that way, but that's what happened. Neil Young went and made his odd, weird albums. Bruce Springsteen broke up the E Street Band. There's a certain point at which you can almost feel the 20-year exhaustion coming, or the 15-year exhaustion, whatever it is. So you could make the case that PopMart was just the point at which America needed to take a little breather from U2, and U2 needed to take a little breather from America.

The core of what U2 do has remained remarkably consistent. The way it's presented to the world has adapted as times have changed. Bono always rails against what he calls the brown rice position, the hippie position on things. But he's got a lot more brown rice in him than he ever wants the world to see. He really does. Look at commercial sponsorship: I know that they've had endless philosophical discussions about it, but in the long run so far they just can't bring themselves to do it. That is ultimately a brown rice position, that's part of what we love about them. Within all of the morphing of the image and the sound and the record production and the way the shows are presented there's this bedrock core of four people who we met in the early 1980s and who we've grown up with. It would be a pathetic thing if they were to come out with the mullets and the white flag doing 'I Will Follow' every night, recreating a moment of glory. But the heart of 'I Will Follow' is alive in all the best work that they've done right down the line. It was certainly alive in the Elevation tour: here's the pure U2. All of their songs can stand next to each other in succession with no trimmings, with the bare stage, with the band walking out in the house lights, and still give you a transcendent experience.

U2 were the first to come up with the B stage on the Zoo tour, the idea of a small satellite stage where they could go out and play an intimate performance after all the hoopla. This kind of staging was immediately adapted by a lot of people – most notably The Rolling Stones, who've done it on every tour since. I remember seeing Mick Jagger in U2 shows paying close attention to the B stage during the Zoo tour.

These days, the tour business is bigger than the record business, and it'll be interesting to see if that turns out to be a good business for U2 in the long run. Touring is extremely unpredictable. It is an interesting moment. And certainly U2 made some very tough decisions before the PopMart tour about cutting their ties with the people they'd always worked with. I think that the biggest problem of all with making PopMart work was that U2 set contradictory goals for themselves. They wanted to do a tour that would be even bigger that ZooTV and Zooropa, more elaborate. They didn't want to be seen as 'Now we're going back to our roots.' They were very, very resistant to that. They also wanted to come home having made some money this time. But they didn't want ticket prices to be nearly as high as comparable bands were charging or to accept corporate sponsorship. When you put all those things together the math doesn't add up. You can probably do two out of three of those things, but you can't do all three. They wouldn't compromise on any of it, and therefore there was probably trouble waiting to happen no matter what had happened with the album or anything else.

The four members of U2 and Paul McGuinness are a sort of fist – four fingers and a thumb – and that's always been at the core of their operation. It seems unlikely to me that anyone new could come along and become part of that core. But at the same time, I don't know another circumstance where 25 years on an immensely successful four-member band has maintained its four members without a change and its original manager. That's very, very, very unusual. Maybe U2 is the only case of that happening. And I think as long as that group stays together, then however much the window dressing changes, U2 will remain the band they were in the beginning.

New York, November 2003

Audience at Zooropa show, Wembley Stadium, London, 1993

Tom Freston

Chairman and CEO, MTV Networks

U2 and I both started out around the same time. We at MTV got the first video from U2, 'Gloria', in 1981. U2 became very proficient video artists over the years and we were involved with them on a bunch of levels, including work on the Amnesty tours in 1986, of which U2 were prime movers and organizers. MTV was the television partner, and we had also broadcast Live Aid. We plugged the Amnesty concert as it toured around the country. The mission of Amnesty International was very clear and it was embraced by the greatest musicians of that generation. MTV had been involved in activities promoting Aids awareness, anti-handgun violence, tolerance, all sorts of things, but one of our earliest support efforts was with Amnesty. I was catapulted into the world of U2, Paul McGuinness and Principle Management, which was just head and shoulders above almost any other organization in the music business. There was a great spirit and care among them all. They were on a real mission, but they seemed to have the greatest interpersonal relationships and feelings towards each other.

When MTV started we were pretty much a music video jukebox. Our programming staple was the music video; there was a great novelty to them and they continue to be the cornerstone of everything we've done. In the late 1980s that formula got a bit stale and we wanted to change ourselves and show that we could do other things. We can produce longer-form programming, not just about the music but about movies, fashion, political issues, and try and keep the channel more interesting. It's a challenge. We have decided not to age with our audience so you always go after teens, young adults, and we've seen a lot of bands sort of pass through us. U2 has been like the consistent player.

Live performances are a lot trickier to do on television than videos. To have a massively successful concert on television has been a difficult undertaking except for the biggest acts. That's not to say that it cannot be successful. Bands like U2 have always looked at how they can use a medium more innovatively. The greatest ideas that we've done with U2 have largely come from them. Paul and the band are very media savvy and are always looking to be seen as innovators. We've always tried to get them to do an 'Unplugged', for example, but U2 will tend to resist something that one would regularly do for anybody.

As a band, U2 loves to tour. Their audience loves to see them. You can look at Jimmy Buffet and The Rolling Stones – they still fill up stadiums and venues – but U2 are still doing it with great new material. You can't find many bands that are producing their best material in their 40s. Most bands have peaked by the time they are in their mid-20s or 30s. U2 are more creatively vital than they have ever been. They are very aware of what goes on in the world. They're incredibly talented and between them they have this unique energy. Their audience loves the fact that the four of them are still together after all these years. That's really something special. On their last tour, all they had to do was walk out into the crowd and they got a standing ovation. A U2 show is like a religious experience. When they played here in New York after 9/11, that was the first night I slept. I thought, 'Wow, I'm gonna get a good night's sleep tonight because I gave it all at that show.' They give audiences love and hope. It sounds really corny, but all those things that you want an artist to do, they were able to do it all and do it with a smile and a sense of humour.

New York, January 2004

U2 pay tribute to the victims of 9/11, Madison Square Garden, NYC, October 2001

Ian Wilson
Radio producer, 2FM Dublin

I remember meeting Bono in 1978. He was asking me about this guy Paul McGuinness, 'You know him, don't you? What do you reckon?' I said, 'Well, he is a very sharp operator, Paul. Just go into it with your eyes open, don't be fooled by any bullshit, but he'll do a good job for you all right. He's a smart man, but don't be too naive about it boys.' Dave Fanning, who was on the pirate stations at the time, really started picking up on new Irish music and started playing it. One of these bands was U2. They had just recorded their first demo and he was playing it and supporting the band. Then McGuinness rings me out of the blue and he says, 'We're going to do a single. We're not sure what to put on the A side.' We came to an arrangement: over the week, we played three songs, and we asked the listeners to send us in a postcard, and a week later we'd say which was to be the A side and which was to be on the B side. So we plugged it and the people voted. The band came in and we said, 'Right. Here they are the votes. They have actually chosen "Out of Control".' The single came out and it was a big hit in Ireland.

Dave Fanning and I gave disproportionate airplay to the band at the time. I just decided it was better to latch on to a couple of artists, pin our reputations on some new Irish acts. There were a number of other acts we supported, people in the North like the Out Casts who were really extreme punk. U2 were one of the first bands to realize the potential of radio, particularly in the South. They realized from the pirate stations that radio play was important, and they were very careful to work with our station. When our station, Radio 2, started it wiped out the pirates because it was new. We had a comprehensive range of programmes and we did a lot of new Irish music.

U2 are funny in a way in that they are Irish, but they are not. They are based in Ireland, but they are quite a mixture of cultures. Larry is very north Dublin, more working class, Catholic, down to earth, speaks with that kind of accent. Bono is from a mixed marriage, Protestant and Catholic, again north Dublin. The Edge is Welsh originally, and his family would have a more Welsh church kind of background, a chapel background. Then on the other hand you've got Adam who is pure Brit, so he's good English Protestant stock. You've got quite a mixture. In terms of Irish, they are a real mish-mash of influences which made them very different over the years. They were not identifiably middle class, they were not identifiably Catholic or Protestant, they were a different culture than most of the other bands in Ireland. One of the things about them was their impeccable loyalty.

There are very serious musicians in the band. The Edge is a very serious musician, Larry is a very serious drummer. The others weren't at all trained musicians, they were self-taught. A lot of the country at the time didn't like them and they had this slight problem that they weren't hard core enough, they weren't working class enough, they weren't Catholic enough. But they were extremely ambitious, particularly Bono and Adam. They were very driven and their ambition marked them out from the other bands.
Dublin, December 2003

Dave Fanning
Radio presenter, 2FM Dublin

In Ireland people often say that three things started all around the same time: U2, *Hot Press* and 2FM, or Radio 2 as it was called then. And they changed the face of the whole thing. U2 were helped big-time by radio. From the very beginning, in May 1979, myself and Ian Wilson worked together. We really just did all the stuff that we wanted to do, and we were away from any play list and any interference.

1978 was the first I'd probably heard of U2 and I got involved because I played their demo tapes, and they were one of those bands that I was trying to help along. I was very much involved in any gigs they might have done. Looking back it's very easy to say, 'Oh, we all knew Bono had it.' No, we didn't. But we certainly knew he was a bit more of a chancer, which is what was needed. When I met them as guys, I really liked them.

I went on the War tour. Mother of God, the War tour was four dates in Ireland! Anyway, we did Belfast, Galway, Cork and Dublin. Album number three was about to be released. I remember on the bus being asked which song I thought should be the single. I said 'Sunday Bloody Sunday' which subsequently became quite a big one for them. But 'New Year's Day' became the single and that was the biggest thing. That was the first song that went straight to number one for U2. In Belfast I remember they were really freaking out at the thought of playing 'Sunday Bloody Sunday'. The reason would be: 'Who's this little pup from middle-class Dublin coming up to Belfast telling us how to live our lives?' I remember McGuinness freaking out about it because he was standing on the balcony and I was near him. He was very pleased there was a huge cheer at the end of it. It went down absolutely fine. Most people who go to a gig, they're not there with machetes and guns, they just want to have a laugh.

It wasn't exactly a massive overnight thing like it is with a million bands. It did actually take its time. It's phenomenal how they've stayed together, and they've never replaced a musician or anything. They really are very together and very down to earth and very capable of being just very good friends and very ordinary. Remember, they grew up together at school. Those kinds of roots are really very important.
Dublin, February 2004

Charity Shows

Ian Flooks
Agent, world outside US, 1982–1997

Around the time of *Rattle and Hum* I was approached by the head of Greenpeace, David McTaggart. He wanted U2 and most of my other bands to play a concert in Moscow to raise money for Greenpeace to start up in Russia, or the Soviet Union, as it was then. Gorbachev was in power. It was 1988. This was two years after Chernobyl and Greenpeace were hoping to start some sort of grassroots environmental movement there. I told McTaggart that it would be pointless to do a concert because tickets would be paid for in rubles and they'd have to pay all of U2's costs and every other band's costs in dollars. They'd lose money. Instead I suggested that they put out an album in the Soviet Union, because no rock albums from the West had ever been released there. But it would be hard to get permission to do that. Sony, EMI and Warner Brothers had been able to release maybe 10,000 copies of a Beatles album at one time, and they probably all went to the politicians, kids. But he came back and said, 'Okay. It's a done deal. We're going to Moscow next week.' So we went to Moscow, met with the head of the state record label, Melodiya, who had obviously been told by Gorbachev that he was to do whatever we wanted. We did a deal. They agreed to produce five million records and give all the proceeds to Greenpeace. And David of course said, 'Well, it was your idea. You have to do it.' So I had six Greenpeace people in my office for two years, and this project took over my life.

The first person I knew I had to go to was Bono. When I came back from Moscow I was on this real high and I went to see them. I

was hoping that they'd give me a track from the last album or something like that, then I could start the whole ball rolling. I hadn't approached any other artists yet. So I went into the studio and Bono was mixing a live version of 'Pride'. I told him the idea and he said, 'You can have that track.' And Paul said, 'Well, we haven't released it yet.' And Bono said, 'That's the track we're putting on.' The net result was that everybody else piled in. All the record companies and the publishing companies gave the tracks for free. In the end, Greenpeace ended up making about $20 million and it started Greenpeace in Russia, where it is now a powerful organization. I took Annie Lennox, Chrissie Hynde, The Edge, Peter Gabriel to the launch. It was the main item on the national news in the UK that day. We had to take our own sandwiches because there was no catering there. I took two hampers on the plane and everyone came around to my room in Moscow for food. It was great fun and the beginning of a strong relationship with Greenpeace. The record was launched and sold out within a day. People queued all night outside the record stores. It was the first Western rock album ever to be released in the Soviet Union. Then it was released worldwide and Greenpeace made a lot of money from it. It was an amazing project. There were about 30 artists in all.

I was asked to be on the Board of Greenpeace and stayed on for about 12 years. U2 then got involved in the Greenpeace campaign to stop the opening of a new reprocessing facility at Sellafield called Thorpe. U2 are strongly opposed to Sellafield. The radioactive discharges from Sellafield wash up on beaches in Ireland. It's outrageous. We did a concert at G-mex in Manchester with U2, UB40, Kraftwerk and The Pretenders. We really wanted to do a concert outside the gates of Sellafield. It was a great concept and Bono was very keen to do it, but then Sellafield got injunctions to stop us. So we had the concert at G-mex instead. We organized an action on the day after the concert. Greenpeace sent one of its ships and took the band to the beach in front of the plant. It's highly radioactive on the beach, a dangerous place to be. They had to wear protective suits. The pictures went around the world. Live Aid was incredible but I think in many ways this Sellafield gig was one of the most effective pieces of political campaigning U2 ever undertook. It was a huge success on every level.

I used to get 10 or 20 applications a week for U2 to do some charity event or other. For every one they agreed to do, a few hundred would be rejected. The band had a very interesting view on these things. They wanted to be what they called 'the silver bullet', which meant that their participation would have to make a sizeable shift in the way that something would happen. They realized that if they went and did every political campaign or every charity, in the end it would just be like, 'Oh, yeah. They're here again. So what?' They realized that their political capital had to be used carefully. And I think that the Sellafield thing was a prime example of using it with great care to great effect. And it was not an easy thing to do.

Bono addresses the crowd during another defining moment – Live Aid, 1985

There were a lot of meetings where it was debated long and hard as to whether they should be doing this. They could have got six months in jail. The high courts don't take kindly to people breaking injunctions.

Bono is an extraordinary person, and he is an astute operator in this field. You only have to look at his work with debt relief. If you're a rock star you can get entangled in lots of issues. But he's smart enough to be able to deal with it and has a calm approach, a more measured approach than others who have done the same thing.

London, September 2003

Jack Healey

Former director of Amnesty International; Conspiracy of Hope

As soon as I became director of Amnesty USA, in 1981, I approached Bill Graham about doing a concert tour in the US. He said, 'Go get the talent and I will do the show.' For all kinds of reasons, though, it didn't happen straight away.

In the summer of 1985, I wired Paul McGuinness and told him I would be in Dublin on my way to an Amnesty meeting in Finland. We met and within eight minutes we had an agreement for U2 to headline the Amnesty tour. Minutes later, literally, I was back in my cab, flew to Finland and told Amnesty of what was to come. No one believed me until I called Bill Graham, and that was enough to make it all go ahead.

Bono recruited Peter Gabriel for the tour. Gil Friesen, of A&M Records, and I recruited Bryan Adams. I recruited Sting over lunch at his apartment. Bill Graham got the Neville Brothers, Joan Baez and others for Los Angeles, including Bob Dylan, Bob Geldof and Dave Stewart. Bill recruited the talent for the big closing show in Giants Stadium, including Miles Davis, Pete Townshend, Joni Mitchell, Howard Jones and others. Speakers were Mohammed Ali, Dick Gregory, Robert De Niro and some other movie people.

When I saw the four guys of U2 on the street in San Francisco the day before the Conspiracy of Hope tour, I followed them down the street. They were not well known then. Bono stopped and asked a young Latino, 'Did you ever hear of Amnesty International?' The answer came, 'Yes, I am alive because of that group.' I think that moment froze the whole band into a brighter light that has lasted.

Special moments on the tour included Bono climbing the musical equipment as a blind man to show the vulnerability of a prisoner of conscience. And he danced an Irish jig with me around the Los Angeles stage to show the unity between his band and Amnesty. They've kept their word ever since. The dance did work! Amnesty International was defined in the USA by this tour. We raised over $3 million and got 45,000 new members at $25 a head within six weeks. We became a household name and the charity of choice. The tour changed American youth, because now there are chapters in colleges and high schools all over the USA.

We human rights people need to understand that anything legal should be used – from pork chops to music to letters to

marches – to stop governmental policies of torture and disappearances. But stop them we must. My personal answer to what I have done with anything in music is to say that the decent need to stop the indecent. I wanted to answer the question 'What can I do?' with a strong and clear message of 'Get busy.' The musicians are the best carriers of that message.

Music, especially rock, is the magical newspaper. Governments cannot stop it; it crosses borders without passports. Through music, our voices become thunder, our candles become bonfires and our spirits and letters ride the wind to victory over so much oppression. It is the least we can do.

Camus spoke of those who receive the lash and those who count the lash. That contract, that relationship, was kept by these tours and told the tale of what Amnesty and other human rights groups were doing to 'count the lash'. The Conspiracy of Hope tour, and others like it, are a symbol of respect between artists and victims. They speak to the victims. They are for them.

Washington, DC, February 2004

Conspiracy of Hope press conference, June 1986. Left to right: Joan Baez, Sting, Bono, The Edge, Lou Reed

Peter Gabriel

Musician, Conspiracy of Hope

Peter Gabriel performing on Conspiracy of Hope tour

What was your involvement in the Amnesty International Conspiracy of Hope tour?

For the 1986 tour it was Bono who contacted me. I had been marginally involved with Amnesty at that point in time, but I'd never done concerts for them, only sort of odd issues. That was definitely part of a process that involved me in human rights. Meeting a lot of the people who had suffered was the inspiration for trying to do something on a bigger scale for the 1988 Human Rights Now! worldwide tour.

Back in 1986, did Conspiracy of Hope break new ground? Do you recall any other instances of people actually touring for charity? Presumably Live Aid paved the way for an international platform and awareness for charity shows.

I don't remember anyone else touring on a charitable front. I think it was more individual shows. And I don't know actually whether they made money, or much money, for Amnesty at the time. Certainly I think it helped raise awareness, and create a climate in which the 1988 tour was possible. The 1988 tour doubled Amnesty's membership. So I think 1986 was as important for opening the doors for 1988 as for what it achieved in itself, which I think was still very helpful. And, for instance, issues like the death penalty, which was extremely unpopular in America, were put back on the discussion platform.

A good indicator of its effectiveness. So, your involvement really was sparked by the Conspiracy of Hope tour?

Yeah. You can trace it back to Bono's hustling capabilities!

Do you have any recollections about the organization of that tour, specifically of Bill Graham and his involvement?

Well, Bill Graham had always been this legendary figure, and it was only through these Amnesty tours that I actually got to know him and really like him. But there were conflicts beginning to surface on the 1986 tour that sort of blossomed on the 1988 tour, between rock managers on Bill Graham's side and the Amnesty side. I mean, it was full of positive idealism, but at the same time not always realistic.

Some individuals, I think, were quite enjoying the sort of excitement of mingling with the names and so it was complicated. All of these charity shows are often marriages of aims and goals. There were some cynics in my camp who tried in some ways not to have me involved with that tour, thinking it was sort of a part of U2 building blocks in the States. But I've always felt that U2 were sincere about what they were doing, and felt very glad to be a part of it.

Bill Graham was absolutely essential in both the 1986 and 1988 tours. I think he was tough and difficult often, but with a big heart. He would sort of try and cut through the bullshit.

I remember when I was hustling everyone I could – I was probably a little less skilled than Bono – for the 1988 tour, and we got Sting in, we got Tracey Chapman. And I said, 'Surely, Bill, we've enough here to go?' and he said, 'Peter, you've given me a plate full of vegetables – now go get the meat!' And that, then, was Springsteen. So I went out to see him. Bill and Jack Healey often had conflicts, but Jack was really inspirational on the 1986 tour,

and he was a great public speaker, a motivator. He's a wonderful man. Mary Daley was the other person. They both worked incredibly hard to get both tours together. Jack is also this sort rabble-rousing preacher, in part, and I think there's probably some seminary link there. He is able to persuade people, much in the same way Bono can, to do things they wouldn't normally do. Amnesty in the US weren't in favour of the rock and roll excursions. They were a bit worried about things being trivialized or sensationalized, and I think he had a real uphill battle. And again, particularly, on the 1988 tour. Both the 1986 and 1988 were, I think, for everyone involved, really powerful experiences, life-changing experiences in the sense that it was an education. We ended up doing these press conferences everyplace and you got all sorts of questions fired at you.

What opportunities are there now, in the current climate, for charity shows?

Well, I think both Bono and I are involved in this Mandela thing at the moment [20 October '03]. Unfortunately it's a currency that can be depleted. The more times your face appears alongside different causes, the less value in some ways you are to that cause. So I think you have to do it carefully and sparingly, and it's probably better for artists to choose which things they most identify with and sort of home in on one cause. And without question you'll be greeted with huge dollops of cynicism. I think it's much better now if they can have a twist, and I think Dave Stewart's idea on this Mandela thing of the phone number that you listen to music on … Instead of giving all the money to the phone company it's going to a charitable cause. That's a smart innovation, and I think we need more of those.

Sting, I think, used to say, 'No act of charity goes unpunished.' And there's a lot of evidence to support that. Rock musicians aren't going to transform the world, but you can introduce subjects to people and you can give them some basic information and emotion through music, which they can then sort of supplement with the TV news or books or magazines. If they feel there's something there that they might want to learn more about, you've done some useful job. And without question, seeing it from the other side, when we've been working with different human rights things since then, it's so much easier to get media coverage with some familiar faces attached. So I'm sure that's gonna continue to be vital. But the actual benefit gig itself, I think, does need looking at.

Record companies and TV companies and the media, as well as the consumers, are pretty tired of being tapped for one cause or another. Once a record company has put out five or ten records where they're not expected to make any profit, their social concern – particularly now in a struggling music business – tends to drift, and similarly with TV. Live Aid had huge viewing audiences; some of the other benefit shows since then haven't. So it's a currency you need to spend wisely.

London, October 2003

Steven Van Zandt

Musician, Conspiracy of Hope

How did it all start? How did you first make contact with U2?
Well, as I recall – and believe me, my memory is a little weird –
it was our [the E Street Band's] first trip to Europe. I mean, we'd
gone briefly in 1975, but in 1980 the River tour was the first time
we really spent time over there. We were very excited about being
there and we would go out to clubs and see what we could see.
I think at this point Frank Barsalona had already made contact and
signed U2. I think he was a bit concerned about the whole thing
because there was no such thing as an Irish rock band.
Van Morrison was somewhere in the background.
Well, he was Van Morrison. His band, Them, didn't make it unfortunately. So there really had been no precedent for an Irish rock
band, exactly. So Frank, I think, was looking to hedge his bets a bit,
him being the smartest and best agent in the world. He called
Bruce [Springsteen], I guess, and told Bruce, 'Go down and see
the boys and if you dig 'em and you like what they're doing maybe
get on stage with them.' And this would help, 'cos we were very hot
at the time. We were just breaking, really. It would get crazy with
Born in the USA four years later. But at this point we broke, we had
our first hit, 'Hungry Heart', and we were selling out arenas everywhere. So Frank figured the association of Bruce hanging out with
U2, that word got back to the States, it would help when U2 came
over for their tour.
And Bruce was happy to do this?
Yeah. So we're out, and we went our separate ways, and the next
day we were talking, and he was like, 'Who did you see?' And I
said, 'I saw a group called U something.' And he said, 'Well, so did
I, but I didn't see you there.' And it turns out he was talking about
U2 and I'd seen UB40.
You don't recall what Bruce said about them at the time?
He said they were great. A good new band. We didn't go into any
great detail about it. But I think Frank's strategy worked, because
by the time U2 came over there was already a vibe going on. And
then I went to see them at their first gig at the Ritz. There was a
good reaction right away, it seemed to me. New York is a bit tough.
*So you were doing your own thing at that time with Bruce ... And
there was no sort of parallel with U2.*
Well, *The River* was the first record I produced and then *Born in
the USA* and then I left. I left in 1982 and started making my own
records. Then I got into the whole political thing.
So you were right at the forefront of that.
Yes. In fact I made it a point: I decided to dedicate my work to politics exclusively, which no one had ever done. We were on tour in
Europe, that same tour, the River, and a kid came up to me in
Germany and said, 'Why are you putting missiles in my country?' I
said, 'Excuse me, but I'm the guitar player in the band. I'm not putting missiles anywhere.' And that stayed with me. And it just bothered me for weeks, because it never occurred to me that I was an
American citizen. I was complete tunnel-vision rock and roll, my
whole life. This was the first sort of, you know, 'Wow. These people
over here, these foreigners, look at us very differently.' We're not
lawyers and guitar players or democrats and republicans; we are

Americans. Honestly, until then it never occurred to me that I was
an American citizen and maybe had some responsibilities or
obligations that went with that. So I thought to myself, 'We're a
democracy, supposedly; therefore if my government does something I am ostensibly responsible as a citizen, right, of a democracy. So therefore I am putting missiles in his country. My God, what
else am I doing?' So I began to study United States foreign policy,
from World War II on, and was quite shocked at what I learned.
Growing up with this impression that we were the stalwarts, we
were the leaders and the good guys, in terms of democracy around
the world. And I found out quite the contrary: we were supporting
every fascist on the planet, and doing very little for democracy in
fact. So it was quite a shock.
*It rocks your world when you think about every school in the coun-
try teaching every child in the country what you've been taught –
and not to question, just to accept.*
And it was all a lie. At the same time we were successful for the
first time in my life. It took me from the age of 15 to the age of 30
to have our first success. Those 15 years were nothing but rock
and roll, fighting for it your whole life until all of a sudden you're on
the top of the mountain. Well the tunnel just starts to fade away.
You start looking around. So that was the second thing. And the
third thing was the incredible feeling, when you go to Europe for the
first time and go to different countries and they're all singing your
lyrics word for word, even though they don't speak English necessarily. That was quite a shock to witness. It was this enormously
profound feeling of direct communication coming from rock and
roll. And I thought, 'Wow. This is too important a medium to simply
be used for escapist entertainment. We have the ability to communicate directly to citizens around the entire world, without going
through our government.' Well, that was a revelation. And I decided
I can't live with this, I must talk about this. I felt like a German
citizen in the 1920s or 1930s. Instead of watching Jews being
killed, or harassed, I was watching it in Latin America. All through
virtually every single country of Latin America was a horror show of
absolute murder. It was a slaughterhouse being accommodated by
our tax dollars. So I made a list of, like, 40 different wars going on
at the time, and looked at how we were engaged in each of these
wars and decided to start writing about that and talking about that.

In 1984 I went to Nicaragua to stop the war; we were about to
invade Nicaragua, so we went to stop it and we did stop it. Then I
made trips to South Africa in 1984, and while I was there I wrote
the record that I would take 'Sun City' from, called *Freedom No
Compromise*. I also had a song on there about hunger, which
talked about the governments in Africa that were causing people to
starve to death. And then Geldof did the Christmas thing.
Did you connect with Geldof at all?
Not then. Later.
*It's interesting. There were all these independent threads.
Different people coming in at the same ...*
Yeah. Yeah. It was a holocaust – I mean, we were killing hundreds
of thousands of civilians, hundreds of thousands in Latin America.
In parts of Africa as well. Once you looked at all the different things
we were involved in with our foreign policy, it was all bad. I mean,
under this ridiculous phoney war against communism, we were

Steven van Zandt
at a sound desk, Artists
Against Apartheid Sun
City recording sessions

justifying murder. Absolute murder. The old we-need-to-burn-the-village-to-save-it thing. And nobody questioned anything. I realized that the only way to stop this stuff is to expose it. So I dealt with many different things at the same time, with Haiti, the Philippines, the southern Morocco war, a lot of things. All the Latin American stuff and South Africa. I spent some time in Algeria, looking at that war, another bad war in which we were supporting the bad guys. It was endless. You could go anywhere and find that we were on the wrong side of the war. It was incredible. But the Nicaraguan thing, I got in pretty deep there. We did a good job there in terms of saving what would have been thousands of lives if the US forces had invaded. So we were able to strategize a way to stop that war. And then I got very, very much into the South Africa thing because it was the one issue that was completely invisible at the time in America. Maybe not so much in England. You couldn't find a book about it here.

The 'Sun City' record, about that whole anti-apartheid thing, was 1985, even into 1986, I think. But the trips I made were pretty much all in 1984. I just happened to go there only because I had never witnessed slavery before that close up. And it was so shocking. But I'm sure the entire anti-apartheid movement saved a lot of lives. The day Mandela got out of jail was just a miracle. You never thought you'd see that. It was like the Berlin Wall coming down. It was like, 'Am I seeing this? In my lifetime?' You get those little victories that keep you going.

What was your objective in getting people to talk?
To learn about what was going on. All my political activity at first was research for the music that I was writing. I didn't mean to get sucked into the actual issues, which I did. I met with dozens and dozens and dozens of groups. I got almost an anxiety breakdown, almost like a nervous breakdown just from seeing the horrors of it all. The little things: you'd be in a taxi and a black guy would step off the kerb and the taxi would try to hit them. You know, just for sport. Something like that happened every 15 minutes. It was an absolute shock to the system until I finally collapsed, because I'm trying to be an objective journalist here at this point. I'm trying to combine journalism and art here, you know, into this new hybrid.

You were devoting a lot of time and energy into translating your feelings, beliefs and discoveries into your own music.
Yeah. I was doing it for me first. I was learning about myself first. Second, I was learning about what goes on in the world. Then you translate that stuff into your music, which is a personal thing, and I knew it was a personal thing. It was intentionally a personal thing, and not a career per se.

Did you have any trouble bringing anybody on board for the 'Sun City' record?
Only a couple of people said no. I wanted one person from every genre of music: a rock guy, a country guy, a jazz guy, you know, and it just sort of grew on its own. It wasn't like the very organized Geldof thing or Quincy Jones thing. For my thing, people would come in at three o'clock in the morning, different people at different times. I would have them usually sing the whole song and then we had to sort it out later. I ended up with 14 reels of 24 tracks, and I had to make a song out of that! Yeah, everything's easy after that.

What about the Amnesty tour?
Bob Geldof and I did a song together. I was involved early on with Amnesty International. When I started doing research it was Amnesty and Greenpeace and the Human Rights Watch, three or four organizations which I was in contact with before that tour. Before I even started fund-raising, I was using them for information and I would have them in the lobby of my shows; I would have them there with tables with information. I also recommended organizations on my album covers and books to read and things like that. You know, all my friends tried to talk me out of this stuff, saying, 'You're ending whatever hope for a career you're ever gonna have!' And I just felt I had to be extreme. I literally didn't write a love song for ten years. I mean, I wrote nothing but political music for five albums. I was completely obsessed. I was insane for a while. I went to war zones and I did crazy, crazy things. I didn't care about anything. As much as I supported the big events, I thought to myself, 'This is not the way it should be, where we just do these big events. Do the little ones, get involved in your community, you know,' I would recommend to people. You don't have to be a big band, just clean up your neighbourhood. Just get involved. Make political involvement a normal part of your day. Do something. Give a little something back.

And so you were approaching other artists about this?
Yes. Make this a normal part of our lives because, you know, it was not such a normal part of our lives that I got blackballed by the industry. They're like, 'He just brought down the South African government – who's next?!' And the corporations, of course, wouldn't put the record out because the South African record companies corporately were saying, 'Stop that record.' When I finally got it out, after everybody passed, I got to the last possible option. When people used to come up to me and talk about politics, I would say, 'Be careful about these things.' In other words, 'I want politics to be a normal part of your day, but you don't have to sacrifice your career for it.' I don't believe in that any more, because the more successful you are the more effective you can be. I discovered that really too late. I got more done than I should have been able to get done in my position. I wasn't really successful at anything, really. I felt successful because of Bruce Springsteen's success.

Can we talk a little about U2 now and your feelings about what they were doing at the same time?
It was very important. I didn't really know they were doing this stuff, really, until the mid-1980s. After that, Bono just really kind of came out, you know, he was a bit quiet until then. Can you imagine? He was a quiet individual back then. And U2 were weird at first for people in the States because there was a rumour that they were a Christian band. I never really talked to them about it, but they had to overcome that, which must have been difficult. When they raised their white flag, or whatever, people wondered, 'Are they proselytizing? Is it a Christian thing? Are they selling that? Or is it a human rights thing?' Which, in the best of all worlds, is the same thing.

And they weren't speaking so publicly. They were only trying to make their way as a young band. It wasn't as though Bono was where he is today and everyone knew what he was saying.

By the time of *War*, it was like, 'Well, it's an Irish thing.' You know what I mean? 'Cos that's how Americans are; we have to categorize. 'Oh, I see – it's not really a Christian thing, it's an Irish thing. Well, we can dig that. So that's okay.' But I just liked them right away, personally.

You supported them on the Joshua Tree tour, you and your band.

Oh, yeah! That's right. That wasn't so much a philosophical thing.

Was it a Frank Barsalona thing?

Yeah. Frank was completely disgusted with me. You know, because I did all this work, worked my whole life to make this band a success, Bruce Springsteen and the E Street Band, and the minute we're successful I leave. So he was just completely pissed of, you know, and just felt obligated to get me a few gigs here. There weren't many, though. There weren't many. I was going around with an 11-piece band for a while.

In the 17 years since you did 'Sun City', how do you think the industry's changed?

I couldn't have done the South African thing now. No way. Because it's 'form your wagons in a circle' time here. Record companies have their own problems now. They can't possibly be concerned with other problems. It's partly why we got away with the whole Iraq thing, you know. You now have two-people households working absolutely full time just to try and come close to breaking even. And really we don't break even because we're in debt. Just to show you, at my age, I remember in the late 1960s it was an absolute given that we were gonna go to a four-day work week. There was no question. It was only a matter of when. Next year? The year after? Four-day work week. And this was with one person working in the household. Okay? Now you've got two people working six days a week, and can't make ends meet. That's how much the dollar has become worthless. We were gonna go to the four-day work week. That was gonna be progress, and it would have been, absolutely.

So, as far as concerts are concerned...

They're still gonna happen. I'm very proud of that fact. As much as I criticize the music business – you know, I used to criticize everything, constantly – I'm very proud of the fact that we have supported more issues, more charitable causes, than any other business. You don't see the oil business doing these kinds of things. They can afford it a lot better than we can. We're not that big a business. You don't see the automobile industry doing these things.

How do you feel about being an American these days?

Well, I've always felt very proud of the idea of America, and I always felt it was a work in progress. We're the only country that will ever exist built on ideas. And it's an idea that has not quite been fulfilled yet, but a great idea. And I am very, very, very patriotic about that. And I criticize my government when I feel it is not living up to those ideals. By this point we should be further along. There shouldn't be any prejudice. There shouldn't be unequal opportunities.

What advice would you give to the next generation?

Get very rich and famous, and then start thinking. But, on your way up, do what you can do in your neighbourhood. Don't bring any attention to yourself in the big picture politically until you're quite rich and famous.

Otherwise ...?

You'll never get there. And you can do a lot more when you're rich and famous than when you're not. A lot more.

New York, November 2003

Friends

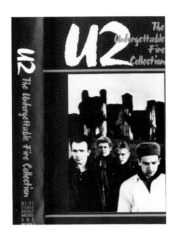

The Unforgettable Fire
Collection *directed by Barry
Devlin in 1985*

Barry Devlin

Video director, screenwriter

Before U2, before Horslips, even, if you were an Irish band and you got to the top of the greasy pole here, you went to England, you lived in a basement eating cornflakes for two years and Decca signed you and put out one album and that was the end of you. Horslips weren't having that. We formed our own record company and we put out our own records. We had the fastest-selling album in Ireland, *Happy to Meet,* until, I think, *The Joshua Tree.* Our manager Michael Deeny was a good friend of Paul McGuinness. They had met in 1971 when Paul was still at Trinity. They worked together for a while as Headland Promotions and together they put on our first festival gig in Dublin. Michael ended up managing Horslips, but Paul always had that little hankering and in 1975/6 he started managing a folk-rock band, Spud.

When Paul came to me in 1978 and said, 'I'm thinking of managing another band', I said, 'You're crazy, I beseech you don't do this. Punk is over, there's about a year left in it.' He said, 'Well, I don't agree with you. I think these guys are very good.' Paul asked me if I'd go into the studio with them, so I agreed. After I came out of the studio I told him: 'Two things: (1) you have to get a proper producer; and (2) You have to mortgage the house.' I'd been in a band. I knew what made bands tick. What defines great bands is the kind of glue between members. There has to be a degree of compatibility, a degree of imagination, but most of all there's their own sense of where they can go together as a unit. That was the single thing that I saw uniquely in them, and I was right. U2 have the same four people in the band that started out back then. No one ever, in the history of the world, has ever done that before. It just hasn't happened. These guys had 'Great Group' written all over them. They were striped like zebras. I really did believe they were remarkable. I was very public about it and I wouldn't have said it if I didn't believe it.

They knew a great deal about what they wanted to do, musically. I mean, before Edge, all guitarists based their riffs around the blues; everybody wanted to be a blues man. But The Edge had this jangle thing, and since then that's what guitar is. In the studio the line of communication was quite clear. Bono could tell Edge what he wanted to do and Edge knew what he meant. What Bono wants is very important, but Bono couldn't do what he wants without Edge to translate it. Separately they're great. Together they're unbeatable.

As a director I worked with them quite a bit in the early years. In 1984 Declan Quinn and I filmed *The Making of the Unforgettable Fire*, the mini-documentary about the making of the album, set in Slane Castle and in Windmill Lane Studios. We cut a video out of that for 'Pride', and the band loved it. It was quite an interesting piece and it was also pretty flattering to them. But they didn't make it easy. They'd agree that I would work all day with them, but then they'd decide they didn't want a crew in the studio so they'd put up a sign saying 'No Entry'. Consequently – it's pathetic – a lot of the stuff is actually shot through glass. People go, 'What a fantastic idea to shoot through the glass so that you're together but you're subtly divided. It's a metaphor, isn't it?' And I'm going, 'Yeah! Metaphor. Definitely.' In fact it was because the bastards wouldn't let me into the studio.

For their shows they've always managed to do the complex without doing the complicated, so their shows were always right for the material. I got involved in a kind of dialectic about what *Achtung Baby* meant, out of which came ZooTV, the greatest, smartest, most ironic touring show that there's ever been. That's an example of how they have always made the stage show correspond to the kind of music on the album. The Joshua Tree show was like a lantern show in a way, which was appropriate, I think, for the feel of the music; those stirring, timeless anthems like 'I Still Haven't Found What I'm Looking For' and 'Streets'.

They're a great band to talk about, because their practice always matches the theory terribly well; but don't try telling them what to do unless you can demonstrate that you know something they don't. U2 inherited a world where bands were given creative control. Groups by and large have an attention span of 38 seconds, and so when they go into meetings, they tend to look at stuff and go, 'Yeah, great, my head hurts now, I think I'll go and have something to drink.' Which is fine. Record companies are quite happy with that kind of control. Not so with U2. No one has ever filibustered them. Ever. Guys come in and they go, 'We'll soon get this passed', and 24 hours later, they've bags under their eyes and the lads are still going, 'Show us that again there ...' Whatever grisly technical detail they need to know – and some that they don't – they'll find out how the process works and tell you how to do it better. They're a bit scary that way, very bright, very focused. Bono's incredibly focused; he genuinely has a commitment to perfection and the detail; he really works at it.

U2 always adhered to a very simple principle, which is: they know what U2 is better than anyone else. They are an extraordinary phenomenon – style and substance, both together. And to their eternal credit, after the experience of PopMart they went, 'No, no, no. For better or worse, nobody knows who we are but us.' And what did they do? They made their best album in ten years! They work very, very hard and they're rather wise. You never find any of them acting in a film. They do one thing. They are U2 and they are the custodians of that. And they love it.
Dublin, February 2004

Dave Kavanagh

U2's first agent, Ireland

I had been the entertainment officer in University College, Dublin and I had been booking gigs there. Paul was working with Spud, the band he managed prior to U2. We worked together for a number of years. My first memory of U2 was Adam Clayton turning up at Paul's door with a tape, and we did one of those, 'We're very busy, can you just leave it on the table?' type of things. We listened to the tape on an answering machine and Paul decided fairly quickly that he wanted to manage them. Soon after that he asked me if I would book the band, be their agent. Actually, I was both their agent and their promoter in Dublin, and for a period of about two years – 1978/9, the period leading up to the recording of *Boy* – I booked the band out in Ireland doing whatever number of gigs they did. This was at the stage when they were attempting to get a record deal, which they were finding increasingly difficult. At least six or seven record companies saw the band and decided they weren't interested.

Compared to a punk band, which at the time was rising in England, they hadn't got that aggression, so if you were looking at The Clash or someone like that in England and then coming to see U2 their music seemed slightly ponderous. They had a very limited amount of material during that period: I think they had eight numbers and repeated 'Out of Control'; they used to start and finish with it! But they were still very, very good live. Record industry people were coming to see them in venues where there weren't that many people in the audience.

We decided to move it out of the pub arena and, in consultation with the band, took on what would have been perceived ludicrous at the time: the National Stadium. It can take about 2000 people and it was the main gig of its day. This decision was based on an extraordinary result in the *Hot Press* Band of the Year poll that year when U2 finished ahead of the Boomtown Rats and Thin Lizzy. I promoted the show for the band. We would have sold around 50 to 60 per cent of the tickets and we Gave away the rest. It was attended by Nick Stewart, the A&R guy at Island Records who was known as the Captain. This was his first time to see the band, and I think it was Bono's idea to take the seats out of the front of the venue, allowing the crowd get close to the stage and create a bit of atmosphere. That night, when they had to deliver, they upped the ante. That ability has been consistent with everything they have done: when they are pushed, they just deliver big-time. That night they were explosive. That was a real momentum change for them. They came off the back of being band of the year, big show, and suddenly they were *the* band. They had a record deal, they were on their way.

They recorded *Boy,* and I did their first tour on the back of the *Boy* album. They played in a very unusual venue called the Television Club, which is no longer there, that held about 1500. We sold out two shows really quickly and they did about eight other shows around the country. They were all packed. There was a real homecoming feel about the whole thing: the band had gone and got substantial reviews in the UK by that stage, and when they came back they were a hot ticket. What struck me when they came back from the UK at the end of the Boy tour and played the Television Club was just how polished they had become and how confident. There was something that they had learnt, having just been away for a short period of time. There is a very famous thing in live music where a band get enough confidence to 'drop the song', where they are able to just drop the song back onto a beat and allow the singer to talk to the audience. This is a thing that's usually associated with hardened bands and takes years to be comfortable with. Well, U2 picked that up really quickly. They were very comfortable live very quickly; that's where they were most at home. When they were able to drop the song, Bono was very good at being able to communicate, and it never seemed corny, which is always that thin line. On the *Boy* album, what I was very pleased about was that they had me ahead of Frank Barsalona [on the sleeve notes]. It was quite a thrill for a young Dublin boy to be on the same list as Frank Barsalona.

I think they could have been born anywhere, but they were born here in Dublin and showed enormous pride in it. Remember they were the first band to stay here, the first band who didn't leave. It was a very personal choice they made: they did stay here and they have significantly contributed to whatever industry has been developed here. They not only developed from a live perspective; they developed themselves, they developed road crews, PA crews, rehearsal rooms, they created a whole mini-industry by staying here, rehearsing here and performing out of here.

I couldn't quantify the absolute contribution they have made to Irish life, forgetting about just the musical aspect to it. I've travelled around the world as Clannad's manager playing gigs in different places, and people would say to me, 'Where are you from?' and I'd go, 'I'm from Ireland.' They'd say, 'Oh, you're the fucking IRA. Aren't you guys over there killing one another?' I remember the significant change which came, that in telling someone where I was from they now said, 'Oh, that's where U2's from.' I thought, 'Jesus, they've passed the fucking IRA in terms of world recognition.' The country suddenly went from being known as a battleground to being the home of U2. That's how important they became, and we got a chance to go out there, be Irish and not just be associated with war. They changed the perception of this country internationally in such a positive way. For that I will always be eternally grateful to them.

Dublin, January 2004

Gavin Friday

Musician

I've known Bono since I was a child, over 30 years, and U2 for maybe 28 years. We even played together sometimes. The first performance by my band The Virgin Prunes was with Guggi, another singer (now a full-time painter), backed by U2 sort of incognito. We then developed our own musicians – one of which was an excellent band called The Hype. Edge's older brother, Dick, became our lead guitarist. One of the very first residencies that U2 had was in Sutton Hotel. They had to play for an hour and a half or two hours, and it was when they were verging on writing originals but still playing a lot of cover versions. Bono used to get tired sometimes, so I used to stand in, sing two or three songs, and then Bono would come back on. There was one song that both bands wrote together, called 'Sad', but it was never recorded. We would play a version of it and U2 would play a version and occasionally Guggi would do vocals with them, and occasionally Bono would do vocals with us. The creative process between us is still intertwined, but much more so. There's no recording I would make or they would make without us throwing our opinions in, because we understand and know each other so well.

When our bands were formed in the late 1970s–early 1980s, from my point of view, what I was doing musically was more con-troversial and avant-garde than straight-up rock and roll. The Virgin Prunes were an avant-garde punk performance band. I was part of the whole punk movement in Dublin. Prior to punk, rock and roll was an elite thing in Ireland. The emphasis was on traditional music and show bands and the only reference to rock and roll, really, was to Van Morrison. With the advent of punk The Radiators from Space and The Boomtown Rats arrived. The young bands of our generation were U2, The Virgin Prunes, The Blades, and it was so hard to get a gig. There were no venues. The country was so conservative.

One of the most open-minded places was across the road: the Project Arts Centre, run by Jim Sheridan, the film director. He was quite open to punk bands playing. The other places were the universities – Trinity College and University College, Dublin. There was one venue called McGonagles, which was infamous as a punk venue, and another, the Dandelion Market, which doesn't exist any more. U2 and Paul McGuinness came up with the idea of doing gigs on Saturdays at the Market. That became quite a legendary U2 show. The Virgin Prunes never played there, though. We were too avant-garde. We'd frighten the locals and I wasn't interested in appealing to the masses.

Before our bands even existed, though, we were all friends. We grew up in the same street, and at the age of 13 and 14 the big love that we had was music, not football, which most teenage boys loved then. We talked about ridiculous things, like we're going to have bands and make movies. Teenage dreams and ambitions. We were very driven kids. When punk came along it did an interesting thing: it gave us the licence to form bands. Before that I had this feeling that you almost needed a degree to form a band. Before punk, music was very mystical: 'Oh look,

Eric Clapton's a genius,' as if the guy was from outer space. But punk rock, that's bare roots, all you need to know is three chords; and for us it was, 'Jesus, we can do this.' We used to share rehearsals and equipment. Best friends becoming bands – a close community. We still have a group of 20 to 30 people who hang out with each other. It's even bigger when you add all the girlfriends, wives and children. It's like a tribe. It's a cultural thing too. At a very early age we all started to travel. When U2 got signed in 1980 and they started touring primarily in America, we started touring primarily in Europe, and you'd lose contact with the next-door-neighbour types or the school types. That travelling kept us in the same boat, though with totally different scales of where we wanted to go. You'd come back after six months on the road and have the opportunity to share all these experiences. Bono's like my brother. Bono and Guggi are my closest friends.

U2's influence is extraordinary because they've been going for so long. They're up there with The Beatles, The Rolling Stones. And it's not over. And what Bono has done as a person is quite extraordinary. And that extends back into the band. You can't separate it, really. Just what they've done musically in the last three, four years is amazing. The real change happened when they reinvented themselves at the start of the 1990s. And then it became profound, because what they did with ZooTV, Zooropa and, believe it or not, PopMart will endure very well. They turned arena rock on its head completely, because arena rock is very lazy ultimately. It's all about selling tickets, but they actually brought in aesthetics and emotion, parody and entertainment, and they sort of turned it on its head. They brought art into music and had a tremendous team on board to help them do that. That changed the course of music history and touring history and stands alone. PopMart was two steps ahead, espe-cially from a North American point of view. Certain cultural things didn't kick in. U2 were feeding off this mid-1990s dance culture that was a euphoria from the late 1980s in Europe. It had a European sensibility. The look of and the album for *Pop* was influ-enced by that. The Americans are only getting into that now. So at the time in America I think it was just a little 'What the fuck is that?' musically as well as visually. But that screen . . . *Wow*, that was great, that was brave. Extraordinary. I think the fact that Bono cut his hair and wore a superhero outfit was just one little step too far for the Yanks. They were still in Zooropa in their head. But U2 kept pushing the boat out. After the massive suc-cess of *The Joshua Tree* they got this kick in the side from the world media for *Rattle and Hum*. After *Achtung Baby* they got dissed for *Pop*. It was a similar kick. But I feel that what they did in Pop was far more radical than *Rattle and Hum*. *Rattle and Hum* was tipping your hat to the legends, you know, B.B. King, the great songwriters and history book of rock and roll, going back to Sun Studios. PopMart looked forward. Sometimes Americans don't like looking forward too quickly.

How the band arrives at these ideas happens quite instinctive-ly. The music usually tells you instinctively. I work a lot on movie scores now and you watch the movie and it tells you: 'Jesus', this is a hard movie, this is about pain, this is fucked up, oh, it's so cold, this needs warmth, this needs strings.' When you work on a movie you look at the visuals first. If U2 are writing or recording, I'll drop in. We drop in as mates and then sometimes as advisers. We'll go for a pint, there's a cassette being played in the car. 'Look at this, it's an idea, what do you think?' When we're sitting down having drinks – we know how to have a good time – always in the back of the head there are lyrics being thrown around, ideas for movies. Seventy per cent is just fantasy, but our way of having a good time is talking: 'I want to do this play, I want to do this film.' You could be in the middle of the recording sessions for ZooTV or *Achtung Baby* and you hear 'Zoo Station' and you just go 'Jesus, that's an opener.' It's just conversation like that. Seeds of ideas are always being thrown around. Everything's in the agenda. Always. Same for the visuals. So there's always a perception of, 'Oh, well, that might look good like that.' Albums and shows are linked together. 'Imagine opening the tour with this, imagine closing the tour with this, imagine this as the middle section, look at this chord to this song, what an emotion, wow!' I remember simple things like, say, 'The Fly'. When that was being constructed in the studio, Bono was like most performers and writers: you take on personas in your head. I remember he wasn't too happy with his persona lyrically and vocally and he went out on the town one night with a few friends. I think Fintan Fitzgerald, who works in wardrobe, got him a pair of sunglasses, which became the infamous Fly glasses. Bono put them on and did the vocal. They haven't come off since. They've just changed colour. He put on these glasses and an attitude came across. So from a musical event this character was invented, the Fly. And then when meetings came to talk about a live show there was already this character. Mirrorball Man was a character in ZooTV. When Zoo came to Europe, he had the Mirrorball character but it was so American that it wasn't going to work in Europe. He wanted something a little bit more European. It was an awkward time in Europe because you had the beginning of the horror in the former Yugoslavia and the world looked like it was bit fucked over here. I helped develop MacPhisto, the Devil, in the Zooropa tour pre-production rehearsals in Holland. That was just, 'Whoosh, put horns on your head.' Well, it was a little slower than that. There's an awful lot of MacPhisto in me, you know.

For the visual stuff, there's a committee, if you want to call it that: the band, obviously, and then Willie Williams, Catherine Owens and myself. Catherine was brought in because she was a visual artist, living in America, and knew a lot of independent video-makers. We'd all respond to ideas from the band. For example, Bono works in essences, smells, you know, and he might see something, or say about MacPhisto, 'No, he can't be a cowboy, can't be American, has to be European, has to be darker.' We take it very seriously. We all work very hard. I know how to stir things up. I'm not afraid of saying, 'I think that's a piece of shite.' I'm sort of a midwife and bodyguard. I remember when they started really going through the roof, with *The Unforgettable Fire*, and suddenly they became icons in America. You're on stage and 70,000 people are in front and everybody says, 'You guys rock – everything is fantastic.' Willie's running around trying to organize 50 million lights and video screens and

whatever and I walk out and I say, 'That's a piece of shite.' I can look out at the stage and see the four boys and protect their ass. 'They're telling you that you look good, and I'm telling you that it looks like shite.' So it's an unpopular role sometimes, but I don't care about anything other than the final show and the band. But I've also known every single one of them since they were kids, so I understand their language. It's weird – I know what humour they're in when they walk on the stage, by their body movement, the way you know someone for 30 years. But they know me, too. Bono and I are mates. If I'm mixing an album then I'll ask, 'Do you like this?' and he goes, 'Get rid of that, repeat that. So we look after each other's asses that way, which is a very treasured and beautiful thing. We know our stuff, we've been around. And I quite enjoy the sort of obscenity of fucking walking into a meeting with 100 executives and bringing a bit of reality to it. But that's the side that gets up everyone's noses – except the band's. But it's not just a sense of loyalty – it's also exciting. Everyone was very excited about the way ZooTV changed and influenced live performance in such a huge way, both obviously and subliminally. I remember days when they were basically still bumming chips and having no money, you know. It took years and years of hard work. And they would put their neck on the line, that's including Paul McGuinness, to pay for a proper lighting rig and a proper sound system. Putting a show on even for the War tour or the Red Rocks gig. It was like: 'We put everything into this, we gamble on this.' They've got this incredible work ethic, incredible seriousness, dedication, drive, and they're always trying to top themselves artistically. There's also humour and parody. One of the funniest people you'll ever meet is Bono, believe it or not. He's a devil in his own way. He's a very chilled and smart man. You can have business with him and you can have a great laugh. I think ZooTV and PopMart showed there was humour. It's taking nothing for granted. I have a theory in my own head: the day that you don't walk in to make an album with the same excitement and the same fears as when you were 18 and you first went into the studio, then there's something wrong. It's about never sitting on your laurels, never taking it for granted, and then actually getting on with it. And a lot of people do take things for granted. They go, 'I've made enough money, I'm successful.' It isn't about money. The work

Gavin Friday and Bono

ethic is huge, but we enjoy life, we're not miserable gits who sit and moan. I think it's a lot to do with the certain practicality about being a Dubliner.

When you start on an album you just don't know when it will get finished. Songs are babies; they tell you, 'I want to come out – that's it.' From what I've heard of the new albumit's very raw so far, very raw – almost like punk meets The Who – and then very sophisticated, like 'Electrical Storm'. I find 'Electrical Storm' to be one of the most sophisticated and beautiful things they've ever written. You really feel that Bono is a man now, as a lyricist and singer – from boys to men. There is a maturity about it which could only have been reached through going through a kind of adolescence and gestation process.

All That You Can't Leave Behind was the most sophisticated album, it was stripped back, songs were more minimal, but also dealing with death and loss. Something starts kicking into your life when you hit 40. Yet they were doing it as a rock and roll band. Most rock and rollers, when they hit 40 or 50, make the big mistake, they run around the stage like they are 14, and shout, 'Get your rocks off baby.' And U2 are talking about death and loss and suffering, but in a very sophisticated way.

Personally, I think if you go into an arena, and play in front of 70,000 fans, it's hard not to go ZooTV, to make a comeback on that scale. Edge's guitar sounds travel very well over a large open space. The way Bono sings, the anthems and the emotion, the songs are almost suited to mass crowds. I think that's one of the reasons why they've become one of the biggest rock bands in the world, because sonically and emotionally it makes sense. He's perfected the art of communication, communicating to the back of the arena. The only other performer I've seen per-form in that way is Freddie Mercury in his prime. He knew how to fucking communicate to the back. And you're talking about the most camp man in the world having football fans as fans. But Queen went for showbiz. U2 go for the heart. It's not just the aesthetics. It's the heart, whether that meant the angst of teen-hood, or losing your mother, or the political and emotional prob-lems of the world. And done without preaching. They've become great songwriters. I think the first few albums were like sound-scapes with emotions and then, suddenly, Jesus, from *Joshua Tree* on, they're writing songs. They've become real lyricists. Big-time.

From the aesthetics to the practicalities of it all, each person in the band has individually carved out their own dynamic and roots. They have remained friends and love each other and that has a lot to do with their longevity. It's passion, formation, and I think this has a lot do with even why we've stuck together as a gang. There's sort of a psychosis about where we come from in Dublin in the late 1970s, a real 'Fuck off and die – you are over.' Culturally we never had a post-war boom like Britain and America did in the 1950s and 1960s. We never had that because we were an independent country that was struggling with all sorts of bullshit. As young teenagers we looked towards Britain and America for influences in music, art, literature and movies while at the time in Ireland it was like, 'You're in the civil service or you're on the dole.' So there was this sort of, 'Let's get rid of all these ridiculous hang-ups the Paddies have.' We were kids when there were the troubles in the North. In the 1970s and 1980s horrific things were happening on these British Isles. It gave us all a certain determination. Now you have kids going into bands because they want to make money and it's a job. Look at 'Pop Stars'. Andy Warhol said, 'In the future everyone will be famous for 15 minutes.' He got that wrong. He should have said, 'Everyone will be famous for 15 minutes and they'll all want to be famous at the same fucking time.' Twenty-five years ago, when we were teenagers, it was like it was a different sort of energy and angst. And I really believe that we were the first generation of Irish that didn't have Catholic hang-ups. Those seeds are in a lot of us our age. You saw why punk was so relevant in Britain and Ireland. The coun-tries were in tatters: racism, unemployment, political problems. It was the dole queue or fuck off. And Maggie Thatcher came in on top of all that. You looked to the sort of tough bands. The Beatles came from Liverpool and Liverpool is basically another suburb of Dublin, except it's across the river. One thing The Beatles have is that sort of Irishness about them – especially John Lennon. Believe me, U2 has a lot of ingrained toughness. *Dublin, January 2003*

Right, Adam Clayton, Paul McGuinness, Larry Mullen Jnr, Bono, The Edge. ZooTV tour, Foxboro, USA, August 1983.

Contributors and Interviewees
U2 Touring Personnel
Special Mentions
Photographers' Credits

Band, management and crew,
Elevation tour, Las Vegas,
November 2001

Contributors and Interviewees

Michael Bracewell
Michael Bracewell is the author of six novels, including *Perfect Tense* and *Saint Rachel*. He has also published two works of non-fiction: a study of Englishness in popular culture, and a collection of essays and journalism, *The Nineties*. He is a regular contributor to *Friez* and the *Los Angeles Times*, has written catalogues for many contemporary artists, and is currently researching a biography of Roxy Music.

Willie Williams
Willie Williams designs and directs multi-media events and has been the principal designer of U2's live shows since 1983. His extracurricular collaborations have included rock tours with R.E.M., David Bowie and The Rolling Stones; performance pieces with the Kronos Quartet and La La La Human Steps; the stage musicals *Barbarella* and *We Will Rock You*, plus permanent installations at Experience Music Project, Seattle and the Rock and Roll Hall of Fame Museum, Cleveland.

Mark Cunningham
Co-founder of the definitive live industry magazine *Total Production*, Mark has also authored books, including *Good Vibrations: A History Of Record Production* and *Live & Kicking: The Rock Concert Industry In The Nineties*. Also an active musician and producer, Mark is a founder member of folk-rock band The Marshmen.

Management:
Paul McGuinness
Manager
Paul McGuinness, born 1951, is the founder of Principle Management. His career has been spent working in the entertainment industry and he is well known throughout the world in both the film and music busi-

ness. He is a director of TV3 Ireland, and Ardmore Film Studios. He was a member of the Arts Council of Ireland for 12 years. He is a government-appointed board member of the Dublin Digital Hub and of the School of Film and Drama at University College Dublin, and is a member of BAFTA. He is married with two children and lives in Dublin.

Ellen Darst
Principle Management, USA, 1983–93
Ellen Darst nurtured the careers of many world-class artists during her three-decade tenure in the music business. While at Warner Brothers she worked closely with widely diverse talents, from Dire Straits to Devo. In 1980 she met up with U2 and over the next dozen years was instrumental in developing them into the internationally known artists they are today. Ellen is currently living in Gloucester, Massachusetts with her husband, Stephen Rainford.

Anne-Louise Kelly
Managing Director, Principle Management, Dublin 1983–97
Anne-Louise Kelly joined Paul McGuinness as his first assistant in 1983, and helped set up the Principle Management offices in Dublin which she ran until her retirement in 1997.

Agents:
Frank Barsalona
Premier Talent, US agent, 1982–97
Frank Barsalona is a legend in the US music industry. He founded his Premier Talent agency in 1964. He was responsible for booking both The Beatles and The Rolling Stones on their first US tours and opening up new markets for then emerging British talent. Barsalona was a founding member of the Rock and Roll Hall of Fame and has been honoured with many of the industry's most prestigious awards. Premier

Talent merged with William Morris Agency in 2002 and he continues there as an active consultant.

Barbara Skydel
Premier Talent, US agent, 1982–97. Senior Vice President, William Morris Agency, NY
Barbara Skydel joined Premier Talent in 1977 and became a full partner in 1985. She helped to pioneer the contribution of women in the music industry, and has been saluted as such, being named as *Performance Magazine*'s Agent of the Year five times. Following Premier's merger with William Morris Agency in 2002, she is now senior vice-president of their music division.

Ian Flooks
Agent: worldwide excluding US, 1982–97. Founder and CEO, Wasted Talent Agency, London
Ian Flooks is an entrepreneur who has specialized in finding new talent, first in the music business and now in film. He started Wasted Talent in 1979 for the new generation of musicians then emerging and represented U2, Talking Heads, The Clash, The Pretenders, REM and Red Hot Chilli Peppers. Later came Texas, Blur and Robbie Williams. In 1994 Wasted Talent was sold to ICM, with Ian diversifying into a record label, music publishing and film distribution and latterly film and TV development. Ian is a long-time director of Greenpeace.

Tour Management:
Dennis Sheehan
Tour Manager: 1982–Present

After playing with various groups in England and Europe until 1965, Dennis Sheehan then worked with Jimmy James and the Vagabonds. From 1968 to 1971 he worked with Cartoone and Stone the Crows as well as with Led Zeppelin until 1979,

Arista Records with Patti Smith, Iggy Pop and Lou Reed and with U2 from 1982 to the present.

Bob Koch
Tour Business Manager: 1984–Present
Bob Koch worked as a club promoter and tour accountant before becoming U2's Tour Business Manager. He has been with the band since the Unforgettable Fire tour.

Sound:
Joe O'Herlihy
U2 Audio Director: 1979–Present
In 1968 Joe started out as the bass player in a band at school in Cork, he then joined local bands Chapter Five, Gaslight and Sleepy Hollow as a backline roadie. From 1974 to 1978, he worked with The Rory Gallagher Band starting as a backline technician and graduating through the ranks to front of house sound engineer. In 1976, he formed a sound company called Stage Sound Hire with partners Denis Desmond and Eamon McCann of MCD, Ireland's leading concert promoter. Joe first met U2 at a UCC downtown campus gig in The Arcadia Ballroom, Cork, at the end of Sept' 1978 when he supplied the sound equipment for that gig. Paul McGuinness was very impressed and Joe has been doing the live concert sound for U2 ever since, with his job progressing over the years from Sound Engineer to Audio Director.

Roy Clair and Greg Hall
Clair Brothers Audio, Littitz, Pennsylvania. Tour sound suppliers, War tour–Present
Clair Brothers Audio began back in the mid-1960s, with the Clair Brothers – Roy and Gene – doing shows at the local college, Franklin and Marshall in Lancaster, PA. Around that time the idea occurred that in order to provide a consistent standard of quality for a live performer from show to show, you could make a

sound system portable – a revolutionary idea at the time. Early touring accounts Elton John, Yes and The Moody Blues are still loyal clients, along with many others. Clair Brothers have since grown to worldwide proportions, and are concert industry leader and trendsetters, having been recognized with many technology and industry service awards.

Production:
Steve Iredale
Backline and Stage: October, War. Production Manager: Unforgettable Fire–Present
Steve Iredale's first job in music was in 1977 with Irish group Horslips. Introduced to Paul McGuinness in 1981 he started as a backline technician on the October tour, moving to stage management for War. In 1984 Steve became U2's long-time production manager, a position he has held ever since. Since forming his own production services company in 1987 he has event-managed three MTV European Music Awards, Woodstock '94 and worked on numerous tours for various acts, including George Michael, Prince, Robbie Williams, Bon Jovi and Frank Sinatra. All between U2 tours.

Jake Kennedy
Lighting Designer: Boy, October. Deputy Production Manager: Joshua Tree, ZooTV. Director: PopMart
Jake Kennedy has over 20 years' experience at all levels of concert touring, event management, TV, video and music-content-driven film projects. The early years of his career were spent as a Lighting Designer working with, amongst others, U2 and Rory Gallagher. He was one of a small group of U2's key personnel who managed all aspects of concert production, set design and touring logistics from 1987 to 1998. He has provided production management services to numerous

events, including the Millennium Celebrations in Stockholm, Ireland's National Day and Expo 2000, Hanover, Germany. He is currently Director of Cork 2005, the company charged with organizing European Capital of Culture events in Cork, Ireland.

Rocko Reedy

Assistant Stage Manager: ZooTV, PopMart. Stage Manager: Elevation

Rocko Reedy was born in Chicago. He got into the music business doing vintage guitar and violin repair, and selling guitars to rock stars such as Yes, Peter Frampton, Kansas, Foghat and Bad Company. He then moved into stage management with his first tour, Styx, going on to work with Survivor, the Kinks, Robin Trower, Bon Jovi and of course U2. In addition there have been many one-off projects such as the 1989 Moscow Music Peace Festival and many other festivals around the world.

Jake Berry

Tour Production Manager: Elevation

Jake Berry started his career after a chance meeting with Rick Wakeman in Devon in 1975 led to work with Yes as a keyboard technician. Jake's first production job was with AC/DC, who he worked with through the 1980s, as well as Metallica and Motley Crue. Since 1994's Voodoo Lounge tour he has been production manager for all The Rolling Stones' tours. He has also worked with Cher, Tina Turner and as a consultant with U2 on PopMart and as tour production manager on Elevation. Aside from these major tours, Jake has found time to tour manage the children's shows, Barney and Bob the Builder.

Design and Staging

Jeremy Thom

Set Designer: The Joshua Tree

Jeremy Thom has been designing extraordinary stage sets and structures for over 25 years. He also has design, site planning, production and project management credits for an array of projects from rock 'n' roll, movies, industrial theatre and trade shows, to ballet, opera and special events with a diverse roster of clients worldwide. Jeremy has practised on both sides of the Atlantic and in countries throughout the globe. He migrated to USA from London in the mid-1980s and now lives and works just outside New York City.

Michael Tait

Tait Towers, Littitz, Pennsylvania US lighting supplier: War, Unforgettable Fire. Set Fabrication: Unforgettable Fire, Joshua Tree, ZooTV, PopMart, Elevation

After graduating from Royal Melbourne Institute of Technology Michael Tait arrived in London from Australia in 1967. He started work at the Speakeasy club before joining the road crew of Yes. Through the 1970s, while touring as Yes's lighting designer, he was responsible for numerous lighting and stage equipment inventions which enabled the live concert industry to grow and develop efficiently. After 15 years on the road, Michael relocated permanently to Pennsylvania, USA, in 1978, eventually concentrating his company, Tait Towers, solely upon set production. His unique skills and experience make him the pre-eminent set builder in the industry.

Rene Castro

Artist, Set Designer: Love Town. Trabant artwork on ZooTV

Rene Castro is a Chilean artist, photographer, curator and teacher. In 1975, Castro was forced into exile in the US from Chile after serving two years in

Chile's infamous detention camps. Since then his designs have been featured on the CDs and albums of many artists including U2, Mercedes Sosa, Inti Illimani, Quilapyun, Carlos Santana and Ruben Blades.

Richard Hartman

Stage Interface Consultant and Engineer: ZooTV, PopMart

Richard Hartman is a theatre technician by profession. He has worked on all populated continents with many people of different backgrounds doing different types of theatrical projects, from touring music groups, the Olympics, Presidential gatherings to running lighting rental production companies. His career spans from pre-Woodstock 1 to the present.

Jonathan Park

Set Designer, ZooTV Outside Broadcast

Jonathan Park, a Yorkshireman brought up on hard work and rugby, moved to London in the late 1960s. Working for Arups as an engineer he soon added architecture and, during the 1970s, taught at the Architectural Association until a surprise telephone call from Pink Floyd. The rest is history – he and AA friend and colleague Mark Fisher formed Fisher Park. They designed sets and shows, famously including The Wall, for the major rock 'n' roll bands of the era, culminating in U2's ZooTV Outside Broadcast. His solo work since then has encompassed lighting, architecture and creative direction.

Mark Fisher

Set Architect: ZooTV, PopMart, Elevation

Mark Fisher is known for his spectacular live entertainment design. He has created some of the most memorable rock concerts ever staged, including The Wall for Pink Floyd, Bridges to Babylon and Licks for The Rolling Stones, and Zoo TV, PopMart and Elevation for

U2. His other designs include the Millennium Show at the Dome, the Queen's Golden Jubilee Concerts at Buckingham Palace and, in the USA, three halftime shows for the NFL Superbowl and the Cirque du Soleil show at the MGM Grand in Las Vegas. His current work includes the design of the opening and closing ceremonies for the Winter Olympics in Turin in 2006.

Lighting

Bruce Ramus

Lighting Director: ZooTV, PopMart and Elevation

Bruce Ramus has been working as a lighting director since the early 1980s with many notable artists, including Bryan Adams, Savage Garden, REM, David Bowie, David Byrne, and with U2 since their Zooropa tour.

John Lobel

Light and Sound Design/Fourth Phase, California. Lighting suppliers, Joshua Tree–Present

John Lobel provides lighting systems for concert tours and special events and has been involved with every U2 tour since the Joshua Tree. Most of John's work is done during pre-production and rehearsal. Although he does not go on tour any more, he attends as many shows as possible. He worked for Nocturne Productions during the Joshua Tree and Love Town tours, Light & Sound Design (LSD) for the ZooTV and PopMart tours, and LSD/Fourth Phase for the Elevation tour. He's a former principal of LSD. John works with the lighting designer and production manager to implement the designer's vision and fit the production's requirements. He now arranges lighting packages for tours and special events, and for fun he travels to remote corners of the world looking for rare and unusual birds.

Show Video Production:

Pat Morrow

Nocturne Productions, Inc., California. Lighting suppliers for Joshua Tree; Video suppliers for ZooTV

Pat Morrow was tour manager for 14 years with Journey, Steve Miller and Tower of Power. Concurrently, for 20 years he was general manager of Nocturne Productions US, whose clients include U2, David Bowie, Madonna, The Who, Michael Jackson, Elton John and many other top bands. Based in Berkeley, California, Pat is still tour managing, while also producing live DVD shoots and consulting to the live production industry.

Monica Caston

Video Director: PopMart Assistant Video Director: ZooTV

Monica Caston's career in music, film and television spans more than 20 years in directing and producing video and film for world tours, concerts, TV specials, multi-format events and documentaries. She has been an integral part of some of the most innovative productions, for example as video director of U2's ZooTV and PopMart, which involved collaborating on the use of cutting-edge technologies in live presentations. Monica also has a wide range of entertainment and corporate clients.

Carol Dodds

Video Director: ZooTV

For the past 20 years Carol has been a visual – lighting and video design – artist doing live multi-camera production for international network specials, webcast, pre-produced playback, location based multi-media shows, spectacles and concert tours. Clients include Madonna, Ricky Martin, The Eagles, Bruce Springsteen, Mariah Carey, Lenny Kravitz, Alan Jackson, Bette Midler and Whitney Houston.

Frederick Opsomer

System Technologies, Belgium. Video screen suppliers: Zooropa, PopMart

Frederic Opsomer, a Belgian national, has been involved in the technical design and engineering of custom video screens for a number of years. In 1995 he established System Technologies, and with his expertise quickly developed relationships with the leading manufacturers of the day, such as Sony and Panasonic. Frederic rose to the challenge of designing and making a 706m video screen for the PopMart tour, a major innovation in the use of LED technology for motion video.

Show Video Content:

Catherine Owens

Artist, Visual Collaborator: ZooTV. Curator of screen imagery: PopMart, Elevation

Catherine Owens' work as U2's creative director of screen visuals has consisted of making video segments in response to the band's musical direction on each tour, and commissioning a series of animations and videos by other artists and film makers. She lives in New York City.

Kevin Godley

Film and Video Director Contributor: ZooTV

Kevin Godley, originally the drummer for 1970s British band 10cc, later formed the duo Godley and Creme with former bandmate Lol Creme. In the early 1980s Godley and Creme moved from performing music to directing music videos. By the 1990s Godley was working solo and his unique style landed him work with the top musical acts of the time. U2 called upon Godley to direct a number of videos for their *Achtung Baby* album, and he advised and directed the ZooTV tour for Channel 4. In addition to his work with U2, Godley has directed music videos for an impressive list of artists ranging from Frank Sinatra to Frankie

Goes to Hollywood, and from The Beatles to Boyzone. Godley's directorial credits also include television commercials and documentaries.

Mark Pellington

Film Director, Contributor: ZooTV

Mark Pellington is an innovative film maker who began his career at MTV in 1984 with ground-breaking explorations in sound/image/text juxtaposition, culminating in the collage programme 'Buzz'. He created the multi-screen image environment for U2's ZooTV tour. One of the world's top award-winning music video directors, he has also directed feature films including *Arlington Road* and *The Mothman Prophecies*. In 2002 he was honored with a Lifetime Achievement Award by the Music Video Producers' Association.

Mark Neale

Writer and Film Director Contributor: ZooTV

Mark Neale is a director and writer with over ten years' experience in the creation of film, TV and new media. His recent work includes the documentaries *Faster*, about grand prix motorcycle racing, and *No Maps for These Territories*, about sci-fi legend William Gibson. As a music video director, Mark earned a Best Director nomination at the 1994 MTV Awards for the U2 video 'Stay (Faraway So Close)', co-directed with Wim Wenders. Mark directed the U2 video 'Lemon' and numerous hits for artists including Counting Crows and Paul Weller. Other credits include: video for U2's ZooTV world tour; two 13-part series for Channel 4 television, 'Mojo Working' and 'Buzz'. Mark left his native England in 1998 and is now based in Santa Monica.

Show Filming:

Malcolm Gerrie

Chief Executive Initial Television, London. Film Producer: Under A Blood Red Sky, U2 Live at Red Rocks

Malcolm Gerrie began his television career as a researcher and presenter of regional programmes at Tyne Tees Television in Newcastle. He produced defining programmes like the live music series 'The Tube', which reinvented live music television in the 1980s, and 'The White Room' in the 1990s. He has worked with artists such as U2, Aretha Franklin and Oasis. For eight years he was the creative drive behind the Brit Awards. Malcolm Gerrie is currently Chief Executive of Initial Television, part of Endemol Entertainment.

Gavin Taylor

Film director, U2 Live at Red Rocks, *1983*

As The Tube live director Gavin was asked to direct a concert in Gateshead with The Police, where the support was a relatively unknown band called U2. Their performance was electric and after the show Paul McGuinness asked if he would direct U2's concert at Red Rocks, Colorado. He went on to direct video concerts around the world with artists such as Janet Jackson, Celine Dion, Stevie Wonder, Whitney Houston, Michael Jackson, Elton John, Rod Stewart, John Bon Jovi, Eric Clapton, Bob Dylan, Queen, Dire Straits, Paul Simon, Bryan Adams, David Bowie, Diana Ross, and Tina Turner.

Ned O'Hanlon

Solo Too, Dublin. Film Producer: virtually all live show performances for U2 since 1992

Between 1991 and 2003 Ned ran a film production company, Dreamchaser, with Maurice Linnane; now he runs his new Dublin-based independent film company Solo Too. Ned's

pedigree in the world of television and music television production is seriously impressive: producer of the first three MTV Europe Music Awards in Berlin, Paris and London; producer of the Annual Rock & Roll Hall of Fame Induction Ceremony in New York from 1998 through to 2002; executive producer on MTV's inaugural ICON show, held in Los Angeles in 2001. He has produced virtually all live show performances for U2 since 1992, winning a Grammy for ZooTV Live from Sydney in the Best Music Video Long Form. Other artists, live concerts and documentaries include: Neil Young, The Rolling Stones, Oasis, Britney Spears, Cranberries, Boyzone, Garth Brooks and Van Morrison, among others.

Maurice Linnane

Video Director, Dreamchaser Productions, 1991–2003

Maurice Linnane has been working in film and television since leaving college in 1984. His debut as a director was at the helm of an MTV Rocumentary on U2, during the band's ZooTV world tour. Since then Maurice has been a frequent collaborator with U2, and has worked with many other Irish artists. Internationally, he has directed work for The Rolling Stones, Neil Young, The Foo Fighters, Garth Brooks, Reba McEntire and Nora Jones. In 1996 he produced and installed a celebratory film honouring inductees into the Rock and Roll Hall of Fame in Cleveland, Ohio. He has also designed and directed installations for Metropolitan Museum of Modern Art in New York. Maurice is currently working on a documentary on Irish music legends Horslips called *The Return of the Dancehall Sweethearts*.

Wardrobe:

Fintan Fitzgerald

Wardrobe assistant: Joshua Tree. Stylist/head of wardrobe: ZooTV. Tour wardrobe co-ordinator: PopMart, Elevation

Fintan Fitzgerald first worked with U2 in 1986 and was their stylist from 1988 until 1996. He lives and works in London as a free-lance stylist on a wide variety of music, TV, commercial, photographic and magazine projects.

Sharon Blankson

Head of Wardrobe: PopMart and Elevation

Sharon Blankson has known U2 since 1978 when they played in the Dandelion Market in Dublin. Chosen by Bono in 1996 to style PopMart, she works with the band to the present day.

Band Crew:

Steve Rainford

Guitar Technician, The Edge: 1983–1986

Stephen Rainford worked with U2 both on the road and in the studio. He enabled their transition from electric to electronic instrumentation during the period of *War* through *The Joshua Tree*. Subsequently, he has worked in film and broadcast television and is currently in the real estate business in Gloucester, Massachusetts.

Dallas Schoo

Guitar Technician, The Edge, 1987–Present

Dallas Schoo has been The Edge's guitar technician since the second leg of the 1987 Joshua Tree tour. As guitar tech to the stars for some 32 years now, he has worked with The Police, The Eagles, Prince, Pearl Jam, Jimmy Buffet and Bruce Springsteen, among others.

Recording:

Chris Blackwell
Founder, Island Records
Chris Blackwell has spent 40 years in the entertainment industry. Of Irish/Jamaican parentage, he launched Island Records in 1959, which became the finest small record company in the world. Blackwell promoted a roster of Jamaican and British artists covering ska, reggae, rock, folk and, later, African pop. Artists included Spencer Davis, Bob Marley and the Wailers, Traffic, Roxy Music, Burning Spear, Third World and many others. In the early 1980s Blackwell signed U2 (after their rejection by the majors). In 1983 he formed his film and distribution company Island Alive. In 1989, Island was bought by the conglomerate PolyGram. Blackwell stayed on to supervise the Island companies. The early nineties saw the creation of his hotel and resort company Island Outpost, and in 1995 he formed Island Black Music. In 1997 Blackwell parted ways with PolyGram, and in 1998 started the audio/visual entertainment company Palm Pictures. He was inducted into the Rock and Roll Hall of Fame in 2001.

Jimmy Iovine
Chairman, Interscope Geffen A&M, a division of Universal Music. Record Producer: Under A Blood Red Sky, Rattle and Hum Jimmy Iovine started as a recording engineer in the mid-1970s, working with John Lennon and Bruce Springsteen, going on to produce hit albums for U2, the Eurythmics, Stevie Nicks, The Pretenders and Patti Smith among others. He has been twice voted Producer of the Year by *Rolling Stone*. He co-founded Interscope in 1990. Universal's acquisition of Polygram in 1999 resulted in the newly comprised Interscope Geffen A&M Records of which Iovine was named Chairman in 2001. Most recently he co-produced the movie

8 Mile and was co-producer of the SuperBowl XXXVII Half-time Show.

Brian Eno
Musician, Record Producer: The Unforgettable Fire, The Joshua Tree, Achtung Baby, Zooropa, All That You Can't Leave Behind *Video Staging Concept: ZooTV* Trained as an artist, Brian Eno's career encompasses visual art, writing, lecturing, teaching and especially music. He has released a series of highly influential albums, and his audio/visual installations have been exhibited around the world. He has worked with U2 since the early 1980s as co-producer with Daniel Lanois on many of the band's albums. He is also a founder member of the Long Now Foundation and a Visiting Professor at the Royal College of Art in London and at the Hochschule der Künste in Berlin.

Daniel Lanois
Musician, Record Producer: The Unforgettable Fire, The Joshua Tree, Achtung Baby, All That You Can't Leave Behind Daniel Lanois was born in Quebec. He has spent his life absorbing the music of North America; blues, rock, country and folk, and has a musical experience matched by few. He has produced for artists such as Bob Dylan, Peter Gabriel, Robbie Robertson and the Neville Brothers, as well as collaborating with Brian Eno on U2's *The Unforgettable Fire, The Joshua Tree, Achtung Baby* and *All That You Can't Leave Behind*. Daniel is also a distinguished solo artist and live performer.

Flood
Recording Engineer: The Joshua Tree, Achtung Baby *Record Producer:* Zooropa, Pop Flood established his career as a recording engineer working at Morgan and Trident studios in London with artists such as Nick

Cave and Soft Cell. At Trident he gained his first production credits working with Depeche Mode and Nine Inch Nails. In subsequent years he gained a reputation for being one of the finest recording engineers in the country, combining the experimental with the commercial for artists such as Polly Harvey, the Smashing Pumpkins and with U2 on *The Joshua Tree, Achtung Baby, Zooropa* and *Pop*.

Cheryl Engels
Partial Productions, Los Angeles Cheryl Engels was director of quality control and mastering for A&M Records, where she worked from 1974 to 1992. In 1993, she founded her quality control and audio post-production services company, Partial Productions. She has QC'd all of U2's records since *Rattle and Hum*, and has supervised the mastering and editing of many U2 projects. Other clients include the Bee Gees, Sting and Melissa Etheridge. She lives and works in Los Angeles.

Graphics:

Steve Averill
Four5One Creative, Dublin. Designer of all U2 record and tour artwork Steve Averill's first job was in an advertising agency, with some time out as a lead singer for punk band the Radiators from Space. He set up his own company in the 1980s, with its present incarnation being Four5One Creative. His longest creative partnership has been with U2, with whom he has worked for almost 30 years. Steve also writes and broadcasts on hardcore country and Americana.

Shaughn McGrath
Four5One Creative, Dublin. Co-designer with Steve Averill of U2 record and tour artwork since Achtung Baby. After qualifying from the National College of Art and Design in

Dublin, Shaughn McGrath joined Steve Averill's design company for a month's trial and never left. He has worked on various design projects for international acts such as Tom Jones, Art of Noise, and Depeche Mode, including recent solo projects for both Martin Gore and Dave Gahan, as well as all Four5One's work for U2 since *Achtung Baby*.

Promoters:

Dennis Desmond
MCD, Dublin, Ireland Denis Desmond first promoted U2 at the Downtown campus in Cork around 1977/78. Since then MCD has promoted numerous concerts by the band, including Slane Castle in '81 with Thin Lizzy, Phoenix Park in '83 with Simple Minds, Eurythmics and Big Country, PopMart at Lansdowne Road and two Elevation shows at Slane Castle in 2001, with an 80,000 capacity for each show. In the 22-year history of concerts at Slane, U2 are the only act to perform two sold out shows in the prestigious venue. A DVD of the concert *U2 Go Home* was released worldwide December '03.

Jim Aiken
Aiken Promotions, Belfast, N. Ireland Jim Aiken has been a promoter for 40 years. He has been associated with major acts, including Pavarotti, Elton John, Garth Brooks, Bruce Springsteen, and Paul McCartney and has had the pleasure of bringing them to Ireland. He is very proud to be associated with U2's great outdoor concerts at RDS and Croke Park.

Tim Parsons
MCP, UK Tim Parsons started MCP with partners in January 1978, went on to originate Monsters of Rock, and co-promoted Live Aid. He started working with U2 in the early 80s, the first show was

support to Talking Heads at Leeds Poly. Tim continued to work with U2 throughout their career until Elevation. He is now retired from the music business, honing his golf handicap, getting a life and buying records!

Don Law
Chairman and co-CEO Music Group for Clear Channel Entertainment Don Law is the founder of the Tweeter Center Boston (formerly known as the Great Woods Center for the Performing Arts) in Mansfield, Massachusetts. Today, the Tweeter Center is one of the premier performance amphitheaters in the United States. Mr. Law co-founded New England Express Ticketing (NEXT), the world's first fully automated, high-volume reserved-seat ticketing system. Law was also the President of Precision Media, a broadcasting company that owned and operated five radio stations in New England, later sold to SFX Broadcasting. In addition, he co-founded and served as inaugural chairman of the North American Concert Promoter Association, an international trade association of the largest talent buyers in North America. Over the past two decades, Don Law and DLC Corp. have been active in numerous non-profit and charitable causes.

Gregg Perloff
Another Planet Entertainment, San Francisco, California Gregg first became involved in concert promotion while attending UCLA and continued booking and producing concerts while in graduate school at UC Berkeley. Joining forces in 1977 with Bill Graham, Gregg continued his tenure with Bill Graham Presents through the next two decades booking and/or producing such notable events as The Rolling Stones 1981 national tour of the US, the first US Festival, Live Aid and WOMAD in San Francisco's

Golden Gate Park – the largest paid concert in the world that year, with attendance of 112,000. He successfully continued Bill Graham Presents' legacy through consolidation and in 2003 embarked on the most challenging role of his long career by starting his own independent concert company: Another Planet Entertainment.

Arthur Fogel
President of Touring, Clear Channel Entertainment – Music
Arthur Fogel began his career as a concert promoter with Concert Promotions International in Toronto in 1981. By 1985 he was responsible for the entire concert division promoting over 200 concerts annually plus world tours for The Rolling Stones, David Bowie and Pink Floyd. CPI was sold in 1995 and Arthur co-founded TNA, dubbed 'the next adventure', promoting Bridges to Babylon and U2's PopMart. TNA was bought by SFX, itself acquired by Clear Channel in 1997, following which Arthur is President of Touring with Clear Channel's Music group.

Michael Cohl
Chairman, TGA Entertainment, Ltd., Toronto, Canada
Michael Cohl began his career in 1969 as a local promoter of concerts. In 1973, he created Concert Productions International and quickly became a driving force in the Canadian Music Industry, putting much of Canada on the map as a viable stop for tours of all sizes. From 1973 to 1988, he worked on projects in almost all fields – music, sports, theatre and film. He has also produced dozens of TV and film specials and thousands of concerts throughout North America. Beginning in 1989 with The Rolling Stones Steel Wheels Tour, Michael developed the concept of 'package' touring. Michael worked directly with the artist to strategize and route the tour and promote the dates. He then helped to develop and exploit

the aftermarket – books, TV shows, videos, films and merchandise. Michael has received the Number One Promoter of the Year award several times from an array of trade publications. He was inducted into the Canadian Music Hall of Fame in 2002 and received the Walt Grealis Special Achievement Award. Michael's new company, TGA, is a multifaceted entertainment entity with a wide range of expertise in all areas of live concert and event production including tour marketing, merchandizing, sponsorship, broadcast and home entertainment.

Media:
Bill Flanagan
Senior Vice President, MTV Networks International, New York, NY
Bill Flanagan is the author of the book *U2 at the End of the World*. He met the band in 1980, when he was a music critic for the *Boston Globe*. From 1985 to 1995 he was editor of *Musician Magazine*. In 1995 he became editorial director of VH1. He is currently senior vice-president of MTV Networks International. Among his other books are *Written in My Soul* and *A&R: A Novel*.

Tom Freston
Co-President and Co-Chief Operating Officer, Viacom, Inc., New York. Former Chairman and CEO, MTV Networks
Tom Freston is part of the original team that developed MTV back in New York in 1980. He has held a succession of jobs with the company since then and has been the Chairman and CEO of MTV Networks since 1987. The company owns and operates MTV, MTV2, VH1, College Television Network, Nickelodeon/Nick at Nite, Comedy Central, Noggin, TV Land, Spike TV and CMT. It operates some 93 networks around the world as well as a portfolio of leading Internet operations. Prior to his career at MTV Networks,

Freston lived in New Delhi and Kabul, Afghanistan for eight years. He currently resides in New York and Los Angeles with his wife, Kathy.

Ian Wilson
Irish radio producer
Ian works for 2FM the music station of RTE, Ireland's national broadcaster, where he looks after music production and alternative programmes (rock, indie, dance, hip hop, etc.). In the late 1970s he started the recording sessions for Dave Fanning and went on to head the EBU's music group, the Euro-sonic Partnership for six years.

Dave Fanning
Irish radio presenter and DJ
Dave Fanning started in 1979, and today Dave is the word on music in Ireland. He has interviewed artists from Eminem to Kylie Minogue to Paul McCartney and Bob Dylan. His connections with U2 date back to his friendship with the band when they formed in the late seventies and to this day he gets world exclusive first play on all U2 releases for his radio show. In addition to his work on 2FM, Dave has also presented 'The Movie Show' on RTÉ TV for the last ten years and currently presents 'The Music Zone' every Friday night on Network 2. He also presents 'Music Express', which is now broadcast in over fifty countries worldwide. He is the movie critic for the *Sunday World*.

Charity Shows:
Ian Flooks
Wasted Talent Agency, London
(see 'Agents')

Jack Healey
Former director of Amnesty International, Conspiracy of Hope tour
Jack Healey is a world-renowned human rights activist. He was active in the civil rights and anti-war movements while a seminarian and a Franciscan priest in the 1960s, and has been an effective

and innovative leader in the human rights movement for over 25 years. Jack helped move the topic of human rights from closed-door diplomatic negotiations to widespread awareness, public debate, and direct citizen action. Jack has brought human rights to the global stage by his creative use of media and enlistment of world-class musical talent. As Executive Director of Amnesty International USA for 12 years, he pioneered new ways to reach youth – the next generation – to deliver the message of human rights. A few events he created include: 1986 Conspiracy of Hope tour, 1988 Human Rights Now! Tour, From a Hug to a Hope two-day concert in Chile, and Free to Laugh, a two-hour show in honour of women's rights.

Peter Gabriel
Musician.
In 1975 Peter Gabriel started a solo career after leaving Genesis (which he co-founded) and he has released eleven solo albums. In 1980 he co-founded WOMAD (World of Music Arts and Dance). In 1987 he founded the Real World group of companies. Human rights work includes concerts for Nelson Mandela in 1988 and 1990; and being coordinator of and participant in the Human Rights Now! tour in 1988 with Amnesty International. He is also co-founder and board member of OD2 (On-line Distribution), which is now the leading European platform provider for the distribution of on-line music.

Steven Van Zandt
You may know Steven from 'The Sopranos' (he plays Silvio Dante) or as the long-time guitarist from Bruce Springsteen's E Street Band, or as the acclaimed record producer for artists such as Bruce Springsteen, Southside Johnny and the Asbury Jukes and Artists United Against Apartheid. In April 2002 he also became known as the coolest DJ in the

USA when Little Steven's Underground Garage started broadcasting on radio across the USA.

Friends:
Barry Devlin
Friend, video director, Horslips member, screenwriter
Barry Devlin was the lead singer and bass player for the Irish band Horslips from 1972–1980. He has directed documentaries and music videos, including U2's 'Pride', 'Bad', 'Still Haven't Found What I'm Looking For' among others. His film credits include writing and directing *Lapsed Catholics* and *All Things Bright and Beautiful*.

Dave Kavanagh
U2's first agent
Dave Kavanagh began his career in the entertainment industry as a concert promoter, bringing many major acts to Ireland including The Pretenders, Ian Drury, The Undertones, Moving Hearts and other international acts. He also set up the Road Runner Agency, which represented U2, the Boomtown Rats, Christy Moore, Thin Lizzy and many other top Irish acts. As manager of Clannad between 1982 and 1996 he steered the band to unprecedented success all over the world.

Gavin Friday
Musician and friend
Gavin Friday was a founder member of the legendary Irish avant-garde punk group The Virgin Prunes. His debut exhibition of paintings 'I Didn't Come Up The Liffey in a Bubble' was in 1988. Since 1985 he has composed, recorded and performed with his longtime musical partner Maurice Seezer and has written several film scores and stage shows.

U2 Touring Personnel / Special Mentions

The interviews in *U2 Show* represent a cross-section of people who have been involved with U2's concerts in different ways. It has not been possible to speak to all those who have played critically significant roles in U2's touring history. There are many other individuals who have been part of the collective effort necessary to put together the shows and tour them, and without whom these shows would not have realised their final level of success. Some people did only one tour, others worked only on a few dates, others have been with the band for ever, but all of them helped to make it happen. These people are the sound crews, the lighting crews, the riggers, the security, mangement staff, accountants, video crews, steel crews, pyro crews, truck drivers, bus drivers, carpenters, caterers, tour technicians, generator crews, promoters' reps, local crews and union crews.

In recognition of these many special contributors, this list has been compiled from recommendations given to the author by Steve Iredale, Joe O'Herlihy and Willie Williams. It is focussed on those who have actively participated in U2's tours.

Band
Bono (vocals)
The Edge (guitar)
Adam Clayton (bass guitar)
Larry Mullen Jr (drums and percussion)

Management
Paul McGuinness p.19, All tours
Ellen Darst p.200, War to ZooTV inclusive
Anne Louise Kelly p.201, War to PopMart inclusive
Sheila Roche, Joshua Tree to Elevation inclusive
Keryn Kaplan, Joshua Tree to present
Susanne Doyle, Joshua Tree ZooTV, PopMart
Sheila 'Holly' Peters, ZooTV, PopMart, Elevation

Tour Management
Dennis Sheehan p.207, 1982 to present
Bob Koch p.209, 1984 to present

Audio Director
Joe O'Herlihy p.210, 1979 to present

Show Designer
Willie Williams pp.15, 1983 to present

Architect
Mark Fisher p.233, ZooTV, Outside Broadcast, PopMart, Elevation

Production
Steve Iredale p.218, October to Elevation inclusive
Jake Kennedy p.222, Boy, Joshua Tree, ZooTV, PopMart
Tim Buckley, Unforgettable Fire to PopMart
Tim Lamb, ZooTV, PopMart
Rocko Reedy p.224, ZooTV, PopMart, Elevation
Sue 'Duchess' Iredale Joshua Tree to Elevation inclusive
David Herbert, ZooTV, PopMart, Elevation
Helen Campbell, ZooTV (wardrobe), Elevation
Jake Berry p.225, Elevation

Band Crew
Tom Mullally (Drums) October to Conspiracy of Hope
Steve Rainford (The Edge) p.258 War to Joshua Tree

Des Broadberry (Keyboards) Conspiracy of Hope to PopMart
Fraser McAlister (Guitars) Unforgettable Fire to PopMart
Stuart Morgan (Bass) ZooTV to present
Sam O'Sullivan (Drums) oshua Tree to present
Dallas Schoo (The Edge) p.259 Joshua Tree to present
Bob Loney (Tech) Unforgettable Fire to Love Town
Colm 'Rab' McAllister (Tech) ZooTV to present

Stage Tech
Gregg Carroll, Unforgettable Fire, Amnesty
Adam 'A.J.' Rankin, Joshua Tree to present

Wardrobe
Marion Smyth, Unforgettable Fire, Amnesty, Joshua Tree
Fintan Fitzgerald p.253, Joshua Tree, ZooTV, PopMart, Elevation
Sharon Blankson p.256, PopMart, Elevation

Sound Crew
Paul Lilley, Boy, October, War
Chris Haywood, Boy, October, War
John Sherman, Boy, October, War
Jo Ravitch, War to present
Dave Skaff, Joshua Tree to present
Don Garber, ZooTV to present
C.J. Patterson, War to ZooTV inclusive
Dave Natal, War, Unforgettable Fire
Dave Wilkerson, Joshua Tree
Tom Ford, PopMart, Elevation
Niall Slevin, Elevation

Lighting Crew
Ian England, October
Lin Scoffin, October
Bob Morbeck, War and Unforgettable Fire
Pete Jennings, Unforgettable Fire, Joshua Tree, Love Town
Lynn Scottin, Joshua Tree
Scott Richmond, Unforgettable Fire and Joshua Tree
Kevin Shirley, ZooTV
Kevin Lecky, ZooTV
Bruce Ramus p.238, ZooTV, PopMart, Elevation
Gary Chamberlain, ZooTV, PopMart, Elevation
Russel 'Bits' Lyons, ZooTV, PopMart, Elevation
Simon Carus-Wilson, ZooTV
Firmin Moriarty, ZooTV, PopMart

Video Crew
Carol Dodds p.241, ZooTV
Monica Caston p.240, ZooTV, PopMart
Bob Loney, ZooTV
David Neugebauer, ZooTV, PopMart
Bruce Ramos, ZooTV, PopMart
Jay Strasser, ZooTV, PopMart
Mike Tribble, ZooTV, PopMart
Stefaan 'Smasher' Desmedt ZooTV, PopMart, Elevation
Mark O'Herlihy, ZooTV, PopMart, Elevation
Kurt Verhelle, ZooTV, PopMart, Elevation

Carpenters
Dragan Kuzmanov, oshua Tree, Love Town, ZooTV
Adam 'A.J.' Rankin, ZooTV, PopMart, Elevation

Riggers
Steve Witmer, Unforgettable Fire, Joshua Tree
Michael Grassley, Unforgettable Fire
Warren Jones, ZooTV, PopMart
Pete Kalopsidiotis, ZooTV, PopMart
Charlie Boxhall, ZooTV, PopMart

Engineering Consultant
Richard Hartman p.230, ZooTV, PopMart

Band Security
Ron McGilvrary, Unforgettable Fire
Bob Wein, Joshua Tree
John Clarke, Joshua Tree, Love Town
Jerry Mele, LoveTown, ZooTV, PopMart
Scott Nicholls, ZooTV, PopMart, Elevation
David Guyer, ZooTV, PopMart, Elevation
Eric Hausch, ZooTV, PopMart, Elevation
Jerry Meltzer, PopMart, Elevation
John Sampson, PopMart, Elevation

Generators
Pete & Andy Wills, Joshua Tree, Europe/MiltonKeynes 1985
Mike Goode, Joshua Tree, Europe/MiltonKeynes 1985
John Zajonc, ZooTV, PopMart
John Campion, ZooTV, PopMart, Elevation
Lawrence Anderson, ZooTV
Mitch Margolin, ZooTV
Anthony Hurlocker, ZooTV
John Ross, ZooTV

Travel Co-ordinator
Lindsey Sheehan, LoveTown, ZooTV, PopMart
Bret Alexander, ZooTV, PopMart, Elevation

Art and Video curator
Catherine Owens p.243, ZooTV, PopMart, Elevation

Tour video contributors
Mark Pellington p.246, ZooTV
Mark Neale p.247, ZooTV
Kevin Godley p.244, ZooTV
Run Wrake, PopMart

Stage Design
Jeremy Thom p.226, Joshua Tree
Rene Castro p.229, LoveTown
Jonathan Park p.232, ZooTV Outside Broadcast

Show filming
Malcolm Gerrie p.248, War (*Live at Red Rocks*)
Gavin Taylor p.250, War (*Live at Red Rocks*)
Phil Joanou, Joshua Tree (*Rattle and Hum*)
David Mallet, ZooTV, PopMart
Allen Branton, ZooTV, PopMart
Ned O'Hanlon p.250, ZooTV, PopMart, Elevation
Maurice Linnane p.252, ZooTV, PopMart, Elevation
Hamish Hamilton, Elevation

Tour and album artwork
Steve Averill p.272, Boy to present
Shaughn McGrath p.274, Joshua Tree to present

Agents
Ian Wilson, 1979–1983
Frank Barsalona p.203, 1980–1996
Ian Flooks p.205, 1983–1996

Promoters
Jim Aiken (Ireland) p.275
Dennis Desmond (Ireland) p.275
John Curd (UK)
Tim Parsons (UK) 1980–1996 p.275
Jack Boyle (USA, Detroit/Washington)
Barry Fey (USA, Arizona/Colorado)
Don Law (USA, Boston) p.276
Gregg Perloff (USA, San Francisco) p.277
Arthur Fogel (Canada) p.278
Michael Cohl (Canada) p.278
Thomas Johansson (Scandinavia)
Marek Lieberberg (Germany)
Leon Ramakers (Holland)
Michael Coppel (Australia/New Zealand)
Mr Udo (Japan)
Fran Tomasi (Italy/Brazil)
Herman Schueremans p.276
John Giddings (Europe)

Publicity
Regine Moylett, War to present
Nigel Sweeney (radio & tv pr) ZooTV, PopMart

Media
Martin Wroe (UK)

Tour Supply Companies
Sound
Stage Sound Hire (Ireland, UK & Europe) 1 O'clock Tick Tock, Boy, October
Panther Sound (Ireland, UK & Europe) Boy, October, War
Delicate Productions (USA) Boy, October, War
Roy Clair & Greg Hall (Clair Brothers) p.215, War to present

Lighting
Peter Clarke (SuperMick/Europe) Boy to Love Town inclusive
Tait Towers Lighting (USA) War to Joshua Tree inclusive
    Nocturne Lighting Inc. (USA) Joshua Tree
Ronan Willson (Meteorlites,Australia/New Zealand) Love Town
John Lobel (LSD/US) p.236, Nocturne: Joshua Tree/LSD, ZooTV, PopMart, Elevation
Terry Lee (LSD/UK) ZooTV, PopMart, Elevation

Video
Pat Morrow (Nocturne USA) p.239 lighting: Unforgettable Fire, Joshua Tree, video: Joshua Tree, ZooTV
Herbie Herbert (Nocturne USA) lighting: Unforgettable Fire, Joshua Tree, video: Joshua Tree, ZooTV)
Frederic Opsomer (Systems Technologies) p.242, ZooTV, PopMart
Fred Jalbout (SACO Smartvision) PopMart
Chris Mounsor (PSL Video) PopMart (XL Video) Elevation
Rene Dekeyzer (XL Video) Elevation

Set construction
Michael Tait p.228, War to Elevation inclusive
Charlie Kail PopMart, Elevation

Staging
Spike Falana (Upfront Staging) Joshua Tree to PopMart inclusive
Hedwig DeMeyer (StageCo) outdoor staging, ZooTV, PopMart
Anne Taylor (Upfront Staging) Joshua Tree to PopMart inclusive
John McHugh (Upfront Staging) Joshua Tree
Henry Crallen (EdwinShirleyStaging) Milton Keynes 1985, Dublin Croke Park 1985

Trucking
Pete Gray (Hippo Trucking) Boy to ZooTV inclusive
Robin Shaw (Upstaging Inc.) Unforgettable Fire to Elevation inclusive
Robert Carone (Upstaging Inc.) Unforgettable Fire to Elevation inclusive
Phil Allen (Eurotrux) Unforgettable Fire to ZooTV inclusive
Shoe Sanders (Atkinson Sanders) ZooTV, PopMart
Brian Higgins (Upstaging Inc.) ZooTV, PopMart, Elevation

Freight
Alan Escombe (Rock-It Cargo) October to Elevation inclusive

Catering
Val Bowes (Flying Saucers/Europe) ZooTV, PopMart, Elevation

Photographers' Credits

The Publishers would like to thank the following sources for their kind permission to reproduce the photographs in this book. We are particularly grateful to U2 and Principle Management for access to their picture archive and wish to acknowledge the following photographers for their contribution. Although every effort has been made to trace copyright holders we apologise for any omissions or errors and would be happy to correct them in future editions of the book.

Page 4: top Redferns/Erica Echenberg; centre Bill Rubenstein; below centre Mark Fisher; bottom Diana Scrimgeour
Page 5: top Bill Rubenstein; above centre, centre and below centre Diana Scrimgeour; bottom Willie Williams
Page 9: Colm Henry
Page 10: Redferns/John Kirk
Page 11: Mark Fisher
Page 12: Rex Features/Brian Rasic
Page 13: Mark Fisher
Page 14: Diana Scrimgeour
Page 15: Willie Williams
Page 17: left Willie Williams; top right and bottom right Diana Scrimgeour
Page 23: Patrick Brocklebank
Page 24: Hugo McGuinness
Page 27: Redferns/Virginia Turbett
Page 28: Colm Henry
Page 29: Hugo McGuinness
Page 30: Colm Henry
Page 31: Redferns/Erica Echenberg
Page 33: Dionne Eskelin
Page 34 and 35: Colm Henry
Pages 36-37: Retna/Geoff Crawford
Page 38: Willie Williams
Page 39: Redferns/Ebet Roberts
Pages 40-41: Courtesy of Red Rocks Associates
Page 42: Paul Slattery
Page 43: Redferns/Ebet Roberts
Page 44: Herman Sell
Page 45: Redferns/Ebet Roberts
Page 46: top Adrian Boot/urban image.tv; bottom Rex Features/Kees Tabak
Page 47: Kees Tabak
Page 48: Res Features/Kees Tabak
Page 49: left Rex Features/Ilpo Musto
Page 50: top Willie Williams
Page 51: Laurens van Houton
Page 52: Jeremy Thom
Page 56: Debra Netsky

Page 57: Willie Williams
Page 58: top left and top right Rene Castro; bottom right and bottom left Debra Netsky
Page 59: Debra Netsky
Page 62: Rex Features/BrianRasic
Page 63: top Jeremy Thom; bottom Rex Features/Brian Rasic
Page 64: Rex Features
Page 65: Redferns/Ebet Roberts
Page 66: Colm Henry
Page 67: Bill Rubenstein
Page 68: top left Bill Rubenstein; top right Anton Corbijn; bottom left, below centre and bottom right Bill Rubenstein
Page 69: top left, top right, below centre and bottom right Bill Rubenstein; 69 bottom left Redferns/Ebet Roberts;
Pages 70-71: U2 *Rattle and Hum* Courtesy of Paramount Pictures. Used with permission
Pages 72–73: Bob George
Pages 74–75: Willie Williams
Page 76: Graeme Horner
Pages 78 and 79: Willie Graeme Horner Page 80: top left, top right and bottom left Garry Brandon bottom right Colm Henry
Page 81: Rob Verhorst
Pages 82–83: Colm Henry
Page 84: Bill Bernstein
Page 87: Billl Bernstein
Page 88: Andrew McPherson;
Page 89: Bill Rubenstein
Page 90: top Bill Rubenstein; middle and bottom Dan Williams
Page 91: Dan Williams
Page 92–93: Stephane Sednaoui
Page 94: top left and centre left Mark Fisher
Page 94: bottom left Bill Bernstein; right Stephane Sednaoui
Page 95: Andrew McPherson
Pages 96 and 97: Stephane Sednaoui
Page 98 and 99: Bill Rubenstein

Page 100: top left and bottom left Mark Fisher; bottom right Bill Rubenstein
Page 101: top Mark Fisher; top right Mark Fisher; bottom left and bottom right Bill Bernstein
Pages 102–105: Mark Fisher
Pages 106 and 107: Bill Bernstein
Page 108: Stephane Sednaoui
Page 109: Andrew McPherson
Page 110: left Bill Bernstein; right Bill Rubenstein
Page 111: Stephane Sednaoui
Page 112: left and centre Stephane Sednaoui; right Bill Rubenstein
Page 113: Bill Rubenstein
Page 114: top left, above centre left and right, below centre left and bottom left and right Andrew McPherson; top right Brendan Fitzpatrick; below centre right Stephane Sednaoui
Page 115: Stephane Sednaoui
Page 116: top Bill Bernstein; bottom Bill Rubenstein
Page 117: Bill Rubenstein
Page 118: left Redferns/Rob Verhorst; right Rex Features/ Brian Rasic
Page 119: Rex Features/Peter Stone
Page 120: left Bill Bernstein
Pages 120–121: Bill Rubenstein;
Page 122: Andrew McPherson
Page 123 and 124 Mark Fisher
Page 129: Diana Scrimgeour
Page 130: Diana Scrimgeour
Pages 131 and 132: Mark Fisher
Page 133: Diana Scrimgeour
Page 134: top left, top right and bottom right Diana Scrimgeour; bottom left Mark Fisher
Page 135: Diana Scrimgeour
Page 136: Mark Fisher
Page 137: Diana Scrimgeour
Page 138: left Mark Fisher
Pages 138–139: Mark Fisher
Pages 140–141: Diana Scrimgeour
Pages 142 and 143: Anja Grabert

Picture credits continued:

Pages 144: Redferns/Ebet Roberts

Page 145: Diana Scrimgeour

Page 146: top left and top right Diana Scrimgeour; bottom Redferns/Ebet Roberts

Page 147: top Anja Grabert; bottom Rex Features/Brian Rasic

Pages 148 and 149: Mark Fisher

Page 150: top left Diana Scrimgeour; top centre, top right, above centre left to right, below centre, below centre right, bottom left and bottom right Mark Fisher; below centre left and bottom centre, Diana Scrimgeour

Page 151: top left above centre left and bottom right Diana Scrimgeour; top centre, top right, above centre, above centre right, below centre left to right, bottom left and bottom centre Mark Fisher

Pages 152–194: Diana Scrimgeour

Page 196: Redferns/Ian Dickson

Page 197: top Redferns/David Redfern; bottom Jim Anderson photog.com

Page 198: Redferns/Andrew Whittuck

Page 199: Redferns/David Redfern

Page 203: Adrian Boot/ urbanimagage.tv

Page 204: Willie Williams

Page 205: Neil Cooper

Page 206: top Jeremy Thom; bottom Rene Castro

Page 208: top left Garry Brandon; bottom right Diana Scrimgeour

Page 209: Diana Scrimgeour

page 210: top right Diana Scrim-geour; bottom left Ellen Darst

Page 211: Willie Williams

Page 212: Andrew McPherson Page

213: top Andrew McPherson; bottom Diana Scrimgeour

Page 214-215: Diana Scrimgeour;

Page 216: Mark Fisher

Page 217: Diana Scrimgeour

Page 218: top Willie Williams; bottom Bill Rubenstein

Page 219 top Diana Scrimgeour

Pages 220 and 221 Diana Scrimgeour

Page 222: Willie Williams

Page 223: Diana Scrimgeour

Page 224: left Andrew McPherson; right Diana Scrimgeour

Page 225: Diana Scrimgeour

Page 226: Jeremy Thom

Page 227: Bill Rubenstein

Page 228: Diana Scrimgeour

Page 229: Rene Castro

Page 230: Graeme Horner

Page 231: top Mark Fisher; bottom Willie Williams

Page 232: Bill Rubenstein

Page 233: Mark Fisher

Page 234: top Mark Fisher; bottom Diana Scrimgeour

Page 235: top Mark Fisher; bottom Bill Rubenstein

Page 236: top Catherine Owens; bottom Neil Cooper

Page 237: Diana Scrimgeour

Page 238: Diana Scrimgeour

Page 239: Peter Stone

Page 240: Mark Fisher

Page 241: top Peter Stone; above centre and centre Bill Rubenstein

Page 242: left of centre and bottom right Mark Fisher; bottom left Diana Scrimgeour

Page 243: top Mark Fisher; above centre Bill Rubenstein; below centre and bottom courtesy of Catherine Owens

Pages 244–245: Mark Fisher

Page 246: bottom Neil Cooper

Page 247: Andrew McPherson

Page 248: Redferns/Erica Echenberg

Page 250: Courtesy of Red Rocks Associates

Page 252: Bill Rubenstein

Pages 253 and 254: Andrew McPherson

Page 255: top Andrew McPherson; bottom Diana Scrimgeour

Page 256: Anja Grabert

Page 257: Diana Scrimgeour

Page 259: top right and bottom left Diana Scrimgeour; bottom right Anja Grabert

Page 260: top Anja Grabert; bottom Diana Scrimgeour

Page 261: Adrian Boot/ urbanimage.tv

Page 263: Mark Fisher

Page 264: Diana Scrimgeour

Page 265: Colm Henry

Pages 266 and 267: Diana Scrimgeour

Page 268: Andrew McPherson

Page 275: Colm Henry

Page 277: top London Features International

Page 277: centre Real Capuano; bottom Bill Rubenstein

Page 278: Diana Scrimgeour

Page 281: Neil Cooper

Page 282: Diana Scrimgeour

Page 284: Rex Features

Page 285: Redferns/Richard E Aaron

Page 286: Corbis/Neal Preston

Page 287: Rex Features

Page 293: BP Fallon

Page 295: Andrew McPherson

Page 296: Diana Scrimgeour.

Page 298: Diana Scrimgeour.

Quotation Sources

Section i
Page 32
Melody Maker
February 6, 1982
'Songs of Praise'
By Lynden Barber

Page 38–39
(Taken from the *U2 Reader,* com-
plied and edited by Hank Bordowitz)
Musician
October 1, 1987
'Luminous Times: U2 Wrestle with
Their Moment of Glory'
By John Hutchinson

Page 44
Melody Maker
January 5, 1985
'The Only Flame in Town'
By Kevin Cummins

Page 49
New Musical Express
February 26, 1983
'War and Peace (War)'
By Adrian Thrills

Page 50
(Taken from the *U2 Reader,* com-
plied and edited by Hank Bordowitz)
The Wall Street Journal,
April 2, 1985
'Keeping the Rock Faith with
Unforgettable Fire'
by Pam Lambert

Section ii
Page 59
Melody Maker
March 14, 1987
'Bringing It All Back Home'
By Colin Irwin

PAGE 75:
The Rolling Stone Files
March 10, 1988
'The Edge: The Rolling Stone
Interview'
By James Henke

PAGE 77
The Rolling Stone Files
March 9, 1989
'Now What? – Having conquered
the world, U2 tries to figure out
what to do next'
By Steve Pond

Section iii
Page 90
From *Details*
September 1992
'U2 anew'
By Sean O'Hagan

Page 98
Source: Willie Williams

Page 102
The Rolling Stone Files
October 1, 1992
'U2 Finds What It's Looking For'
By David Fricke

Page 110
The Rolling Stone Files
October 1, 1992
'U2 Finds What It's Looking For'
By David Fricke

Page 118
New Musical Express
June 13, 1992 (ZooTV tour)
Rock and Roll
By Stuart Bailie

Page 120
Vox
August 1993
'The Lord of the Fly'
By Chris Donovan

Section iV
Page 130
Source: Willie Williams

Page 135
PopMart programme notes
By Bill Flanagan

Page 144
Hotpress Annual 2002
'The Hotpress Interview'
By Niall Stokes

Page 146
Details
September 1992
'U2 A New'
By Sean O'Hagan

Section V
Page 160
Revolver
December 2000
'Raw Power: Never Mind the
bollocks, Here's U2 – and They
Want Their Rock and Roll Crown
Back' by Anthony DeCurtis

Page 162
New Musical Express
June 6, 1987
'The Band of Holy Joy'
By Sean O'Hagan

Pages 178–179
The Rolling Stones Files
March 4 1993
'Behind the Fly – Bono the Rolling
Stone Interview'
By Alan Light

Page 190
New Musical Express
February 26, 1983
'War and Peace (War)'
By Adrian Thrills

This paperback edition published in
2006 by Orion Books
First published in hardback in 2004
by Orion Books an imprint of the
Orion Publishing Group Ltd
Orion House,
5 Upper St Martin's Lane,
London WC2H 9EA

A CIP catalogue record for
this book is availablefrom the
British Library

ISBN-10 0 75287 393 8
ISBN-13 978 0 75287 393 0

Consultant, Robert Violette
Designed by Katy Hepburn
Picture Research by Emily Hedges
Project Assistant, Rhonda Goldstein

Printed and bound by
Printer Trento S.r.l.

The Orion Publishing Group's policy
is to use papers that are natural,
renewable and recyclable products
and made from wood grown in
sustainable forest. The logging and
manufacturing processes are
expected to conform to the
environmental regulations fo the
country of origin